Pete
scie
Scie
at t
(KA
free
boo
Und
(Cas
and

er
er
or
y
a
e
ue
rs
n

DIGITIZED

The science of computers and how it shapes our world

Peter J. Bentley

OXFORD
UNIVERSITY PRESS

OXFORD
UNIVERSITY PRESS

Great Clarendon Street, Oxford, OX2 6DP,
United Kingdom

Oxford University Press is a department of the University of Oxford.
It furthers the University's objective of excellence in research, scholarship,
and education by publishing worldwide. Oxford is a registered trade mark of
Oxford University Press in the UK and in certain other countries

First Edition published in 2012
First published in paperback 2013

Impression: 1

Published in the United States of America by Oxford University Press
198 Madison Avenue, New York, NY 10016, United States of America

British Library Cataloguing in Publication Data

Data available

ISBN 978–0–19–969379–5 (hbk)
ISBN 978–0–19–967876–1 (pbk)

Printed in Great Britain on acid-free paper by
Clays Ltd, St Ives plc

CONTENTS

Acknowledgements   xi

List of Illustrations   xiii

000   Introduction   1

      Computers uncovered   4

      The science of computers   8

001   Can You Compute?   13

      Understanding the impossible   16

      Turing's unstoppable machines   21

      Turing's legacy   25

      Complexity is simple   29

      Does P = NP?   34

      Oracles and other complexities   38

      Theoretical futures   41

010   Disposable Computing   43

      Thinking logically   45

      Building brains   49

      Anatomy of a digital brain   54

      The end of the beginning   58

      The Law of Moore   62

CONTENTS

	The future is many	67
	Beyond von Neumann	71
011	Your Life in Binary Digits	74
	Learning to program computers	80
	Climbing higher	85
	Bases for data	91
	Software crisis	95
	Virtual futures	102
100	Monkeys with World-Spanning Voices	104
	Diverse connections	108
	Inter-networking	112
	Addressing for success	119
	Spinning webs over networks	123
	Weaving tangled webs	129
	Webs of deceit	134
	Digital lives	137
101	My Computer Made Me Cry	140
	The birth of friendly computing	145
	Seeing with new eyes	149
	Photos and chicken wire	153
	Waking dreams	156
	It's not what you do but the way that you do it	162
	My pet computer	168
	Human–computer integration	170
110	Building Bionic Brains	173
	Teaching computers how to play	175
	The birth of intelligence	179

CONTENTS

The seasons of AI   182

Intelligence from feet to head   190

Adaptation by natural selection   195

Learning to learn, predicting the predictors   201

Complex futures   205

111 A Computer Changed My Life   209

Computer creativity   210

Computational biology   218

Computer medicine   225

Computer detectives   233

Endnotes   241

Bibliographic Notes   263

Index   285

ACKNOWLEDGEMENTS

ozkurt, Nicolas Courtois, Norm Matloff, Pere
b Pefferly, Robert van de Geijn, Sam Gan, Selim
ar, Spyridon Revithis, Stefano Levialdi, Susan
, Vagan Terziyan, William Buckley.
and of proof-readers, distracters, and loved ones
u are): Soo Ling Lim, John Bentley, Sue Black,

ot have been possible without the support of the
uter Science, University College London. Many
ady listed above) were generous enough to pro-
is book, and check the accuracy of the content.
like to thank the cruel and indifferent, yet aston-
cesses of natural evolution for providing the
rk. Long may it continue to do so.
nank my mother who passed away suddenly in
ture my love of books and writing throughout
e was perhaps the biggest fan of my own books.
d. We miss you, Mum.

In 2010 the Department of Computer Science, University College London, celebrated its 30th anniversary. May it celebrate many more!

Klopotek, Mustafa
Villez, Peter Lewis, R
Aki, Sitharama Iyer
Stepney, Tim Weyric

Thanks also to my
(you know which y
Arturo Araujo.

This book would
Department of Com
UCL researchers (alr
vide their words in t
(As usual), I would
ishingly creative pr
inspiration for my w

Finally I'd like to
2009. She helped nu
my childhood, and s
She was also my frie

Thanks to all th
be interviewed
ments on the co
Sue Black, An
Crowcroft, Bru
Handley, Mark
Hogeweg, John
bands, David Jo
Jon McCormack
son, Angela Sas
Philip Treleaven

Many thanks
Computer Scien
Sasse, Ann Bla
Moret, Bruce D
Christian Dresc
ton, David Clark
Brostow, Ged Ri
rina Falkner, Ma
Sewell, Mateusz

LIST OF ILLUSTRATIONS

1. Alan Turing (far left, on the steps of the bus) with members
   of the Walton Athletic Club, 1946.
   By kind permission of the Provost and Fellows, King's
   College, Cambridge   27

2. Shannon's Boolean logic AND and OR switches. Adapted
   from 'A symbolic analysis of relay and switching circuits',
   by C. E. Shannon, Thesis (M.S.), Massachusetts Institute of
   Technology, Department of Electrical Engineering, 1940   47

3. The Electronic Numerical Integrator and Computer (ENIAC).
   Left to right: PFC Homer Spence; Chief Engineer Presper
   Eckert; Consulting Engineer Dr John Mauchly; Betty Jean
   Jennings; BRL–Upenn Liaison Officer Captain Herman
   Goldstine; Ruth Licterman, 1946.
   © Bettmann/Corbis   53

4. John von Neumann and the first computer at the Institute
   for Advanced Study (IAS), 1951.
   Photo by Alan Richards, from The Shelby White and
   Leon Levy Archives Center, Institute for Advanced Study,
   Princeton, N J, USA   59

5. Sir Maurice Wilkes in front of the oldest working electronic
   computer (originally built for the Atomic Energy Research
   Establishment in Harwell in 1951) at the National Museum
   of Computing, Bletchley Park, 2009.
   © John Robertson/Alamy   90

6. Peter Kirstein in front of racks of modern computer servers
   in the machine room of Computer Science, UCL, 2011.
   © Peter J. Bentley   119

7. Claude Shannon and 'Theseus' the Maze-Solving Mouse,
   moved magnetically by his maze-solving machine, 1952.
   © Time & Life Pictures/Getty Images   176

Introduction

They obey our instructions with unlimited patience. They store the world's knowledge and make it accessible in a split second. They are the backbone of modern society. Yet they are largely ignored.

Computers. They comprise our crowning achievements to date, the pinnacle of all tools. Computer processors and software represent the most complex designs humans have ever created. The science of computers has enabled one of the most extraordinary transformations of our societies in human history.

You switch on your computer and launch the Internet browser. A one-word search for 'pizza' finds a list of pizza restaurants in your area. One click with the mouse and you are typing in your address to see if this restaurant delivers. They do! And they also allow you to order online. You choose the type of pizza you feel like, adding your favourite toppings. The restaurant even allows you to pay online, so you type in your credit card number, your address, and the time you'd like the delivery. You choose 'as soon as possible' and click 'pay'.

Just thirty-five minutes later there is a knock on your door. The pizza is here, smelling delicious. You tip the delivery guy and take the pizza to your table to eat.

Ordering pizza is nothing unusual for many of us around the world. Although it may seem surprising, this increasingly common scenario with cheap prices, fast delivery, and access to such variety of food for millions of customers is only possible because of computers. In the situation above you might have spotted just one computer. If we take a look behind the scenes, the number of computers involved in bringing your pizza is astonishing.

When you switched on your computer, you actually powered up many computers that all work together to make the display, mouse, keyboard, broadband, and main computer operate. Your computer linked itself to the Internet—which is a worldwide network of computers—with the help of computers of the phone company and Internet service provider. When you searched for 'pizza' the request was routed between several computers before reaching the search engine computers. These special machines keep an up-to-date index of the Internet and search this summary to provide near-instant results for you—a list of links to pizza restaurants. When you clicked on a link, your computer was directed (through another chain of computers) to the restaurant computers, which provided details of their products back to your own computer. The pizza toppings you selected on your computer were sent to their computer so it could calculate the price. When you clicked 'pay', your computer talked via a secure encrypted link to another computer, which talked using more secure links to the bank and transferred the payment from your account into the account of the restaurant.

With the payment completed, the main computer of the restaurant chain then sent your order to the computer of your local restaurant. The kitchen received the order just thirty seconds after you paid online and they began making your pizza. It's a good restaurant so they made it from scratch using ingredients such as cornmeal, wheatflour, tomato sauce, mozzarella cheese, pepperoni, olive oil.

But there is a contradiction—the restaurant has very cheap prices and yet it uses good quality ingredients. It can only have this fine selection of Italian ingredients because of highly accurate stock-keeping which minimizes waste, and high-volume ordering which reduces the price. To achieve this, the restaurant's computer keeps track of the sales and stock levels each day (combined with data gathered over the last two years), automatically preparing a proposed order for the manager to approve or amend.[1] The approved order is then sent to the main computer of the restaurant chain, which in turn places the combined orders from all its restaurants to the various food suppliers. The orders cause a ripple of computers to talk to each other in distribution companies, food-processing factories, shipping companies, and food production companies, all over the world.[2] The mozzarella may have come from Italy, your pepperoni from Ireland, your cornmeal from USA. Every company relies on its computers to maintain and enable their accounts, salaries, schedules, stock, communications, and many use computer-controlled machines in their factories.

Just ten minutes after you clicked 'pay' on your computer, your pizza had been made using those fresh ingredients. The chef then placed it on a computer-controlled conveyer oven designed to be energy efficient and fast. It rolled in raw and less than ten minutes later it rolled out perfectly cooked. The delivery man then packed the pizza in a box (which had been manufactured by a computer-controlled cardboard-cutting machine a few days earlier). He collected several deliveries together into a bag designed to keep the food hot, and went to his vehicle.

In your case, since the restaurant services a large area, the delivery man used a car. Like most modern cars, his was packed full of computers to make the engine run efficiently, provide traction control, anti-lock braking, climate control, and even make his radio work. The radio signal he listened to had originated in a studio a split second earlier, and yet another chain of computer-controlled communication had brought the radio signal to his car. He was new to the job so he used a GPS gadget to find his way—a computer which listened to signals beamed from orbiting satellites produced by their computers (and calibrated by yet more computers).

Unknown to you, he still managed to become lost. Thirty minutes after you clicked 'pay' he was using his mobile phone to call the restaurant to check your address. The device used its tiny internal computers to send a special wireless signal, which was received by several computers in nearby cellular receivers. They negotiated with each other and his phone, calculating the best way to route his signal to the restaurant, and dynamically changing the route based on signal strength and capacity of each receiver. His conversation was successful thanks to this constantly changing network of computers, and he realized he'd typed in your address incorrectly.

Five minutes later he arrived at your home. He took out your pizza from his bag and knocked on your door.

Computers uncovered

Look at any common activity in the modern world and you'll find more computers lurking behind the scenes than you ever imagined. Our computers are hidden to such an extent that most of us are completely oblivious to their existence. If they could feel emotions,[a]

they'd be feeling quite unappreciated right now. Computers are cam-
ouflaged but we don't need to wear Safari clothes and use binoculars
to find them—we can just look a little more deeply at any common
activity. Switch on a light and your room is brightened because computers in the power station enable the right flow of electricity at the
right times. Call a friend on your phone and you initiate an extraordinary network of computers talking to each other so that your voice
can reach the ear of your pal. Watch television and you're seeing
images decoded in real-time by a computer, which were transmitted
using computers and recorded digitally with computers. Computers
are our invisible helpers, discreetly enabling almost every aspect of
our lives.

I can't help being astonished at the impact of computer science on
people. Just a few short years ago it was only computer scientists like
myself who spoke the obscure language of emails, Web pages, directories, and operating systems. Today I can sit on a train and hear people, from toddlers to Grandmothers, using these words—and using
them correctly. Gossip and fashion magazines now feature articles
about computers, and the same magazines can be read online or on
tablet computers. The technology that was once confined to our computing labs has spread across the world like wildfire. Imagine if a similar revolution had happened in biology. We'd all be using complicated
words like plasma membranes, ribosomes, and cytoskeletons.

Twenty years ago I remember seeing prototype videophones and 3D
television in the depths of computer labs—technologies that are now
becoming mainstream consumer products. I remember the first optical character recognition (OCR) programs, which struggled to read
anything correctly. Now fifteen (and rising) per cent of all books ever
written have been digitized using OCR technology, allowing us to

perform instant searches for occurrences of phrases or words through their 500 billion words.[3]

I recall the beginnings of the World Wide Web very clearly.[b] When I saw my first Web page, I couldn't see the point of it. Why would anyone want to wait ten minutes for some text and an image? Twenty years later and my television can browse the Internet and play movies provided online by television companies. My phone can browse the Internet and show me a satellite picture of my exact location anywhere on Earth. I can buy almost any product online from almost any country in the world and have it delivered direct to my home. In the next twenty years it is hard to predict what we will be able to achieve. I suspect the technology will be cheaper, faster, and more impressive than anything we might imagine today.

Whatever you do, no matter which job or recreational pursuit, you will be using a computer of some kind, whether you are aware of it or not. They are so useful, and so cheap to make, that we use them for every conceivable activity. Industries centred on computers are predicted to be the fastest growing of all for the foreseeable future, with only medical services matching this growth.[c,4] The industries that are growing the most did not even exist a few decades ago: information technology consulting, Internet hosting and publishing, cable and satellite programming, computer systems design, software publishing. It's no co-incidence that many of the world's richest people are in the computer business.[5] Who would have guessed that computers could outsell oil, steel, food, or fashion? Whatever your ambitions, you need to understand computers (or at least how to use them effectively) in order to succeed in the modern world.

Today to say that you are working with computers is meaningless. We all do. The question is what do you use the computer for? Are you an artist or musician? A writer or blogger? Are you a financial trader or salesperson? A product designer or engineer? A surgeon or nurse? A supermarket assistant or fast food cook? A college or school student? Computers are such a fundamental part of our lives that it's hard to understate the importance of computer literacy. Your whole working life (or your children's lives) is likely to involve using these electronic machines.

In this book I'll reveal the secrets of computer science that are not taught in schools or colleges, but which enable our computer-filled world to function. We will go on a journey through the hidden labs of computer scientists. I'll introduce you to many of the researchers (and one or two self-made millionaires) who have developed and are still developing the technological miracles that surround us. With their help we will see how computers are used in myriad different applications.

I'll show you that computers are fundamentally very simple to understand, and how you can use that knowledge to excel in your work and play. Together we will explore how this young discipline grew from its theoretical conception by pioneers such as Alan Turing, through its growth spurts in the Internet, its difficult adolescent stage where the promises of artificial intelligence were never achieved, and the dot-com bubble which grew until it burst, to its current stage as a (semi)mature field, now capable of remarkable achievements. We will see the successes and failures of computer science through the years with the help of leading researchers and pioneers, and discover what innovations may change our world in the next twenty years.

I am an enthusiastic guide, for I am a computer scientist myself. You can't grow up building robots and programming computers without having a fascination for the subject. They may be our silent slaves, performing every instruction blindly, but I believe that computers have much to teach us about our world and ourselves.

The science of computers

The pizza story may have helped you to spot computers living in the wild. Yet the physical devices and the software that they run are just the tip of the iceberg. There is so much more to computers than a bunch of silicon chips and programs. There has to be—for otherwise computers could never have become so widespread.

Computer science is the music of mathematics and engineering. Just as it is impossible to understand the diversity and complexity of music from a few instruments or popular songs, it is not possible to learn about computers from a few specific examples of computers or software packages. Music has a rich history and tradition, controversy and emotion. It is filled with ideas and theories, methods and instruments, virtuoso performers. Computer science is the same. Its history may be much shorter, but there is plenty of it. Computer science has its traditions, its controversies, and emotions. At its core are theories and ideas, which are built into methods and performed using computing instruments. There are virtuosos in computer science, although they may never wear tuxedos or perform in front of audiences, and they rarely receive rapturous applause from the general public, despite transforming the lives of millions. More likely they are ordinary-looking people who work in jeans and drink too many soft drinks or too much coffee.

Ask members of the public what they think about computer science, and you hear some interesting replies. Here are a few I've heard when I asked this question:

Computer science has to do with hardware and software.
Computer science is messing about with computers.
Computer science is mainly programming, engineering, and maths.
Computer science is as wide as the food industry.

These answers are not wrong, and perhaps you agree with them. But I hope that by the time you reach the end of this book your answer might be a little different.

Computer science is the mysterious field from which all computer technology originates. Its practitioners often work in university laboratories or technology companies. But some may be found in unlikely places such as cancer research laboratories, banks, computer games companies, art studios, car manufacturers, or publishers. If you are a computer scientist you could be working on almost anything, anywhere—it's one of the joys of working in the field.

The discipline of computer science is so new and diverse that some prefer to call it a branch of engineering or mathematics. Perhaps surprisingly for a professional discipline, computer science has something of an identity problem. Biologists have a pretty clear idea of what their area includes and what it does not. Physicists are even more precise. But ask some leading computer scientists for their personal definition of computer science and the result is a little different. Their diverse answers provide a fascinating snapshot of the mixture of research and development that takes place in this field. To show you what I mean, I sent out the question, 'What is your personal definition of computer science?' to mailing lists, social networking sites, and chat groups used by computer scientists. (If you want to talk to computer scientists, it's best to use the computer.) Here are just a few of the responses I received, kindly sent to me from computer scientists all over the world. We will meet some of these people again in later chapters.

Prof Angela Sasse, who specializes in human-centred technology and information security at UCL, replied: 'Computer Science is the science of how to design & build systems that are fit for purpose, value for money, and improve individual & collective well-being.'

Prof Barry Fagin, based at the United States Air Force Academy and working on computer hardware including robotics, said, 'Computer science is about the discovery and creation of what can be computed, what should be computed, and how to do so efficiently.'

Prof Derek Hill is founder and CEO of IXICO, a company specializing in medical imaging services for the pharmaceutical industry. He replied, 'Computer Science uses innovative technology to tackle unsolved scientific challenges and turns new scientific discoveries into life-changing technologies.'

Pere Villez, a lecturer at the University of Portsmouth who focuses on music and sound technology replied, 'Computer science is about producing new social trends with technology.'[d]

One response (from PhD student Michael Firman who works on processing laser range finder data at UCL) encompasses the variety within computer science very aptly: 'Branding disciplines as diverse as Medical Imaging, Artificial Intelligence and Bioinformatics under the banner "Computer Science" because they happen to use a computer can sometimes seem as illogical as grouping English, Law and Sociology into "Pen Studies" because they happen to use a pen.'

Some might see this diversity and apparent disagreement as a problem. In reality it is the secret of the success of computer science. Our labs are not filled with spotty geeks who do nothing but write obscure code that is meaningless to anyone else.[e] They have some of the brightest people from all over the world, building solutions to real problems. We have researchers modelling cancer, or predicting the effects of new drugs on the body. Some use virtual reality in order to help people with phobias. We have people creating new secure systems to enable online banking, car remote fobs, or credit cards to work. There are scientists perfecting new medical imaging systems to make scanning ever more accurate. Others work on mobile devices, enabling ever more reliable wireless technology. Some work to produce the best interfaces or peripherals, enabling us to use computers more naturally. We have researchers building better financial systems to help keep our economy working.

Computer science is diverse, and becoming more so by the minute. A computer scientist may be an engineer, mathematician, or scientist; they may specialize in theory, experiments, or applications; they may work only with hardware, software, or people. But whatever they call themselves and whatever they do, together they create the technology we all use every day.

This book celebrates the diversity and success of the ever-changing community that makes up computer science. We cannot look at every area, every innovation—they are being invented faster than I can write—but I will show you some of the highlights that I find exciting.[f] By the time you reach the end of this journey I hope that you will understand why we computer scientists find computers so compelling. There is no other technology that can touch the lives of so many in so many positive ways. Our first stop on this futuristic journey is perhaps the most fundamental of them all, the foundations of the whole technology. We must visit the grand pillars that support all of computer science, the birthplace of the automatic computation machine.

The nice thing about the computer is that behind all those flickering lights, whirring disks, and rows of chips and wires, there is an elegantly simple idea. This idea has nothing to do with transistors, operating systems, networks, or word processors. It cannot, because it predates all of these. The idea was created by a twenty-four-year-old man called Alan Turing in 1936.

001
___

Can You Compute?

Created by pioneering mathematicians and engineers during times of political unrest and war, computers are more than electronic machines. Underneath the myriad complicated circuits and software glows a mathematical purity that is simplicity itself. The maths at the root of computers illuminates the nature of reality itself.

Today explorers of the impossible still compete to find the limits in our universe. With a revolution in mathematics and technology and a million dollars at stake, who can blame them?

It was 1926 and the General Strike was taking place in England because of disputes over coal miners' pay. There were no buses or trains running. Fourteen-year-old Alan Turing was supposed to be starting at a grand boarding school: Sherborne in Dorset. Yet he was living in Southampton, some sixty miles away. Many children would have simply waited for the ten-day strike to finish and have a longer holiday. Not Turing. He got on his bike and began cycling. It took him two days, with a stay in a little hotel halfway, but young Turing made it to his new school on time.

Turing's independence may have stemmed from the fact that he and his older brother John had seen little of their parents while growing up. Both parents were based in India, but decided their children should be educated in England. The boys were left with friends of the family in England until their father retired and returned in 1926—just as Turing made his way to the new school.

It was an impressive start, but Alan Turing didn't do very well at his new school—he never had in any previous school. His handwriting was terrible, his written English poor. His English teacher said, 'I can forgive his writing, though it is the worst I have ever seen, and I try to view tolerantly his unswerving inexactitude and slipshod, dirty, work…' The Latin teacher was not much more approving. 'He is ludicrously behind.'[1]

The problem was that Turing didn't pay attention to the curriculum being taught. Instead he spent more time following his own interests. He performed his own experiments in chemistry, and worked out his own solutions to all the maths problems he was given. Somehow he managed to win almost every mathematics prize the school offered with his wildly original methods. Unknown to his teachers he was even reading about Einstein's ideas of relativity and the latest theories of quantum mechanics in a book given to him by his grandfather. His headmaster was not impressed with Turing, saying, 'If he is to stay at Public School, he must aim at becoming educated. If he is to be solely a Scientific Specialist, he is wasting his time at a Public School.'[2]

From an early age and throughout his life, Turing wore his dark hair in a characteristic side parting on the left. As he grew older his voice never deepened very much and he had something of a stammer, giving him a deceptively unimposing manner. He had few friends at school, and was clearly unhappy, according to his mother. Another pupil once drew a sketch of him watching the daisies grow in the middle of a hockey field—during a hockey match. But although he was a dreamer, he was also athletic. He took up running and was to become a proficient marathon runner. He finally received some recognition at the school by building a replica of the Foucault pendulum[a] in the dormitory stairwell to show the Earth's rotation.[3]

As Turing entered the Sixth Form of the all-boys boarding school, he developed his first important friendship with an intelligent boy called Christopher Morcom. They challenged each other with chemistry and mathematical problems, and it was Christopher's influence that made Alan apply for a scholarship at Trinity College, Cambridge. They travelled to the interview together and Christopher was successful, but Turing was not. Then tragedy struck. Christopher fell ill with Bovine Tuberculosis—a type of TB that can be caught from infected cattle if the milk is not pasteurized. He did not survive the illness. The eighteen-year-old Turing was devastated. The loss made him think deeply about how life and physics related—subjects that he would revisit for much of the rest of his life. He became determined to remember his friend by continuing the work they loved, so he retook his exams and tried again at Kings College, Cambridge, the next year. This time his application was successful.

Suddenly Turing was in a different world. At Cambridge he was free to explore his ideas and his unconventional nature was encouraged. He developed socially, taking up rowing and continuing his long-distance running. He read further about quantum mechanics, mathematics, and logic. At the Moral Science Club he read a paper on mathematics and logic. Turing's views on the topic were summarized at the time by one of the other members.[b] 'He suggested that a purely logistic view of mathematics was inadequate; and that mathematical propositions possessed a variety of interpretations of which the logistic was merely one.'[2] In other words, Turing thought there may be more to maths than logic.

Turing graduated in 1934 with a distinguished degree, and continued his studies at Cambridge taking an advanced course in the foundations of mathematics. He wrote a fellowship dissertation in which he proved the Central Limit Theorem[c] in statistics—and then discovered it had already been proven many years earlier. This kind of thing was fairly common for Turing, and for good reason, as his colleague James Wilkinson described many years later. 'Turing had a strong predilection for working things out from first principles, usually in the first instance without consulting any previous work on the subject, and no doubt it was this habit which gave his work that characteristically original flavour. I was reminded of a remark which Beethoven is reputed to have made when he was asked if he had heard a certain work of Mozart which was attracting much attention. He replied that he had not, and added, "neither shall I do so, lest I forfeit some of my own originality".

'Turing carried this to extreme lengths and I must confess that at first I found it rather irritating. He would set me a piece of work and when I had completed it he would not deign to look at my solution but would embark on the problem himself; only after having a preliminary trial on his own was he prepared to read my work. I soon came to see the advantage of his approach. In the first place he was really not as quick at grasping other people's ideas as he was at formulating his own, but what is more important, he would frequently come up with some original approach which had escaped me and might well have eluded him had he read my account immediately.'[4]

Understanding the impossible

In the advanced course at Cambridge, Turing learned of a topic that was destined to reveal his genius to the world. The subject suited his nature for it was a big and significant issue at the heart of mathematics, and this time it really did not have a solution.

The course was run by Max Newman, a famous mathematician at Cambridge (who would become a great friend and colleague of Turing later in his life). It focused on ideas exploring the limits of mathematics—could everything and anything be proven in maths? Could everything even be calculated? These puzzling ideas were new, unsolved, and very exciting. Mathematics was supposed to be the formal language of the universe—our way of describing everything and calculating what would happen next. Science, engineering, and economics simply could not happen without maths. If our mathematics were found to be incomplete then it would have major implications about what we could and could not calculate in the future. These ideas captured the imagination of Turing immediately.

One such example of a flaw in mathematics had been discovered some thirty-four years previously by another Cambridge-based mathematician called Bertrand Russell. Russell's work had been enormously successful—he had shown how all mathematics could be reducible to logic—that is all mathematics findings could be rewritten as logical expressions. (This was the same work Turing was to present to the Moral Science Club many years later.) The work was great, for it helped us understand all those fundamental truths that mathematics is built upon. But Russell had later discovered a problem. He had found a paradox—something that seemed to be both true and false at the same time. Mathematicians often look for paradoxes, for if you believe something to be true and false then your belief must be faulty, so it is possible to show that various ideas are wrong in this way. Russell's paradox was much more serious, for it seemed to imply that the whole of mathematics was faulty.

Russell's paradox is quite similar to the Barber's paradox. Think about this:

> There is a barber who shaves precisely those people who don't shave themselves. Does he shave himself?

If he doesn't shave himself, then he must shave himself. But if he does shave himself, then he will not shave himself! The only way this makes sense is if he shaves himself and does not shave himself at the same time—but that's logically not possible. That's why it's a paradox.

Russell's paradox is similar, but it's about sets, or groups of things. Russell knew that if you can have, say, a set of plates, and a set of bowls, then you could have a set of sets of plates and bowls. If you also have a set of cups, then you could have a set of sets of cups, plates, and bowls (a dinner set). In other words the concept of 'set' is a useful mathematical notion, and we can group sets inside other sets. Many proofs of basic arithmetic operations such as addition and subtraction are made using ideas of sets of numbers, so they form some of the fundamental building blocks of mathematics. Russell knew that it is possible for some sets to be inside themselves. One example of this is the set of all non-empty sets. If you have a set of anything, then it's in this set. But because there's something in this set, it is a non-empty set itself, and so must be included in the set of non-empty sets. So it's inside itself. Or, as we say in set theory, it's a member of itself.

So far so good. No paradoxes here, just some slightly weird ideas. But Russell thought of a very special kind of set, which was perfectly acceptable in mathematics yet made no sense at all. Russell's paradox[5] asks:

> There is a set of all sets that are not members of themselves. Is the set a member of itself?

This set will contain itself only if it does not contain itself. But if it does not contain itself, then it will contain itself. Like the Barber's paradox, the only solution that makes sense is if the set both contains itself and does not contain itself at the same time, which is logically impossible.

The reason why mathematicians found the whole thing so appalling was because it identified what seemed to be a flaw in the foundations of mathematics. Centuries upon centuries of mathematical ideas and proofs were all built upon a series of basic, fundamental truths. Even the behaviour of addition and subtraction had been proven using sets and logic. But Russell's paradox suggested that no proof could be trusted any more. The notion that mathematics was the only area where truth could be known absolutely, as Descartes had believed, was no longer valid.[6]

Russell's paradox was just the start. In 1931, just four years before Turing took his advanced course, a mathematician proved once and for all that mathematics would always be incomplete. His name was Kurt Gödel.

Gödel's most memorable work became known as Gödel's incompleteness theorems.[7] The first and perhaps most celebrated theorem was similar to another paradox, known as the Liar paradox. Think about whether this is true or false:

This statement is false.

If the statement is true then its assertion that it is false must be true, so it must be false. If the statement is false then its assertion must be false so it must be true. Gödel's first theorem can be written in a similar way:

G = 'This statement cannot be proven to be true in theory T.'

If G were provable within T, then T would have a theorem, G, which effectively contradicts itself, and so the theory T would be inconsistent. This means that if the theory T is consistent then G cannot be proved within it, and so the theory T is incomplete. So the assertion made by G is correct: G is both unprovable and true. Something can be true whether it can be proven or not.

From this mind-twisting riddle emerges a massive result. We cannot prove everything using mathematics. Some truths are not possible to prove.

It was a devastating result, for it showed that the quest by hundreds of mathematicians over millennia could never succeed. It would never be possible to create a fully complete system of mathematics in which everything from the lowest axioms to the highest, most complex proofs could be shown to be unequivocally true. It didn't matter how perfectly the foundations of mathematics were laid, there would always be some truths that could never be proved.

Turing was also taught about a related idea. It was a very recent challenge posed by the German mathematician David Hilbert in 1928.[d] The challenge was called the *Entscheidungsproblem*, which translated as the 'Decision Problem'. Hilbert wanted to know whether it was possible to decide the truth of statements automatically. He asked whether there was some kind of method or procedure that would always tell you if something was true or false, for a given mathematical language. So you might tell this mysterious machine that your language was logic and that you wanted to know if the following statement was true or not: 'If all sisters are female and Sarah is your sister, then Sarah is male.' Then the machine would have a little think and output 'False'. Or you might tell the machine that your language was arithmetic and you wanted to know whether the statement 'any integer greater than 1 can be made by multiplying prime numbers together'. And the machine would have another think and output 'True'.

It sounded like a very useful thing to have, but the challenge was: could such an automatic method or machine ever exist? It seemed quite possible for simple statements, but would it still work for really difficult statements in complicated mathematical languages? Was this kind of universal truth-sayer possible?

Turing's unstoppable machines

Alan Turing spent the next few months working on this problem. He may have only been twenty-three years old but his wildly creative brain was soon coming up with some fascinating ideas. The first problem he faced was how to think about this mysterious process or machine. This was a time before electronics, a time when the most complex electrical systems were the new automatic phone exchanges—machines big enough to fill a large hall. It was a time when a machine did one thing: the thing it was designed to do. Yet Hilbert's challenge required a general machine. Some kind of machine that could look at any mathematical language and any statement in that mathematical language. To achieve these tasks it needed to be able to perform any possible mathematical operation, in any order, and you needed to be able to change your question. Reprogram it.

There was no machine that could do these things. So Turing imagined a machine that could. He imagined a theoretical computer.

In 1935, if you looked up the definition of a computer in the dictionary, the definition said 'someone who computes'. Young Alan Turing had just thought of a device that could automate all the computations that people had always performed manually.

The machine envisaged by Turing behaved like someone playing a board game—say Monopoly. It had a memory, rather like the positions of pieces, houses on the board, and money of the players.[e] It could be in different states, like different stages of the game. In each state it could change to another state, as though the game was progressing according to the rules. It required input from outside and followed rules to make it change state, like throwing the dice, landing on the 'go to jail' square, and moving your piece to 'jail'.[f] But unlike a board game, the rules behind Turing's Machine could change. In fact the rules could be given as input and would be stored in memory (as if we wrote new rules on the board itself). As the machine changed state, those rules could change further (a square might say 'Cross out the "Free parking square" and write instead: "Landing here means you lose"'). Playing a board game where the rules of the game change as you play would clearly be tricky! But if you can change the rules, you can imagine that it would be possible to convert a game of Monopoly into a game of Snakes and Ladders, or a game of Chess into Checkers.

Of course Turing did not talk about board games. Instead of a board, he imagined a machine that looked at a tape. Depending on the instruction currently being read, the machine could spool the tape left or right, and read or write to the tape. But regardless of the metaphor used to understand the Turing Machine, its abilities are the same. This is a theoretical computer. Because it can perform every possible mathematical operation, his machine can do everything modern computers can do (albeit considerably slower).

His strange new machine only existed on paper, but that was enough, for he wanted to use it as a way of solving Hilbert's challenge in theory. Perhaps ironically, having just created the idea of this generalized computing machine, Turing did not want to prove that his machine could solve the Decision Problem. He wanted to prove that the problem was impossible to solve. He wanted to show that there are some problems that are *undecidable* in mathematics.

Turing imagined that his little computing machine was performing a calculation, following the symbols on its tape. He then asked the question: is it possible to tell if this machine will get stuck in an endless loop and calculate forever, or if it will stop calculating and give an answer? It would be quite possible for it to calculate forever, for example, if its tape said at point A, 'spool to point B' and at point B it said, 'spool to point A'.

This is a very relevant question today, for if our computers were to become stuck in an endless loop, they might 'freeze' and do nothing useful. For example, we would very much like our cash machines to give us the money after we've entered our PIN, and not sit there forever doing nothing!

Turing figured that if it was possible to tell if his machine halted or not, then another Turing Machine should be able to do it, for he knew that his imaginary machine could theoretically do any mathematical calculation. So he imagined a second Turing Machine[g] that would examine the first and halt, outputting 'won't halt' if the first would never halt, or just running forever if the first machine did halt.

Now for the clever bit. Turing imagined what would happen if the second machine looked at itself, and tried to decide if it would stop calculating or not. Suddenly there was a paradox: if the machine ran forever then it would stop; but if it stopped then it would run forever. This is logically impossible and so proves that there exist some Turing Machines that are undecidable—we will never be able to tell if they halt or not.

Although this may seem like a very obscure and unlikely situation, it turns out there are a very large number of undecidable or *uncomputable* problems—a fact that has been causing problems for computer programmers ever since. Turing's result showed that the power, speed, or amount of memory of your computer doesn't matter; there are some things in mathematics that no computer can work out.

As the young Turing prepared this exciting work for publication in 1936,[8,9] he came across the just-published work of an American mathematician called Alonzo Church. At the time there were several mathematicians around the world all working on Hilbert's *Entscheidungsproblem*, and some, like Gödel, had begun to show important results. Church's approach was very different from Turing's, and involved the creation of new mathematical notations and languages to represent the idea of functions and processes. He had used his new language (called lambda calculus) and extended Gödel's work to show that there was no computable method that could decide whether any two lambda expressions were equivalent or not. This meant that there were some things in mathematics that could never be decided—the *Entscheidungsproblem* was not possible. Church had beaten Turing to the answer, by just a few weeks.[10]

Over the following few years the different ways of describing computation were shown to be directly equivalent. Church's lambda calculus was refined and became an invaluable tool in computer science for making formal proofs about software, even today. But the Turing Machine was the clear conceptual winner. Perhaps because of its simplicity, Turing's idea of a computer became known as the foundation of theoretical computer science. Today even the definition of computability is defined in terms of his idea. The universally accepted 'Church–Turing thesis' states that everything that can be computed is computable by a Turing Machine.

Turing's legacy

In 1936, because of their shared interests, Turing decided to join Church in Princeton, USA, and there he completed his PhD under the supervision of Church.

Alonzo Church was himself a somewhat unusual character. Blinded in one eye at high school in an airgun accident, he later was knocked down by a trolley car coming from his blind side and was to marry the nurse who took care of him in the hospital. Polite, neatly dressed, and deeply religious, he was known for his somewhat eccentric habits. He enjoyed and collected science-fiction novels, although he would pencil amendments into their table of contents pages if he found errors, or write to the authors with corrections. Before beginning a lecture Church methodically erased the blackboard spotlessly in even rows, often using soap and water, and then waited patiently for it to dry before beginning. He spoke in long paragraphs as though reading from a book and would pause awkwardly if interrupted. He rarely spoke without using a logical argument.[11] It is said that Church even had a logical way of eating breakfast: 'First pour the milk into the empty bowl. Next pour in the proper amount of sugar. Stir the mixture with the breakfast spoon. Then pour in a spoonful or two of cereal. Eat that. Then pour in another spoonful or two, eat that, and so on. The sugar is dissolved and evenly distributed, and the cereal never has a chance to get soggy.'[12]

Turing never developed the neatness of Church, but he developed some equally logical and sometimes strange habits. Back in England after completing his doctorate, he would frequently wear a gasmask while cycling to avoid hay fever. If he noticed that the chain on his bike often slipped after fourteen revolutions he would stop to adjust it every thirteen turns.[3]

In 1938, shortly after returning to England, Turing was invited by the Government Code and Cypher School to help them in their work on breaking the German Enigma codes. When war was declared in 1939, Turing started working full time at the School in Bletchley Park. He enjoyed the challenge and the environment, and by 1940 had created a machine called the Bombe, which was successfully decoding all German Enigma messages from the Luftwaffe. By the middle of the next year his work enabled all the Enigma coded messages from the German Navy to be decoded as well. Turing spent November 1942 to March 1943 in America helping with decoding; although the Germans upgraded their codes, it was Turing's ideas that proved to be the most helpful in cracking the codes again.

It has been estimated that the work shortened the war by two years. With around eleven million people a year dying, it was an astonishing achievement. Indeed it is claimed that Winston Churchill said Turing's work was the greatest single contribution to victory in the Second World War.[13] Not bad for a slightly awkward geek! He was awarded an OBE for his work by the King, although his efforts were to remain top secret for another three decades.

Turing (Figure 1) continued his imaginative and groundbreaking research after the war. He proposed the design for one of the first computers, the Automatic Computing Engine (ACE), and when his old tutor Max Newman became a professor at Manchester University, Turing joined him there as a reader. He continued to work on maths, but also broadened his interests and investigated neuroscience, morphogenesis in biology, and quantum theory. Turing was one of the first to think about artificial intelligence (and we will revisit several of his ideas in later chapters). He was elected a fellow of the Royal Society of London in 1951 for his work on Turing Machines. Unknown to

Figure 1. Alan Turing (far left, on the steps of the bus) with members of the Walton Athletic Club, 1946.

his colleagues at Manchester, he continued to work for GCHQ on decoding problems as the Cold War began.

In 1952, Turing reported a burglary to the police. He admitted that the culprit was a friend of a man with whom Turing had previously had a relationship. But homosexuality was illegal and so Turing was charged and prosecuted for gross indecency. At his trial his old friend Max Newman testified on his behalf. It made no difference. Turing was convicted; his punishment was either prison or 'chemical castration' with injections of the female hormone oestrogen. He chose the latter, and then was forced to suffer the side effects, including the development of breasts. His security clearance was removed and he was no longer permitted to work for GCHQ. Every move he made—his holidays, his collaboration with foreign scientists—was scrutinized by the security services.

Turing continued his research, publishing more on morphogenesis, quantum theory, and relativity. He travelled, visiting Paris, Athens, and Corfu. But he was unhappy. In 1954, he was discovered dead in his home, a half-eaten apple by his side. He had been conducting electrolysis experiments and the apple was found to have traces of potassium cyanide on its surface. His mother and several of his co-workers at Bletchley believed it was accidental. An inquest found the cause of Alan Turing's death to be suicide.[2]

Turing's work was never forgotten, and he is regarded as the father of computer science by most academics. Yet public recognition has been patchy at best. In 1998, a Blue Plaque was unveiled on the side of the house where he was born. It would have been his eighty-sixth birthday. Sir Roger Penrose wrote at the time, 'The central seminal figure in this computer revolution was Alan Turing, whose outstanding originality and vision was what made it possible, in work originating in the mid-1930s. Although it is now hard to see what the limits of the computer revolution might eventually be, it was Turing himself who pointed out to us the very existence of such theoretical limitations.'[14] A memorial statue, situated in Sackville Park, Manchester, England, was unveiled in 2001. It depicts Turing sitting on a bench with an apple in his hand.

Today Bletchley Park is home to the National Museum of Computing in the UK. Its facilities, including the hut where Turing worked, are open to visitors.[15] Turing's mug is still chained to the radiator there (nobody quite knew why he liked to chain it up). Most recently they have obtained rare copies of Turing's papers for the collection. Sue Black is a computer scientist who vigorously campaigns on television, radio, and social media on their behalf. Through her work and the work of others like her, Bletchley receives sufficient publicity and funding from companies (such as Google) to enable it to stay open.

Black speaks passionately about Turing. 'The fact that he was treated in the way that he was—persecuted, prosecuted and the fact he had to choose between going to prison and chemical castration—and he chose chemical castration…What an inhumane thing to do to somebody. To think he is one of the greatest people of that century and he was treated so poorly.

'We can't change what happened to him,' says Black, 'but we can celebrate the great things he did now. Hopefully the story of what he did and who he was will help motivate other people that they can achieve great things even if they don't receive great recognition at the start.'[16]

Thanks to the upwelling of support from scientists and the general public, a petition for a government apology in 2009 was successful. Prime Minister Gordon Brown wrote a heartfelt message and ended, '…on behalf of the British government, and all those who live freely thanks to Alan's work I am very proud to say: we're sorry, you deserved so much better'.[17]

Complexity is simple

The Universal Turing Machine became the theoretical blueprint for all electronic computers in the world. It told us how computers needed to behave, and helped us design them and make them real. Because of this theory we have always known that any computer can perfectly simulate the behaviour of any other computer (given enough time and memory). We've known this even before the first electronic computers were made.

The Turing Machine is still one of our best theoretical tools for understanding what can and cannot be computed. Some computer scientists believe that these two categories of things may give deep insights into the nature of our universe. Mark Herbster is one such researcher at UCL. 'I think ideas of computability are stronger than many physical laws,' he says. 'You can get down to foundations of what is and what isn't. They are fundamental categories of reality. I think they're built into our universe and any possible conceivable universe.'[18]

There are also very practical applications of the theory: working out how long a particular computation may take. Even if a computation is theoretically possible, that doesn't mean we have computers powerful enough to do the job.

Theoretical computer scientist Robin Hirsch has studied these ideas. 'There are three types of things,' he says. 'First, there are things that are theoretically impossible. They can never be solved. Second, there are things that are practically possible (so must be theoretically possible). Third, there are things that are theoretically possible but practically it seems not. In theory they could be possible but it usually takes longer than the lifetime of the universe to do it or something ridiculous like that. So in practise we can't solve these things. Most of the interesting problems in computer science fall into this category.'[19]

It's an extraordinary idea. Regardless of our technology, these three categories of things will always exist. Undecidable problems like Turing's Halting Problem fall into the first of these types of things. They are impossible to solve, no matter what kind of computer you use.[h] The second type, practically possible problems, consists of those things that are fairly easy to demonstrate working. We can clearly produce word processors, spreadsheets, or computer games, so they must be possible to compute. But the third kind of things comprises those problems on the edge of possibility. They are much more difficult. Sometimes such a problem may seem impractical, but we were just trying to do the computation in an inappropriate way. Sometimes it may be practically impossible—we could never create computers big enough or fast enough to solve the problem. But how to tell the difference? We don't want to waste our time trying to solve impossible problems, but we'd happily spend time trying to improve our ability to solve very, very hard problems.

The difference usually comes down to scale, or how the difficulty changes with scale. Imagine you're an obsessive school teacher and you want your class of thirty pupils to stand in order of height. Smallest on the left and tallest on the right. To figure out where to tell them to stand, you need to compare heights between pairs of pupils, which can take a minute or two with your measuring tape. You don't want to spend all day doing this, so you'd like to compare as few heights as you can. How many comparisons must you make?

Of course the answer depends on how they are standing to begin with. If they are standing in a perfectly sorted order already, then you only need to make twenty-nine comparisons. (Remember you are obsessive, so you need to check each pupil stands to the right of a smaller pupil.) It is possible to show that if you have a clever sorting method, the average number of comparisons needed would be about forty-four. In the worst case, if you are a bit stupid and you compared every child with every other child you would need to do $30 \times 29 = 870$ comparisons. (And if each comparison took one minute, then this would take you 14.5 hours.)

In computer science we usually use the word *algorithm* instead of method. It just means a description of a method or process that we

31

intend to program into a computer later, which gives all the steps of that program.[i] So a sorting algorithm is a method you follow to sort something into order. One algorithm could be an insertion sort: start with one pupil, pick another pupil, and compare with each existing member of the line in turn, inserting him or her into the line when you find the right place, and repeat until all pupils have been inserted. It's not a very quick method, but it would work. Another algorithm could be to play musical chairs with them (without the chairs). Tell them to run around, shuffling themselves randomly. You then stop them and measure the line. If they are in order, you're done. If they are not in order, tell them to run around again, randomly, then measure them again, and so on. This is a particularly stupid way to sort, because in the worst case it might take forever. They might never arrange themselves in order.

So a stupid algorithm takes a stupidly long period of time to run. A more efficient algorithm will be much quicker to run. Of course, all sorting algorithms will also depend on how many things are being sorted, but a stupid sorting algorithm could take infinitely longer than an efficient one. Clearly we generally like to find the efficient algorithms—those with the lower time complexity.

There's a friendly way in which computer scientists write down the time complexity of algorithms. We call it the big-O (pronounced big-Oh) notation.[j] If we say n is the number of things being sorted (n was 30 in the example above), then if the time to finish simply depends on that number alone,[k] it has time complexity of $O(n)$. If you always compare every item with every other item then it has time complexity $O(n \times (n\text{-}1))$. We usually ignore the constants and other lower-order terms as their effects tend to disappear when n becomes huge, so we'd say it has time complexity $O(n^2)$.

The very best sorting algorithms have average time complexity $O(n \log n)$ which is much better than $O(n^2)$. You can work it out for yourself. The fast sorting algorithm called Quicksort has average time complexity $O(n \log n)$. A slower algorithm called Bubblesort has average time complexity $O(n^2)$. If each comparison takes one minute, then when sorting ten items Quicksort takes about ten minutes, and Bubblesort takes over an hour and a half. Sorting 100 items, Quicksort takes about three hours and twenty minutes, but Bubblesort takes nearly a week. Sorting 1000 items, Quicksort takes two days, but Bubblesort takes nearly two years!

But as bad as Bubblesort sounds, it could be even worse. If we had a Slowsort algorithm which had time complexity of $O(2^{n^2})$ then the numbers really start to become scary. Now its time to run has become exponential in a big way. Sorting just ten items with the Slowsort algorithm would take 2411,816,210,479,888,000,000,000 years. That's 175,405 billion times the age of the universe.[1]

Even if we speeded up that comparison (perhaps using some super-ultra-parallel computers) so that instead of taking a minute to do each one it took the smallest theoretically measurable amount of time, one Planck time (5.316×10^{-44} seconds), we still cannot sort more than thirteen objects before the Slowsort algorithm takes a crazy period of time again. Another approach to speeding things up is to use more memory[m]—but then the space complexity increases: the amount of memory needed may become greater than the amount of matter in the universe.

It should be clear why this form of theoretical computer science[n] is so important. Not only does it tell us how we can make our software more efficient, it can tell us which classes of problems are practically solvable or intractable. Sorting is quite an easy problem for computers to handle, even for large numbers of items, because we can design algorithms with speedy time complexities like the Quicksort algorithm. But for some problems we really cannot do better than the Slowsort example.

At least, we think we can't.

Does P = NP?

In the year 2000, American businessman Landon T. Clay announced seven key mathematical challenges to the world. His new Clay Mathematics Institute in Cambridge, MA, USA, would award a prize of a million dollars for each solution.[20,o] A decade later and just one of the problems had been solved by mathematician Dr Grigoriy Perelman of St Petersburg, Russia. Despite his work being called a 'crowning achievement' of the area, he refused to accept the money (and several other extremely prestigious awards offered by other organizations). Nevertheless, there are plenty of other academics very eager to accept a million dollars and awards for solving one of the other problems.[20]

One of the remaining six problems is perhaps the most succinct. It asks: does P = NP?

It refers to classes of problems with different computational complexities. A problem is in class P when it can be solved with an algorithm of polynomial-time complexity. In other words, a problem that can be solved with an algorithm of $O(n^x)$, whatever x might be, is considered to be in this class. Sorting is an example of this type of problem. Even the very best sorting algorithms are still, in their worst case, $O(n^2)$. So the problem of sorting is in class P.

A problem is in class NP when a candidate solution can be checked in polynomial time, but calculating that solution seems to take much,

much longer—often exponential time. The Slowsort algorithm illustrated just how slow that can be.

Taking longer to find a solution compared to checking it may sound a little strange, but think about the following problem. You are in charge of welfare housing for homeless people. You have space for 100 people in a block of flats. The social services have provided you with a long list of pairs of people who are incompatible and must not be housed in the same accommodation block. There are 400 people who have applied for spaces. Which do you choose?

For every solution that you try, it is very easy to check whether it is valid or not. You need exactly 100 people and you just need to check that your list does not contain any pair that is also on the social services list. But figuring out the right 100 people to choose turns out to be massively difficult. The total number of ways of choosing 100 people from the 400 applicants is greater than the number of atoms in the known universe.[21] So this problem is in class NP. We can quickly check if a solution is right or not, but it is very, very hard to find a perfect solution.

It turns out that there are a lot of problems in class NP. The popular computer game Minesweeper is in NP.[22] Routing delivery vehicles to many different cities, while trying to minimize the overall distance travelled, is in NP. Packing your suitcase to maximize the free space, if you have many different-sized possessions, is in NP. Deciding the order to do your chores from a list within a limited time is in NP. Even choosing the smallest number of coins needed to make a specific total is in NP.[23] All of these problems may seem trivially easy at first glance, and for small numbers they are. But try routing a vehicle to 100 cities, or packing 500 items, or using 1000 coins, and the time needed to find the solution seems to increase exponentially.

So the question of whether P = NP is really asking: for all those NP problems that we find so difficult to solve, can they actually be solved by some polynomial algorithm after all? Are we just using stupid algorithms for these problems like Slowsort? Is there some clever algorithm, like Quicksort, that would suddenly make these problems seem easy?

Many computer scientists have tried to prove or disprove P = NP over the years. By chance, one is a colleague of mine at UCL, who I first met when he was still an undergraduate student. His name is Daniel Hulme.

Daniel had developed an interest in the P = NP problem, and in his spare time had thought of a clever algorithm. By exploiting methods normally used to satisfy constraints he was able to solve some NP problems in polynomial time. He was focusing on Boolean Satisfiability (SAT) problems. These are so-called 'decision problems' framed using logical ANDs, ORs, and NOTs (the maths equivalent of electronic circuits, as we'll see in the next chapter). One application for SAT problems is the verification of circuits. The decision problem might be: will the circuit work for all inputs it might receive? Or, is there a set of inputs for which it will not work?

SAT problems are NP-hard. This means they are at least as hard as the hardest problems in NP. They are also NP-complete. This means that if you have a way of solving these problems in polynomial time then you have a way of solving all NP problems quickly, for they can all be rewritten as a SAT problem,[24,p] So if Daniel's clever algorithm could solve all SAT problems in polynomial time, then he would have proven that P = NP.

Daniel's story is fascinating. 'Originally my PhD was to do with understanding how bumblebees see, using computers to model their vision,' he says. 'But in my spare time I was interested in the P = NP problem. I was trying to convince myself that P does not equal NP. It was silly, I know. I like a challenge! I got some interesting results and my PhD supervisor allowed me to continue working on this idea for my PhD. I built some algorithms that were practical and that I thought were very good and could solve problems better than what was already out there.

'I took a certain SAT problem and showed that my algorithm could solve the problem better than many SAT solvers. I'd managed to solve all of the benchmarks that many other algorithms couldn't. So I went to my supervisor and said, look I've got a practical algorithm that's polynomial, that's solving these problems. Please can you help me understand whether its sensible or not.'[25]

Daniel's supervisor Bernard Buxton passed the problem to Robin Hirsch. 'He thought he'd proved P = NP,' recalls Hirsch, 'so Bernard asked me to have a look at this. We got into some debates and with great difficulty I did find that, no he didn't prove P = NP. The algorithm wouldn't necessarily work in every case. But Daniel didn't quite believe me.'[19]

It was difficult news for Daniel to hear. 'At the time, my algorithm, which was polynomial, was able to solve hard problems faster than many algorithms submitted to a major SAT competition. I was very excited because this basic polynomial algorithm was able to beat SAT solvers. I thought this is definitely the direction we should be going.'[25]

Robin was forced to prove his point to Daniel. 'I had to construct a pathological example—which was very difficult for me to do, but I did eventually do it—which showed that his algorithm was not correct. But it was really good research as it turned out, because it was so close to correct that it ends up being I think comparable to the best in the world in terms of solving this. I think it's good work.'[19]

Of course the result was disappointing for Daniel, but he realized that his algorithm was still very useful. 'Robin showed that if you increase the problem by a certain amount then my algorithm will not solve it. That was when I realized I'd built a very good pre-processor. It's not a solution to the P = NP problem—unfortunately!'[25]

Daniel was awarded a PhD for his work on the topic, and went on to create a company based in Silicon Valley. Its name: *Satalia*[q] (a combination of SAT and *alia*—Latin for difference or other). In the UK the subsidiary company was named *NP-Complete*. Their aim is to find good solutions to NP-complete problems for industry. But in addition to his business goals, Daniel is still lured by the mystery of P = NP. 'Our brains are computers as far as I'm concerned,' he says. 'They evolved, probably are not optimal. But it might be that the brain will find the solution to the P = NP problem, who knows? It might even be hardcoded in there already and maybe one day we will be able to unlock that.

'My personal ambition is to be financially independent enough to have an office with a whiteboard so I can be free to do research on the P = NP problem.'[25]

Oracles and other complexities

NP problems are clearly very difficult to solve, but even in 1936, Turing had ways of thinking about such hard problems.[8] One way is to think about a special kind of Turing Machine known as a non-deterministic Turing Machine. If we could make such a machine, it would be able to run NP problems in polynomial time. It's non-deterministic[r]—we can't predict what it will do, but it will always find the fastest way to solve the problem.

Imagine you are searching for a needle in a haystack. You know instantly whether you are looking at a piece of straw or a needle, but figuring out where to look is a big problem. You have many choices about where to look. The question for this problem is: 'which choice should I make that will lead me to the solution?'

A non-deterministic Turing Machine is much the same. It asks: 'Is there any one set of instructions that I could follow that will lead me to success? If there is it will say "yes!" and follow the instructions, finding the solution in the fastest time. If no possible set of instructions can lead to the solution, it will say "no" and fail.'

Exactly how this clever kind of Turing Machine might figure out what to do is somewhat mysterious. There are two ways in which people think about it. You can have a magical Oracle, which knows everything and just tells you: this is the best choice to make.[s,26] The other way is to think of it is as a form of parallelism or concurrency. You imagine that this non-deterministic Turing Machine is actually doing all of the choices at once.[t]

These strange ideas originated with Turing and other pioneers at the same time, and have developed into a rich theoretical field of research known as computability theory (sometimes also known as recursion theory). In this area, researchers try to understand non-computable functions, trying to figure out just how non-computable they are—perhaps some are more difficult than others even if none can be computed. It may all sound a little fanciful, but there are several very important findings for practical applications. One example is Rice's theorem,[27] which tells us that it is undecideable whether a particular language used by a Turing Machine has a non-trivial property. When applied to programming languages it means that there is no general method to decide non-trivial questions about a language. This basically means we can never write a program which will be able to debug automatically other programs perfectly. And that means we are likely to suffer buggy software forever.

Another important idea is a notion of complexity of strings. In computer science a string is a list of characters or numbers, such as 'abcdefg123456hijklmnop7890'. This could represent anything from an English sentence to an image or even a piece of music. The Kolmogorov complexity[28] of a string tells us how complex the string is. It's defined in terms of—you guessed it—Turing Machines. If a Turing Machine M with a given input of w is able to generate the string, and it uses the smallest, most compact, and efficient way that the string could be generated, then the Kolmogorov complexity of the string is the size of M and w combined. This means that the Kolmogorov complexity of something is not related to how complicated it may appear, it purely depends on how difficult it is to create that thing.

A fractal is a nice example. The Mandelbrot set[u] is infinitely complicated—you can zoom in and see more and more detail forever—and images of its mathematical diversity are very pretty to look at.[29] They can resemble coastlines, organic structures, or networks of rivers. But all of this infinite variety stems from the very simple equation: $x_{t+1} = x_t^2 + c$, so the Kolmogorov complexity is very low. We can generate the Mandelbrot set with very little information.

If you use computers then you will be familiar with the effects of Kolmogorov complexity, although you may be unaware of it. Try compressing any file (using a compressor such as gzip) and you will find that some appear to shrink in size far more than others. An image with very few elements will compress to a smaller file than an image full of complicated details. This is because the decompressor program needs enough information to generate the original image, and a more complex image, by definition, needs more information for it to be generated.

There are theoretical limits as to how small something can be compressed, and we gain clues about what those limits are when using the clever compression programs. Perhaps ironically, however, there is no general function that can calculate the Kolmogorov complexity of an arbitrary string. That function is uncomputable.[24]

Whether we can calculate it or not, often we want our files compressed beyond the theoretical limit, so lossy compressors are used. MP3 is one such example—because it compresses music beyond the theoretical limit, information is thrown away and so the music doesn't quite sound the same when played back compared to a pure, uncompressed CD file. The compression format is designed only to throw away those sounds we probably will not notice, but play the MP3 and CD versions one after the other and you should be able to hear the difference. The same thing applies to jpeg and tiff formats for images. Professional photographers always save their files as uncompressed tiff images because jpeg compression throws away information and the quality is not so good. Look closely at the detail in a jpeg version and it may seem fuzzy or blurred. But the difference in file sizes is so dramatic that most of us prefer jpeg anyway.[30]

Theoretical futures

The theoretical foundations of computer science, and many would argue, the field of computer science itself, began with the pioneering work of Alan Turing and his contemporaries. The tragic loss of Turing has not prevented his work from flowering into a hugely important body of knowledge that tells us what we can and cannot achieve with computers.

Theoretical computer science may sometimes seem a little mind-twisting, but it has never been more relevant. The ideas of computability and complexity that began with Turing are becoming ever more important as computers are used more. As we'll see in later chapters, the Internet is becoming an interconnected web of information and relationships, and querying it in order to retrieve complex patterns of information is very hard. Our software is becoming massively complicated, and debugging it—and making it work with all the other software you already have on your computer—is also very hard. A deeper theoretical understanding of computation will help us solve real problems better. 'Today we are dealing with vast amounts of data at such a large scale that the need to solve theoretical problems is greater,' says Hirsch. 'So looking for alternative models of computation which would allow us to process larger amounts of data in reasonable amounts of time…probably it means that the theoretical questions are more important now than they ever have been.'[19]

The challenge of P = NP is also still a real driving force for many people. Mark Herbster has no doubts about its significance. 'The most important idea in theoretical computer science today is the construction of time complexity classes and their study, leading to the key question of P = NP. It's one of the most important open problems in mathematics and computer science.'[18]

Had he lived, perhaps Turing would have already solved the question of P = NP for us. But the Millennium Prize of one million dollars is still available, and a revolution in new, more efficient computers would be created if anyone found the answer.

010

Disposable Computing

A billion times improved, what once filled large halls and cost millions are now so small and cheap that we throw them away like empty sweet wrappers. Their universal design and common language enables them to talk to each other and control our world. They follow their own law, a Law of Moore, which guarantees their ubiquity.

But how fast and how small can they go? When the laws of physics are challenged by their hunger and size, what then? Will they transform into something radical and different? And will we be able to cope with their future needs?

A high-pitched voice cut through the general murmur of the Bell Telephone Laboratories Cafeteria. 'No, I'm not interested in developing a powerful brain. All I'm after is a mediocre brain, something like the President of American Telephone & Telegraph Company.'[1] Alan Turing was in town.

Turing was visiting the Bell Labs towards the end of his American visit, in early 1943. He was there to help with their speech encipherment work for transatlantic communication (coding the transmission of speech so that the enemy could not understand it). But the visit soon became beneficial for a different reason. Every day at teatime Turing and a Bell Labs researcher called Claude Shannon had long discussions in the cafeteria.[a,1] It seemed they were both fascinated by the idea of computers. But while Turing approached the subject from a very mathematical perspective, Shannon had approached the topic from a different angle.

Claude Shannon was four years younger than Turing. Born in a small town called Petoskey, MI, USA, on the shores of Lake Michigan, his father was a businessman, and his mother was the principal of GayLord High School. Claude grew up in the nearby town of GayLord and attended his mother's school. He showed a great interest in engineering and mathematics from an early age. Even as a child he was building erector sets, model planes, a radio controlled boat, and a telegraph system to his friend's house half a mile away (making use of two barbed wires around a nearby pasture). He had a job delivering papers and telegrams, and also repaired radios for a nearby department store. His childhood hero was Thomas Edison who he later discovered was actually a distant cousin—they both were descendents of the colonial leader John Ogden.[2]

Although shy, Shannon was fascinated with tricks of balance such as unicycling and juggling. His practical skills meant he always looked for ways to exploit his mathematical ideas, perhaps by building a juggling machine or a strange type of unicycle.

By the age of twenty this modest and unassuming American had graduated with two Bachelors degrees in electrical engineering and mathematics from the University of Michigan, Ann Arbor. He then worked as a research assistant at the prestigious Massachusetts Institute of Technology (MIT), helping with their differential analyser machine. This was a mechanical device of cogs and wheels (and had a complex electromechanical circuit to control it) built a few years previously by Vannevar Bush, MIT's dean of engineering. It needed several days of effort to be reconfigured in order to calculate each new equation, and since Shannon was known as a tinkerer, he was given this task.[b,2]

A year later Shannon was an intern at the Bell Telephone Laboratory, learning about the automatic switches used in the telephone networks. While he was working there he realized something important. The young Shannon had recognized that two apparently very different things were actually the same.

Thinking logically

Claude Shannon returned to MIT to develop his new idea. It was still six years before he and Turing would lunch together (Turing was completing his PhD with Church, 250 miles away).

Shannon already knew about a type of mathematics called Boolean logic (named after a British mathematician called George Boole). Instead of worrying about numbers, in Boolean logic we only worry about two values: true or false. Logical operators such as AND, OR, and NOT are all you need to describe any logical statement you like. This statement might be an English sentence, e.g. 'I will take my umbrella when it's raining and it's either overcast or it's calm.'

We can turn this sentence into Boolean logic by looking at all the possibilities. If we're deciding whether to take our umbrella, let's call the decision Q. When Q is true, we take it, when Q is false we leave it at home. Since we're worrying about three things, let's label them too: A (raining), B (overcast), C (calm). So for every possible value of A, B, and C, there must be a value for Q (a decision about the umbrella). If we list them all, we draw a *truth table*:

A (raining)	B (overcast)	C (calm)	Q (take umbrella)
false	false	false	false
true	false	false	false
false	true	false	false
true	true	false	true
false	false	true	false
true	false	true	true
false	true	true	false
true	true	true	true

We can use the table to create a corresponding Boolean expression. Q is true on only three occasions: when A = true, B = false, C = true; or when A = true, B = true, C = false; or when A = true, B = true, C = true. Which can be written in something a little closer to Boolean algebra as:

Q = (A and not B and C) or (A and B and not C) or (A and B and C)

If we were a little silly, we could write that out and try to use it: 'I will take my umbrella when it's raining and not overcast and calm or when it's raining and overcast and not calm or when it's raining and overcast and calm.' But there are lots of handy rules for this kind of algebra that allow us to simplify this expression step-by-step, until we reach:

Q = A and (B or C)

which if you look carefully, perfectly represents our sentence about the umbrella earlier. So Boolean logic allows us to describe logical expressions and manipulate them in the same way that we can manipulate numbers with mathematical functions (and as we saw in the last chapter, all maths can be reducible to logic).

Shannon's breakthrough was that he had noticed how logic and electric switching circuits were equivalent. He had taken Boolean logic and used it to define electric circuits using electromechanical relays (electrical switches). He also showed how any arrangement of the switches could be written down as a logical expression. Figure 2 illustrates how Shannon drew the switches.[3]

The principle is very simple. If a switch is 'on' then that can be seen as equivalent to 'true' in Boolean logic. If the switch is 'off' then it's 'false' in Boolean logic. If you want to create a circuit with your switches that behaves like the AND operator, connect the switches in series (the output of the first one connected to the input of the second). Now the only way the circuit input is connected to the circuit output is when both switches are on. This matches the AND operator (sometimes written as a '+') because X AND Y is true only if both X is true and Y is true. If you want to create a circuit with your switches that behaves like the OR operator in Boolean logic, then wire the switches in parallel to each other (both connected to the same input and output). When either the first switch or the second switch (or both) is on, then they will make the output the same as the input, oth-

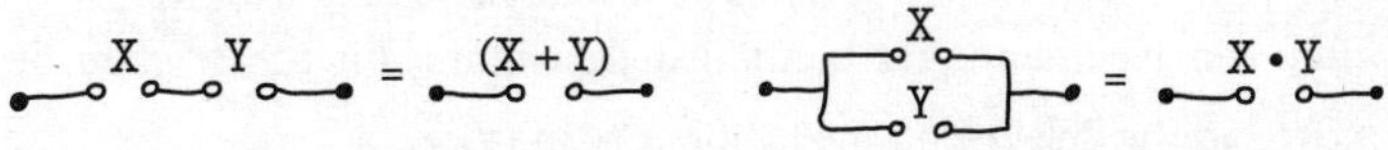

Figure 2. Shannon's Boolean logic AND and OR switches.

erwise the output is zero. This matches the OR operator (sometimes written as a dot), because X OR Y is true only if X is true or Y is true or they are both true. Shannon showed how entire circuits could be written down in Boolean logic and how manipulating logical expressions could be used to simplify and improve circuit designs.[a,4]

This was a time when the very first electrical computing machines were being built, so the ability to design a compact and efficient circuit from a logical mathematical expression was tremendously useful. And because all mathematics can be reduced to logic, and all logic could be performed using electrical switches, Shannon had shown how electric machines could be designed that could calculate any computable mathematical function.

Shannon decided to publish his idea in a paper entitled 'A Symbolic Analysis of Relay and Switching Circuits'. The work was a huge breakthrough. His paper formed the basis for his Master's thesis at MIT, which he completed soon after. The thesis has been described as 'possibly the most important, and also the most famous, Master's thesis of the century'[b,5] and he was awarded the Alfred Noble American Institute of American Engineers Award. Shannon himself remained modest, simply saying, 'I just wondered how things were put together'.[6]

Shannon went on to do his PhD on algebras describing genetics and evolution at the age of twenty-four, before spending a year at the prestigious Institute for Advanced Study (IAS) at Princeton as a National Research Fellow. There he was able to interact with some of the best minds in the world: Hermann Weyl, Albert Einstein, Kurt Gödel, and John von Neumann. He continued developing his ideas when he moved to the Bell Telephone Laboratory in 1941.

Two years later in the Bell Labs cafeteria, and Turing was tremendously excited by his discussions with Shannon—enough to exclaim loudly and distract others nearby. Here was a way that his Turing Machine could become a reality! When he left, Turing purchased an introductory book on electrical circuits, which he read during the dangerous sea voyage back to England.

Building brains

By chance, just as Turing returned to England in 1943, a mathematician called John von Neumann was visiting England from the USA. Von Neumann was the youngest member of the Institute for Advanced Study at the time (he had been one of the first five professors appointed, another being Einstein). He was very well connected. He knew Turing, for he had asked Turing to stay in Princeton after the Englishman had completed his PhD in 1938 and become a research assistant. Turing had turned down the offer, instead choosing to return to Cambridge, UK. Von Neumann had also met Shannon in 1940 at the IAS when Shannon worked there as a research fellow.

In England von Neumann was asked to try to mathematically predict the patterns of German magnetic mines being laid along the convoy routes to Britain—something he was able to do with ease.[7] While there, he also designed his first numerical procedure on a cash register NCR 3000 (an electrical adding machine) at the Nautical Almanac Office in Bath.[8] (He may have visited Turing,[8,7] but there is no clear evidence of such a meeting.) He wrote home, '...I have also developed an obscene interest in computational techniques.' That interest was to develop into something he never could have predicted.

Johnny von Neumann (as he was known to his friends) had always been exceptional. Born as János Neumann in 1903 in Budapest, Hungary, he became a child with extraordinary abilities. His father would show little Jancsi off at parties, for he could memorize a complete page of a phone book in seconds, then correctly recite names, addresses, and phone numbers. Von Neumann's father was a top banker (and bought the title in 1913 that added the 'von' to their name). János learned languages from his French and German governesses, and in 1911 entered the prestigious Lutheran Gymnasium. There his excellent mathematical skills were nurtured with additional tuition.

Von Neumann showed amazing abilities in mathematics at school, but at the request of his father, who wanted him to study something that would lead to a good job, he chose to study chemistry at the University of Berlin. (As a banker, his father had wanted his son to study business, but chemistry became the compromise.) He studied there from 1921 to 1923 before moving to the University of Zurich. In his spare time he attended mathematics courses, where his genius was quickly recognized. One mathematician who taught him later admitted, 'Johnny was the only student I was ever afraid of. If in the course of a lecture I stated an unsolved problem, the chances were he'd come to me as soon as the lecture was over, with the complete solution in a few scribbles on a slip of paper.'[9] He graduated with a Chemical Engineering Diploma in 1926, but in the same year received his doctorate in mathematics from the University of Budapest, showing clearly where his real interests lay. From 1926 to 1931 von Neumann lectured at several different universities, before being appointed Professor at the new Institute for Advanced Study in Princeton in 1931. He was working in quantum mechanics and had created the foundations of much of the mathematics in the area. By this time he was known as a young genius by other experienced mathematicians, gaining him celebrity status.[10] He regularly visited the nearby Princeton University, where Turing was to do his doctorate research with Church.

In the 1930s there was increasing interest in the creation of automatic computing machines. Mechanical machines using nothing but cogs and wheels had been around for centuries. Von Neumann was fascinated by these devices (especially a very impressive mechanical machine designed by Charles Babbage in the 1820s, which had many design features that resemble modern computers today). With the creation of electrically controlled switches called relays[c] came the possibility of using electricity to do the computing. There was no shortage of engineers creating their early computing machines. One of the earliest was created using relays by a German called Konrad Zuse, in Berlin.[d] This giant machine, known as the Z3, was slightly limited by the lack of conditional branching (it could not choose to do different things depending on the result of a calculation—it always had to do the same calculations in its program). It was also slow, because the relays had moving parts to switch the electricity on and off.

Much faster computers used valves (vacuum tubes)[e] which had no moving parts. In USA, in the 1930s, John Atanasoff at Iowa State College spent several years developing an electronic computing machine to solve linear algebraic equations. Working with his student Clifford Berry, they built the Atanasoff–Berry Computer, or ABC, a small and rather unreliable computer containing about 300 valves. Meanwhile British engineer Thomas Flowers developed his own valve-based switching system in 1934, which was put into service at the end of the decade. In his design more than 3000 valves were used for the British telephone exchange, and for simple data processing.

In 1943, after returning home, Turing encouraged Max Newman to approach Flowers and have him improve their existing relay-based decryption machine at Bletchley Park. By the end of 1943, Flowers had built Colossus I—an electronic computer containing 1600 valves. Ten were eventually built, each containing 2400 valves, but they were not general-purpose machines and had to be reprogrammed by plugging in different cables.[11]

By now von Neumann had also returned home to the USA from his visit to England. Because of his fame, he was invited to join the Manhattan Project where he would help design the explosive outer jacket for the atomic bomb. The mathematics involved were tremendously difficult and von Neumann realized he needed a computing machine far superior to anything currently available.

A chance meeting was to change everything. In the summer of 1944, he bumped into former mathematics professor Lt Herman Goldstine at a railway station in Maryland. Goldstine was now an army liaison to the Moore School of the University of Pennsylvania, where an amazing new computer was being built. Goldstine recalled the occasion: 'The conversation soon turned to my work. When it became clear that I was concerned with the development of an electronic computer capable of 333 multiplications per second, the whole atmosphere of our conversation changed from one of relaxed good humour to one more like the oral examination for the doctor's degree in mathematics.'[12]

Von Neumann immediately arranged to visit the designers: John Mauchly and J. Presper Eckert. Their design was the first general-purpose computer: the Electronic Numerical Integrator and Computer – ENIAC (Figure 3). It was to become a goliath with over 17,000 valves and 1500 relays, able to compute far quicker than anything before. It was also massive in size: 8.5 by three by eighty feet, and weighed about thirty tons. Von Neumann was soon visiting the Moore School regularly and was invited to join the group.

Progress on the ENIAC was slow and so before it was completed, the army commissioned the construction of a second, faster computer. The

Figure 3. The Electronic Numerical Integrator and Computer (ENIAC). Left to right: PFC Homer Spence; Chief Engineer Presper Eckert; Consulting Engineer Dr John Mauchly; Betty Jean Jennings; BRL-Upenn Liaison Officer Captain Herman Goldstine; Ruth Licterman, 1946.

successor to ENIAC was called the Electronic Discrete Variable Automatic Computer (EDVAC) and a certain Johnny von Neumann became a member of the design team. The design of the EDVAC continued for many months, and involved many new ideas and technologies. The idea of a memory to store data and instructions for the computer proved challenging—could they be stored using some version of radar or even television tubes? Von Neumann also investigated *instruction sets*—which functions should the computer be able to carry out? By June of 1945, von Neumann wrote a summary of the ideas from the Moore School group. It was just a first draft, and had only his name as the author. But a final version was never written. Instead, Goldstine encouraged the report to be distributed widely, with the result that the ideas were soon known by researchers and engineers worldwide. The report was called 'First Draft of a Report on the EDVAC'. It was the first publically available, coherent description of how to make a computer, and it was revolutionary.

Anatomy of a digital brain

Even though he was describing a work of engineering and mathematics, von Neumann wrote the report using language that almost anybody could understand. Here are some of his words, as he handwrote them on a train in 1945:[13]

In analyzing the functioning of the contemplated device, certain classificatory distinctions suggest themselves immediately.

First: Since the device is primarily a computer, it will have to perform the elementary operations of arithmetic most frequently. These are addition, multiplication and division. It is therefore reasonable that it should contain specialized organs for just these operations...a central arithmetic part of the device will probably have to exist and this constitutes the first specific part: CA.

Second: The logical control of the device, that is the proper sequencing of its operations can be most efficiently carried out by a central control organ...this constitutes the second specific part: CC.

Third: Any device which is to carry out long and complicated sequences of operations (specifically of calculations) must have a considerable memory...this constitutes the third specific part: M.

...The three specific parts CA, CC and M correspond to the associative neurons in the human nervous system. It remains to discuss the equivalents of the sensory or afferent and the motor or efferent neurons. These are the input and the output organs of the device.

Significantly, the design had five logical elements: the central arithmetic unit where all the work was done, the central control unit which determined what would happen next, the memory for storing the program and the results from the program, the input devices such as keyboards, and the output devices such as printers.

We can think of the working of von Neumann's design as being a little like five friends having a conversation. Let's say their names are Connie, Albert, Mary, Ian, and Oliver. Connie is very bossy. She likes to tell everyone what to do. Albert is a bit obsessed with his codebook. Although it may only contain a limited repertoire of codes, he always works out what everything means and gives his friends the results. He can also remember a few things briefly. Mary has a wonderful filing system. Ask her for any information and she'll provide it after a quick dig around. Finally, Ian and Oliver are talkative fellows. Ian is forever telling Mary to remember things and Oliver likes to chat to everyone he can.

Our five friends always play the same roles in a conversation. Here's an example of the kind of thing they say to each other:

Connie: 'Mary, Ian has something he wants to tell you.'

Ian: 'Mary, please keep the following seven numbers for me in your filing cabinet: 100, 010, 001, 101, 110, 110, 000.'

Mary: 'OK, Ian.'

Connie: 'Albert, why don't you start doing something?'

Albert: 'OK. Mary, can you tell me the first number that Ian gave you?'

Mary: 'It's 100, Albert.'

Albert: 'Thanks, Mary. Well that's interesting. According to my codebook, that means *add the next two numbers together*.'

Connie: 'Mary, Albert wants the next two numbers.'

Mary: 'The next two numbers are 010 and 001, Albert.'

Albert: 'Right, well according to my codebook, the sum of 010 and 001 is 011. I'll remember this result briefly.'

Connie: 'Albert, don't be lazy, do something again!'

Albert: 'Mary, would you tell me the next number, please?'

Mary: 'It's 101, Albert.'

Albert: 'Right, according to my codebook, that means *store the last result in the place given by the next number*.'

Connie: 'Mary, Albert needs the next number.'

Mary: 'It's 110, Albert.'

Albert: 'Thanks, you two. I need to store 011 in the file 110.'

Connie: 'Mary, Albert wants to store 011 in the file 110.'

Mary: 'OK, Albert.'

Connie: 'Albert, I want you to do something again!'

Albert: 'Yes, OK Connie. Mary, could you give me the next number, please?'

Mary: 'It's 110 again, Albert.'

Albert: 'Hmm... according to my codebook, that means *tell Oliver the last result*.'

Connie: 'Oliver, Albert has a number for you. It's 011.'

Oliver: 'Is it really? Thank you Albert.'

Connie: 'Albert, I want you to do something again!'

Albert: 'Yes, Connie. Mary, could I have the next number please.'

Mary: 'It's 000, Albert.'

Albert: 'Well, according to my codebook, that means *stop*.'

Connie: 'OK, everyone stop!'

At this point, all conversation usually ceases.

Connie, Mary, Albert, Ian, and Oliver correspond to the logical elements in von Neumann's design. Connie is the control—she tells everyone what to do, based on what Albert figures out.

Albert is the *arithmetic and logic unit* (ALU) and *registers* (von Neumann's central arithmetic unit).[f] This electronic device produces various electrical outputs (results) that depend on electrical inputs. The behaviour of the ALU is fixed and unchanging, determined by its Boolean logic circuits. It has temporary storage areas called registers that work in the same way as the memory (but access is considerably faster) designed to hold the results from the ALU and the memory.

Mary is the *memory*. Information in the form of binary 1s and 0s is stored by 'high' or 'low' voltages. In modern computers this kind of memory is often called RAM, or random access memory. The cryptic acronym just means that we can access *any* snippet of information instantly, without needing to spool through vast amounts of other data, as we would have to with magnetic or paper tape.

Finally, Ian is the input circuitry, which provides the interface from input devices such as keyboards and Oliver is the interface to output devices such as monitors and printers.

The 'conversation' provided above was an example of a *computation*. The seven numbers provided by the input circuits (Ian) and stored in the memory (Mary) comprised the program: a combination of instructions and data. The 'fetch–execute' cycle then began. The processor (Connie and Albert) requested each number in turn, decoded the instruction and executed it, with Albert doing the work and Connie controlling what everyone did. The results of execution could be anything from storing or reading numbers in the memory, the result of a calculation, or sending a result to an output peripheral device such as a monitor. The fetch–execute cycle only ends when an instruction tells the processor to stop.

Many aspects of the design (such as the use of a central memory to store data and instructions) are clearly influenced by the Turing Machine. One of von Neumann's colleagues, the Los Alamos physicist Stanley Frankel, knew how important Turing's work was at that time. 'I know that in or about 1943 or '44 von Neumann was well aware of the fundamental importance of Turing's paper of 1936…Von Neumann introduced me to that paper and at his urging I studied it with care.'[14]

Von Neumann was also well aware of Shannon's Boolean logic and how it could help, writing in his report:[13]

> An important part of the machine is not arithmetical, but logical in nature. Now logics, being a yes-no system, is fundamentally binary.

Von Neumann's draft report was to influence the world. Once the document had been made public and distributed by Goldstine, the effective and efficient design was copied by everyone. The von Neumann architecture, as it became known, has been used as a template for almost every computer ever since.[8,15,16] We may not refer to the elements as 'organs' or 'neurons' any more, but the same five logical, centralized, and serial elements are hidden within just about every computer in the world.

The end of the beginning

It was not until 1951 before the EDVAC was built. Although smaller than the ENIAC, the EDVAC still required 6000 valves (vacuum tubes) and consumed fifty-six kilowatts of power, needing an industrial-strength air-conditioning unit to keep it cool.

Nobody managed to build a useable general-purpose computer in time for the war. In fact some acrimony formed between von Neumann and the original designers, Mauchly and Eckert, who were not happy about the lack of recognition for their ideas, and wished to patent and commercialize their designs. Von Neumann (Figure 4) abandoned the EDVAC and instead decided to build a different computer at the Institute for Advanced Study, and this work soon inspired many other computers.[h,8]

Bruce Damer is the curator of the Digibarn Computer Museum in Santa Cruz and has studied the early history of computer science in some detail. 'John von Neumann's electronic computer project (ECP)

Figure 4. John von Neumann and the first computer at the Institute for Advanced Study (IAS), 1951.

at the Institute for Advanced Study was a fundamentally more fully-formed system than all of its predecessors,' he says. 'The overall system was exceedingly fast, capable of running programs with significant data input and output (H-bomb test calculations, weather predictions, artificial life simulation) for long periods of time without faults. The ECP progress and design was shared widely. IBM learned how to build its nascent computer business (700 series) through its association with the ECP. We live in a von Neumann world today with modern systems only exhibiting variations of the themes pulled together at Princeton by 1952.'[17]

But there was not just one pioneer of computers, and some people today regard the von Neumann architecture as something of a misnomer. For example, Maurice Wilkes at Cambridge University demonstrated the first practical stored-program electronic computer, using valves, back in 1949. Although inspired by von Neumann's report and lectures by Mauchly and Eckert at the Moore School, this machine was completed two years before von Neumann's IAS computer (and the EDVAC), and researchers working with Wilkes were to help von Neumann's team with their computer. Wilkes also helped invent many important ideas, such as microcode.[18,i]

Soon talented engineers in many universities and large corporations around the world were building their own massive computers. The machines were all huge, power-hungry goliaths, using thousands of valves. Many used punched cards to input the data and instructions. But these goliaths were expensive to build and frequently broke down. To make them more powerful, they needed more valves, which meant they needed to be even bigger, more power-hungry, and less reliable.

A new technology was needed, and in fact a new technology had just been invented. Just two years after von Neumann wrote his report, a device known as a 'transfer resistor'—quickly abbreviated to transistor—was invented in Bell Laboratories.[19] At a theoretical level the transistor could do exactly the same job as the vacuum tube, but in practice it had the enormous advantage that it could work many times faster, needed far less power, and was much smaller.[j]

The first computer made from transistors was built by a postgraduate student named Dick Grimsdale at Manchester University in 1953.[20] This began a flurry of activity, with over a hundred new transistor computers built in the following fifteen years around the world. But just five years after the first transistor computer had been demonstrated, electronics engineers were already facing a 'tyranny of numbers'—to make their computers more powerful they needed more transistors, but more transistors meant more expense in manufacture and maintenance as each component needed to be soldered into the circuit board by hand.

The problem was short-lived. In 1958, a new employee at Texas Instruments, Jack Kilby, thought of a revolutionary idea.[21] Why not create all the components at the same time? By etching a wafer of germanium, all the different components of a circuit could be integrated onto one tiny area. A few months later in 1959, another researcher called Robert Noyce independently came up with the same idea, this time using a wafer of silicon. The integrated circuit (IC), or silicon chip,[k] was born.

The invention came too late for von Neumann. He had been enormously busy producing an extraordinary array of work including quantum physics, game theory, nuclear physics, fluid dynamics, and computer science. His political views were robust—he remained a strong advocate of nuclear weapons and the pre-emptive strike. He also enjoyed a full social life—the parties of Johnny von Neumann and his second wife were legendary.[12] But in 1955, von Neumann was diagnosed with cancer. His colleague Eugene Wigner later remembered his friend's suffering. 'When von Neumann realized he was incurably ill, his logic forced him to realize that he would cease to exist, and hence cease to have thoughts…It was heartbreaking to watch the frustration of his mind, when all hope was gone, in its struggle with the fate which appeared to him unavoidable but unacceptable.'[22]

Another colleague and friend, Edward Teller, also recalled those final days. 'I think that von Neumann suffered more when his mind would no longer function than I have ever seen any human being suffer.'[23]

John von Neumann died in 1957, just three years after Turing, and two years before the invention of the silicon chip.

The Law of Moore

Robert Noyce and colleague Gordon Moore continued to develop the technology of integrated circuits at their company, the Fairchild Semiconductor Corporation, until 1968, when they founded a new company called Intel.[l.24] Their work and the work of many other pioneers around the world resulted in a transformation of electronics. While early integrated circuits only had a few hundred or thousand transistors, steady improvements in manufacturing techniques allowed more and more transistors to be placed on one chip. (Much of the early growth in the 1960s was driven by the American missile and Apollo Space programmes.)

The growth in complexity of integrated circuits led Gordon Moore to make a prediction in 1965,[25] when he noted that from the invention of the IC in 1958 to 1965, the number of transistors on a chip had doubled each year. He predicted that this trend would continue for at least another decade. He later revised this to say that the number of transistors on a chip would double every two years.[26] In 1970, the Caltech professor Carver Mead coined the term 'Moore's Law' for this prediction.

Remarkably, the 'law' appears to have held ever since.[m] By the mid-1970s, there were 10,000 transistors on a single chip. By 1986, we could fit more than one million transistors on one chip. By 2005, we could fit a billion transistors on a chip. Although there are frequent predictions that Moore's Law will soon break down because the tiny sizes of transistors are now approaching the limits allowable by the laws of physics, so far the improvement of this remarkable technology continues unchecked.

Computer technology has always embraced the very latest in electronics, so the amazing improvements in silicon chips corresponded to an equally amazing improvement to computers from the 1960s. A colleague of Moore at Intel, David House, estimated that Moore's Law meant that computer performance would double every eighteen months. He was nearly right—for many years, computer power has doubled about every twenty months. As Moore was to joke later: 'House said 18 months, not me.'[27]

Berkeley Professor Dave Patterson is a modern expert on computer architecture, author of most of the main textbooks on the topic, and former president of the Association for Computing Machinery. He also has strong links to the history of computer science. Not only did he co-invent the RAID hard disk technology,[n] his PhD advisor Gerald Estrin worked with von Neumann at IAS during 1950–6. (Indeed, von Neumann was intending to join Estrin at UCLA in the 1950s, but the move was sadly never to take place.)

Patterson speaks emphatically about Moore's prediction. 'Moore's Law was a big idea in computer science. Shortly after the first paper where he made the prediction, he wrote a paper explaining what the implications would be if Moore's Law were true. His paper has all the stuff we have today. It's got computers for individuals when at the time only banks or universities could own their own computer. It's got computers in cars. He extrapolated the consequences of the bold predictions that he'd made. That's astounding.

'Because of Moore's Law,' continues Patterson, 'because of this doubling every year or two of transistors, things are a billion times better than they were in the 1950s. We improved the speed and dropped the cost simultaneously. It's astounding what happened in hardware. And that's why computing technology is everywhere in the world today. That's why more than half the people on the planet have access to a cellphone (which I think of as a computer with wireless communication). Moore's Law let that happen—it made them faster, made them cheaper. The miracle was integrated circuits and the rapid increase of transistors. It's an amazing thing.'[28]

Because of the extraordinary miniaturization of electronics, our computers became smaller, cheaper, and more powerful every year. They began as giant mainframes, which many people needed to access through remote terminals (many keyboards and screens for the same big computer). Soon we had minicomputers, then personal computers—a computer for every desktop. These were then shrunk as more functionality was placed onto a single chip, until we had portable PCs, or laptop computers. These shrank further into netbooks, tablets, and palm devices such as smart phones. They became small and cheap enough to provide complex functionality in children's toys or even music in greetings cards, and be thrown away without a thought.[29]

There is no sign yet that the incredible shrinking computers will stop becoming smaller and cheaper.

But just because we can have more transistors for less money does not mean that computer scientists have stopped creating innovative new methods to make computers faster. Far from it. Although every one of our computers shares the same logical design elements that von Neumann described in his report, they also have a large diversity of very clever design optimizations to make them compute more quickly or more efficiently. For example, since the birth of computers it has always been the case that you need to sacrifice speed if you want more storage. We can make small memories very fast, but massive memories are always slower. We all experience something similar in everyday life—it's quick and easy to write a short shopping list and find a specific item that you wrote down. But write twenty years of detailed diaries of your life, and then try to find a specific item on a shopping list for one day—it takes much longer. So the solution is to use many different types of storage in combination. Computer processors today usually have a small number of super-fast internal memories called registers, a very fast internal cache memory (possibly a second, slightly larger but slower cache), a slower but larger external memory, an even slower but much larger hard disk, and perhaps a still-slower and even larger backup store (tape or hard disk). By swapping data and instructions from the slower storage into the faster storage at exactly the right time (like copying details you know you will need from a diary onto a piece of paper), your computer can find things quickly and run faster.°

Another typical optimization used in modern processors is known as pipelining.[30] The idea is remarkably similar to the factory production line. For example, it might take a day for a factory to build one car, yet the factory can churn out a new car every minute. The production line achieves this by dividing up all the tasks involved in making the car, and then running them all at the same time for different cars. For example, part of the process might involve welding the doorframe, followed by attaching the doors, followed by connecting the electric windows wiring. So car 1 will have its welding done, while car 2 (which is one stage ahead) has its doors attached, while car 3 (which is another stage ahead) has its electric windows connected. Then all the cars move along the conveyer belt to the next stage. A new car will have its welding done, while car 1 will now have its doors attached, and car 2 will have its electric windows connected. In computer processors, exactly the same principle is used. Instructions or sets of instructions are broken into separate tasks and as many of those tasks as possible are carried out in parallel. The more pipeline stages that a processor has, then the more instructions it can potentially carry out in parallel.[p]

Pipelining is not the only way for a computer to execute instructions in parallel. Other methods include using a vector processor that can perform vector calculations (manipulate lists of numbers instead of one number at a time) or simply to have many processors running at the same time in parallel. There have been many 'supercomputers' over the years that work according to these principles. By late 2010, the Chinese Tianhe-1A supercomputer[q] was the fastest in the world. It had 14,336 six-core processors and 7168 448-core processors,[r] which is like having 3297,280 processors in one computer. Even in this modern era of cheap, tiny, throwaway computers, the Tianhe-1A cost eighty-eight million dollars to build, twenty million a year to run, and took up 100 square metres of floor space. It could calculate over two and a half thousand million million floating point operations per second (2.566 peta-

FLOPS), making it one of the first petascale computers (but not likely to be the last).[5]

These massive computers are marvels of design, but in fact today even individual computer processors comprise some of the most complicated designs humans have ever created. They are so monstrously complex that other computers are used throughout the design process to help us. No-one designs where to place individual transistors on a chip any more—indeed most of the time no-one designs much of the low-level circuitry on a processor. The design details of tomorrow's computers are calculated and tested by today's computers.

The future is many

The advances in our computer technology seem limitless, and indeed Moore's Law might make you think that we can just keep making processors smaller, cheaper, and faster forever. But no exponential growth can last forever. In fact, we've already hit a problem.

Professor of computer architecture, Dave Patterson, explains. 'What's happened was in the last ten or fifteen years we increased how much power you burned on a chip every time you had more transistors. We ran into the limit of what you can economically dissipate. That's about 100 watts and we ran into that limit in about 2003. Since then rather than having very inefficient single processors on a chip, we have made a transition to multiple, much more efficient processors. It's not because we had a breakthrough in programming. It's because power limits us. If we wanted to take advantage of Moore's Law, the only way we could get more performance was parallel computers. This means we change the programming model, which is one of the biggest changes in the last sixty years of computing.'[28]

So the problem is not Moore's Law. It seems that we will continue the trend to place more and more transistors on silicon chips for many years to come. The problem is that a big complex processor gets hot when it works. Nobody wants third degree burns from their laptop—nor do we want our processors melting their own circuit boards. The only solution is to create smaller, simpler processors that individually use less power and then place many of them together on the same chip. This transition in processor design has already begun. It's why when you buy a new computer today, its clock speed (which is how quickly it looks at each new instruction) may not have got any faster, but the number of 'cores' inside its processor may be considerably more.

But there is a problem. Writing software to make effective use of parallel or multi-core processors is still extremely difficult for programmers. We have the hardware already, but the software often does not exploit all of the computing power available. Patterson agrees. In a recent article he wrote that, 'the switch to parallel microprocessors is a milestone in the history of computing.'[31]

'It's a risky milestone,' he explains. 'We turn this corner and we're not sure we can make this work well yet. And yet nevertheless we're on the path. I believe we're in the next shift of computing.

'It wasn't like there was a breakthrough that made parallel programming easy,' says Patterson. 'We were desperate—there was no other viable path forward for us. And so we have taken that path and are hoping that people will be able to write good parallel programs that take advantage of the hardware.

'I use the analogy of a Hail Mary path,'[32] continues Patterson. 'In American football where you throw the ball forward at the end of the game where there is no hope, you kinda close your eyes and throw the ball as far as you can and hope somebody catches it. That's the analogy. And it's pretty easy to throw the ball. Closing your eyes and throwing it and saying a prayer is easy. It's the catching that's the hard part. I'd say the ball is in the air and we're going to see whether people can innovate and somebody is going to catch this. The industry is betting that somebody will. It's a very interesting time.[28]

There are many computer scientists attempting to catch Patterson's Hail Mary ball, but for now the problem remains unsolved. We still haven't figured out how best to write parallel software that exploits the new architectures. How do you write a parallel word processor? Or a parallel email program? Thankfully, however, some applications are already naturally parallel. One example is perhaps the most visible—the amazing computer graphics we see on every modern computer. Computer graphics often comprise many thousands of little flat-sided shapes called polygons, glued together, with photograph-quality images stretched over the top. It's like making models out of chicken wire and then wrapping them with perfect photos to make them look completely real.[i] When the computer animates a character in a game, or shows a car driving on a track, or even just displays windows and icons, it is changing the position of those thousands of polygons and images at once, each in very similar ways. It's therefore very easy to perform all those calculations in parallel and speed everything up. In fact, it is so easy to parallelize graphics that today the most advanced multi-core computer architectures are the graphics processing units (GPUs). These processors already have hundreds of cores, all computing in parallel. So most games consoles, PCs, and even small portable computers use parallel GPUs to make their graphics smooth and realistic. Graphics processing units are becoming so fast, with so many cores, that they now form an important part of many supercomputers.

The trend towards parallel processing is not only apparent inside a single chip. A new paradigm called cloud computing provides a dynamic virtual architecture that may change our perception of computers. It enables computer users to buy processing time, use of software, and storage on multiple computers elsewhere, without needing to know any details about where those computers are physically located or how any of the components work. Conceptually, cloud computing treats computers like a resource—for example, we all use electricity and water and need have no knowledge about where it was generated or processed. Cloud computing provides the ability to use the latest software, perform intensive calculations, host Web pages, while the physical computers are located elsewhere, and are upgraded and maintained invisibly. The online bookstore Amazon was a key innovator in cloud computing. It realized that often only about ten per cent of its large data centres were being used, so in 2006 the company began selling its spare capacity as Amazon Web Services.[33] Other companies can buy access to all the computing, software, and storage they need without needing to maintain or update any computers. This idea is gaining popularity and it looks likely that the future for many businesses may be to buy their computing needs from a 'cloud' rather than build and maintain their own internal computer systems. It may also be a method for users to perform parallel processing across many computers in a cloud without needing to worry about how the tasks are divided up—as long as the cloud software is clever enough to figure out how to do it.[34]

Our cars are another example of easy-to-achieve parallel processing.[u] A modern car may have more than 100 microprocessors all working together to keep the engine and transmission running smoothly, control instrument panels, door locks, parking sensors, radio, GPS, lights, wing mirrors, seat adjustments…Indeed most cars have their own computer networks so that the computers can collaborate effectively. You may have experienced the result of your car's computer network when the volume of the radio automatically increases as the engine works harder. Some clever cars link together the airbag accelerometer, parking lights, GPS navigation, cell phone, and door locks so that if you have a nasty accident, the car calls an emergency number, sends your GPS coordinates, unlocks the doors, and flashes the car's lights.[35]

Beyond von Neumann

But some people believe that even these amazing advances are not enough. Professor Steve Furber of Manchester University began his career designing the thirty-two-bit ARM32 microprocessor[v] for Acorn. It's a massively popular design, with over twenty billion ARM cores now shipped—that's more processors (which are worth more) than Intel's chip sales.[36] For many years more than ninety per cent of mobile phones used at least one ARM core. But despite Furber's conventional computer design background, in 1998 he decided he would change direction. He had realized that biological brains seemed to have much superior computing and memories to those of our computer processors. 'In the end I threw in the towel,' says Furber. 'Blow this, what I'm interested in is neural networks.'[36]

Furber is now one of a growing number of computer designers working on biologically inspired computers. His ambitious design is called *SpiNNaker*—a universal spiking neural network architecture based on many hundreds or thousands of ARM microprocessors working in parallel. He is not the only computer scientist with the same idea. Processors that resemble the neurons in our brains, cells in our immune systems, or genes within individual cells are now all being designed. Some researchers are even attempting to move away from silicon and use other materials to process information. Can we create computers by storing information in strands of DNA and allowing them to mix? Can we create computers by genetically modifying bacteria? Can we create quantum computers that calculate using the weird quantum effects in physics?[w,37]

Professor Andy Tyrrell of the University of York is a computer engineer who specializes in bio-inspired computers. He believes that in the near future the architecture of computers will still resemble the classic von Neumann design. 'But one might imagine small "pockets" of computer engineers creating new (and hopefully exciting) architectures, possibly manufactured with different (or mixtures of) media, such as molecular devices, memresisters, bio-electrical mixes, different chemical structures (Liquid Crystal has already been tried) or probably something that we don't know about yet.'

Tyrrell believes nature can teach us something about how to make computers work better because they provide good examples of managing complexity with high levels of reliability. 'The difficult question is how do we map from one medium to the other and continue to keep the important characteristics? Biology appears to be able to create systems with many more components (and more complex) than we could imagine. So the big challenges seem to be how do we make such systems, what might they be made of and how do we harness their power?'[38]

We may not have solved all the problems yet, but there are few fields of research that move quicker than computer science. No technology has ever been improved faster and more effectively than the computer.

You can be sure that tomorrow's computer architecture will be faster, cheaper, and more parallel.

From the earliest pioneers to today's electronics engineers and computer designers, some of the world's best brains provide the imagination and hard work to build the extraordinary computer-filled world we enjoy today. If you design computers, you change the world.

Your Life in Binary Digits

Your ideas, money, memories, and entertainment are dreams in the minds of computers. But the thoughts of each computer are not simple, they are layered like our own minds. Their lowest, most primitive layers are the instincts of the machine. Middle layers perform more general functions of its silicon mind. Higher layers think about overall concepts.

Unlike us, the computer has languages for every layer. We can teach it new ideas by changing any one or all of its layers of thought. We can tell it to consider vast and convoluted concepts. But if we make a single mistake in our instructions, the mind of our digital slave may crash in a virtual epileptic fit.

When our silicon students are so pedantic, how can we engineer their thoughts to make them reliable and trustworthy assistants? And if their thoughts become more complicated than anything we can imagine, how can we guarantee they will do what we want them to?

Light poured in through the large windows of the lecture room. The sound of scratching pens from nearly thirty distinguished engineers and scientists accompanied every word spoken by John Mauchly. One fellow by the name of Gard from the Wright Field's Armament Laboratory seemed to be especially diligent, writing hundreds of pages of notes.[1]

It was Monday morning, a warm mid-summer day of 1946, some three years after his stimulating tea-time discussions with Turing. Claude Shannon was three weeks into the eight-week course at the Moore School of Electrical Engineering, in the University of Pennsylvania. It had been an honour to be one of the select few invited to hear lectures on designing electronic digital computers. This was the first ever course to be taught on computer science, and Shannon was finding many of the ideas highly stimulating. He'd recently learned a new word from Mauchly: 'program' used as a verb.[2] To *program* an electronic computer was an interesting concept. He was also hearing about some of the politics: apparently two of the lecturers, Mauchly and his colleague Eckert, had resigned from the university just four months ago because of some form of disagreement. Another lecturer, Goldstine, was apparently moving to the Institute for Advanced Study (IAS) to join Shannon's old colleague John von Neumann. And while von Neumann was supposed to be giving a lecture in two weeks time, it seemed that he might not show up, because of a prior engagement.[3]

The chair creaked as Claude Shannon shifted position. He glanced around the room. John Mauchly's voice was clear and confident as he gave his latest lecture. Today the subject was the conversion between binary and decimal number systems. Although Shannon knew the topic very well already, it was of particular interest to him because of his cryptography research.

Shannon had already published some of his recent work on cryptography at Bell Labs in a classified paper.[4] It was a continuation of ideas from his MSc project on switching circuits, but now focused on the maths behind cryptography. He was beginning to realize that decoding a scrambled message was much the same thing as correcting errors in a transmitted message. For example, it is much easier to decode a message that has repeated information—perhaps it contains many common words such as 'the', 'a', 'and'. Because we know that these short words are commonly used in sentences, even if all the letters are scrambled we can figure out which words are likely to be which, and that may lead to much of the code being cracked. So to make coded messages harder to crack, you need less redundant information. However if you wish to preserve as much information as possible, perhaps with a memory storage system that commonly causes errors, then it is better to have lots of redundant information. One method with binary numbers might be to have an extra 'parity' bit at the end of each chunk of bits, which is 1 if the total number of '1's in that chunk is odd (making it an even number of 1s), and 0 if the number of '1's is already even. Then if a chunk of bits including the parity bit contains an odd number of '1's you know there has been an error, and the information should be reread. (The method was introduced into computers from the early 1950s, with other more advanced methods soon following.)

Back at the Moore School Lectures, Shannon learned how important binary was for computers, how they also needed to transmit their binary numbers between their internal components, and store and retrieve the information without error. In later years, Shannon would coin the term *bit* for binary digit, and explain exactly how information could be measured, transmitted, encrypted, compressed. and corrected.[a]

But Shannon was not the only computer pioneer to attend the lectures. Maurice Wilkes was another—although he very nearly missed them. On the day Shannon heard Mauchly's lecture on binary and decimal systems, Wilkes was still in England.

Born in Dudley, 1913, Wilkes suffered from ill-health as a child. Asthma and allergies affected his life so much that he was placed at the bottom of the lowest form in his first school, at age eight. His headmaster wrote, 'handicapped by absence' in red ink on his end-of-year report, and Wilkes was one of a handful held back a year. But second time around, Wilkes found himself doing much better, and from that moment never looked back. His excitement at entering the main school four years later was borne out of a love of mathematics and science. Wilkes had always enjoyed the subjects. 'I cannot remember a time when I did not know I would be a scientist or engineer,'[5] he says. His favourite toys were mechanical, and he spent many hours as a child tinkering with batteries, bulbs, bells, and later building crystal radio sets and teaching himself electronics by reading *Wireless World*. He studied physics and mathematics in sixth form, before entering Cambridge to read mathematics. He and Alan Turing both studied the same course in Cambridge at the same time, but somehow never noticed each other. While Turing went on to do an advanced mathematics course with Max Newman in 1934, Wilkes joined the Cavendish radio group and performed research on the propagation of very long radio waves in the ionosphere. Wilkes also continued his practical interests, modifying a model differential analyser machine made out of Meccano[b] parts so it could be used for differential equations. Before long he became the main technician involved in procuring and installing a large mechanical differential analyser machine in the university's new Mathematical Laboratory. He also obtained his MA, followed by a PhD by 1939.[5]

As war looked ever more likely, Wilkes was introduced to the secret work on radar in the UK. Wilkes's experience in radio and practical mathematics made him a natural to join the teams installing the new radar sets along the coastline of Britain to detect ships. Radar became his occupation during the war years. Wilkes first worked on experimental radar in the Air Defence Experimental Establishment in Christchurch. By 1943, he had moved to the Royal Air Force's Telecommunications Research Establishment in Worth Matravers, Dorset, where he helped with the radar used by bombers for targeting. Shortly after the war was over, Wilkes volunteered to go into war-ruined Germany and interview prisoners taken in several different German scientific centres, to learn of their war research. He then returned to Cambridge to work.

Back in familiar surroundings, Wilkes realized that there was a real need for automatic computing machines. He had heard of the work by Eckert and Mauchly as they built the ENIAC in the USA, and wrote a report for the Faculty in February 1946. 'There is a big field out here, especially in the application of electronic methods which have made great progress during the war and I think Cambridge should take its part in trying to catch up some of the lead the Americans have in this subject.'[5]

Just three months later and Leslie Comrie, an expert on mechanical computation, came to visit. He had come from the USA, and he had a copy of a report entitled 'Draft Report on the EDVAC' by a mathematician called John von Neumann. Wilkes had one night with the report. With no photocopiers in existence, he could only read and take notes. Wilkes was immediately inspired. 'I recognized this at once as the real thing,' he says, 'and from that time on never had any doubt as to the way computer development would go.'[5] With these ideas still fresh in his mind, Wilkes suddenly received a telegram from Dean Pender of the Moore School, inviting him to attend a course on electronic computers, starting in just a few weeks time. Travel was still tightly restricted, so Wilkes feared he would not receive permission to travel. The course began on 8 July, but it was not until 23 July that he finally was given clearance to sail on a small ship that would leave at the beginning of August. Wilkes agreed—he had no other option.

The journey was not a smooth one. Although the food was excellent, conditions were cramped with thirty-five people staying on a cargo ship designed for twelve. To make matters worse, the ship's engines broke down several times during the voyage. They finally reached New York on 15 August, and Wilkes made it to Philadelphia on the 18th. He had missed two-thirds of the course, but luckily for him, it had mostly been introductory material. He arrived on Monday 19 August just in time to join the class who were in the middle of a detailed study of the ENIAC, complete with circuit diagrams.

Wilkes made the most of his visit, having a private view of the ENIAC with Mauchly and discussing constructional details. He also arranged to meet Goldstine, since he had arrived too late for Goldstine's lectures. Over dinner they discussed more details of von Neumann's ideas for the logical design of the new computer to be built at the IAS. Wilkins also travelled to Boston to meet other designers of computing machines: Aiken and his Automatic Sequence Controlled Calculator and his relay-based Mark II under construction. He also met Caldwell at MIT, who had designed an improved mechanical differential analyser with electrical gearboxes.

He returned to Cambridge with a head full of ideas, and some key advantages over the Americans. While they were reorganizing themselves and forming new companies and research groups after the split from the Moore School, Wilkes was now the Director of the Mathematical Laboratory at Cambridge, which had achieved the status of a full university department, and had plenty of funding.

Wilkes decided it was time to build a useable stored program computer. Before long he was lucky enough to receive funding and technical personnel from catering giant J. Lyons and Company who were looking for computers to handle accounting and payroll. Progress was fast, especially with Wilkes's experience in radar, which helped them produce a working memory system for storing numbers.[c]

As he continued to build his machine, Wilkes attended a couple of lectures by Turing on Turing's ideas for his Automatic Computing Machine. But he and Turing did not see eye to eye on the design of computers. Turing believed the computer should be built by producing an optimal design around the mercury memory system. Wilkes had a contrasting opinion. 'I took the view that it was only a matter of time before mercury memories would be replaced by truly random access memories. I argued therefore that in a situation in which there was obviously so much to be learnt about programming, it would be a mistake to divert effort into developing techniques which could only be of short-term value.' Turing also did not think highly of Wilkes's designs, writing in a memo that one of Wilkes's ideas was 'much more in the American tradition of solving one's difficulties by means of much equipment rather than by thought'.[5]

But Wilkes's approach was proven to be the most pragmatic. The Cambridge EDSAC computer became operational on 6 May 1949,[d] and remained in continuous use until 1958. It was the first practical stored-program computer in the world.[e,6]

Learning to program computers

The EDSAC was more than a pioneering machine. Because it stored its own program in a memory rather than being reconfigured through plugging in different wires, it also necessitated many foundational aspects of software. Wilkes and his researchers such as David Wheeler helped to invent or improve many of the ideas now considered mainstream in computer programming.

But programming was not easy. All the early pioneers soon realized that having a stored-program computer meant one thing—you had to work extremely hard to write the program that the computer would then follow. If every program was nothing more than a set of binary numbers which triggered mathematical or logical circuits (as we saw in the last chapter), then writing software would be a nightmare—and indeed it was. Wheeler recollected his first realization of this in June 1949. 'I was trying to get working my first non-trivial program. It was on one of my journeys between the EDSAC room and the punching equipment that "hesitating at the angles of the stairs" the realisation came over me that a good part of the remainder of my life was going to be spent in finding errors in my own programs.'[5]

It was clear that some new ideas were needed to simplify and improve their ability to program computers. One idea by Wilkes (which was to come a couple of years later), was to expand the set of instructions available to the programmer by a trick called *micropro-gramming*. Partly inspired by a computer being built at MIT called the Whirlwind, Wilkes realized that it was not necessary for every low-level instruction, such as divide, to be implemented as electronic circuits. Instead, more complex instructions could be built from combinations of simpler ones, and microcode—little low-level programs—would act as the interface between the binary machine code and the hardware. The idea was to prove enormously useful, and complex instruction set computer (CISC) processors to this day still use the same idea in order to enable highly complex operations to be performed. (Reduced instruction set computer or RISC processors do not use microprogramming.)

But even with microcode, programming computers still involved writing long lists of numbers—the machine code instructions. The early programmers were also hampered by the extremely limited memory of these pioneering computers. The EDSAC only had about two kilobytes[6,7] (today even a mobile phone may have memories many millions of times this size). So to tackle these problems, another trick was invented by Wilkes's team[8]—the subroutine. They realized that many programs needed the same operations—they needed to take the square root of a number, or perhaps perform some other more complex operation with some numbers. If the square root code had to be repeated every time the operation needed to be performed, then programs would become unnecessarily large and filled with repeated code. In English it would be like writing a definition of every word. Instead of writing:

> The cat sat on the mat.

we'd have to write:

> definite article used before a noun with a specifying or particularizing effect, noun meaning a small domesticated feline carnivore, a simple past tense and past participle of verb meaning to rest or lie, preposition meaning so as to be or remain supported by, definite article used before a noun with a specifying or particularizing effect, noun meaning a piece of fabric made of plaited or woven material used as a protective covering on a floor.

Wilkes's trick was to create libraries of subroutines—common functions that only needed to appear once in a program, like the definitions of words in a dictionary. Then whenever a program was written that used one of the functions, the computer could 'look up the definition' in the library and execute the appropriate subroutine code, sending input values and receiving the results back.

In this respect, Wilkes was ahead of most. When von Neumann dropped by for a surprise visit, Wilkes recalled how their approaches differed. 'He thought that the instruction sets of computers might come to include a square root operation…My own standpoint was somewhat different, since I had come to regard subroutines as providing an extension to the basic instruction set and did not feel there was any longer a case for built-in special functions.'[5]

Because the Cambridge team were pioneering the writing of software so early, they also began to invent the art of programming. Von Neumann at Princeton liked to draw 'flow diagrams' to show how programs should work—basically a series of steps with arrows between them to show the flow of control.[h] However, Wilkes's best programmer David Wheeler believed other approaches were needed. 'We were particularly interested in making it easy for the users to get results, and we concentrated on that quite a lot,' he says. 'The programming styles were modularized very early on. That was the way we taught. We certainly knew, for example, about von Neumann's flow diagrams. These were never used, except possibly as an explanation of what had been done. We discovered that if you basically took the problem, decomposed it into subroutines, and put these under the control of the master routine, this more or less forced you to think modularly and enabled you to do all these programs without going to the flow diagrams, which in my own personal opinion contributed more to bad programming than almost anything else. This is not to say that they don't have their place, but if they're used as a substitute for thought in the preparation of your program, they don't work.'[7]

Ideas of programming with subroutines are now so well established that almost every programming language ever created makes use of the same concept. Modern programmers make use of libraries of functions, just as they did back in 1949 with the EDSAC. Today it would be inconceivable to program a computer in any other way.

Wilkes's team had also anticipated other difficulties that programmers might face. Although the computer only understood numbers, they realized right from the start that few people could just write programs as lists of numbers and understand what the computer would do. Our brains are used to reading words and symbols, not lists of numbers. Wheeler believed that the IAD computer built by von Neumann compared poorly to their solution because of this. 'It struck me by being remarkably primitive,' he says. 'The programs, I think, were input in binary. At Cambridge we started out very early by having an "assembler". It essentially converted programs as they were written, went from decimal to binary, used mnemonics, had a reference scheme, allowed compartmentalization, allowed for automatic positioning of library routines, and had various other facilities built in as well. This was all from, roughly, the day we started. This made it very much easier to put programs together.'[7]

So instead of writing binary numbers, programmers were able to write programs using little words that looked a little like English words:

```
cmpl    $7, -4( %ebp)
jle     .L6
jmp     .L4
```

which means: compare the value of a variable[i] to the number seven; jump to another region of the program marked with label.L6 if the variable is less than or equal to seven; otherwise, jump to label.L4.[j]

This strange and obscure-looking language is considerably easier to read and understand than writing lists of binary numbers. It's not that different from the low-level codes used by the processor: each word (or command) in the language (such as 'cmpl' or 'jmp') corresponds directly with an instruction in machine code. To convert your assembly language program into the corresponding machine code, another computer program called an assembler is used. The assembler reads in the text written in assembly language and outputs the binary machine code.

Assembly language was so important that whole programs were written in assembly into the 1990s. For many decades two common types of program were written exclusively in assembly language: computer games (because programmers wanted their games to run quickly and squeeze in lots of gameplay) and operating systems.[k] Even today, if programmers want to write extremely fast and compact code, they may write some of it in assembly language.

Climbing higher

By 1951, computers were being clothed in several layers of software. The first layer (microcode) fitted the electronics precisely. The next layer was slightly more general (machine code). The layer above was slightly more readable (assembly language).

To program the computer—to tell it which of those logical and arithmetic circuits it should be using—programmers could write their code using assembly, which as we have seen looked *slightly* like English words. These would then be assembled into machine code, which defined microprograms that were translated into the combinations of instructions within the electronics of the arithmetic and logic unit (ALU).

But assembly language was still much too much of a challenge for many programmers. If you wanted to process more complicated ideas and concepts, dealing with individual memory move or jump instructions was just slowing you down. And what if you wanted your program to run on a completely different processor? Higher-level programming languages were needed; computer languages independent of the underlying hardware.

In 1953, with many of the new electronic computers up and running around the world, the topic of more abstract programming languages was on everyone's minds. Maurice Wilkes was asked to chair a session on the topic (then called automatic programming) at the Association for Computing Machinery (ACM) meeting in MIT. Wilkes remembered the discussions clearly. 'The participants in the session divided quite sharply in their opinions. There were those who felt that all attempts to sidestep the real and eternal difficulties of programming were misguided, and that more progress would be made if programmers kept to their real job of application programming. On the other hand, there were those who saw the new techniques as having a real and very practical value.'[5] (It is still possible to identify the same kinds of opinions amongst computer scientists to this day.)

Already many researchers had been experimenting with newer, easier languages. John Mauchly had invented a language called Brief Code, later renamed as Short Code, back in 1949. While much easier to use, it was interpreted—in other words, the computer had to translate the language into machine code, on the fly, each time it ran the program. This meant that programs in Short Code would run about fifty times slower compared to their machine code equivalents.[8,1] Meanwhile in Manchester, UK, a researcher called Alick Glennie had invented something different for their computer.

It was an easy to use language, and programs written in this language could be converted automatically into machine code by another program, giving the advantage of simpler programming with fast execution. He called it *Autocode*. Here's a fragment of a real Autocode program:[9]

```
n1 = 0
13) PRINT v(300 + n1), 4024
n1 = n1 + 1
-> 13, n1 # n20
TEXT
NUMBER OF LIQUID MOLES =
PRINT v215, 4040
STOP
```

It was clearly considerably easier to write programs in Autocode compared to assembly language. Some statements in Autocode corresponded to several machine code instructions, but the programmer did not have to worry about the machine code. By using another program called a *compiler*, the nice English commands of Autocode were simply translated into machine code. This was the first ever compiled high-level programming language.[m,10]

In the years following the meeting at MIT, more and more computer scientists realized that programming had to be made easier. By 1957, John Backus at IBM had produced another compiled high-level language called FORTRAN (meaning formula translation). This was even more advanced, and enabled the programmer to write more complicated programs. Its compiler was also extremely clever, designed to produce very efficient and compact machine code. Here's an example FORTRAN program—a sorting subroutine:[11]

```
1          SUBROUTINE SORT (A, N)
           DIMENSION A (150)
           DO 4 J = 2, N
           SMALL = A (J - 1)
           DO 4 I = J, N
           IF (A (I) - SMALL) 3, 4, 4
3          SMALL = A (I)
           A (I) = A (J - 1)
           A (J - 1) = SMALL
4          CONTINUE
           RETURN
5          END (2, 2, 2, 2, 2,)
10         DIMENSION ALPHA (150), BETA(100)
```

Before long FORTRAN compilers had been written for many other computers, allowing the same FORTRAN program to be compiled into the specific machine code of each machine. From that moment on programmers could write 'portable' code—the same program could be executed on completely different computers. Many other languages soon followed, such as ALGOL, LISP, and BASIC. They were steadily improved as computer designers began building transistor-based machines.

Soon computer scientists were able to analyse programming languages and formalize them using mathematics—including the lambda calculus of Church (from the second chapter). Programmers were able to write more abstract concepts in their code, without needing to worry about the tricky lower-level details underneath. Different types of programming language were invented. While the early languages were *procedural* (the programmer told the computer what to do step by step), later languages used other approaches. In object-oriented languages,[n] data and methods for manipulating the data are encapsulated into 'objects' in order to help modularize the code and stop accidental damage to data ('side-effects' in programs). In functional programming languages,[o] the computer is told what to do by the use of a series of functions (rather than a series of changes in states as defined by a procedural language). Yet more programming language types were created for parallel computer architectures.

Many of the early pioneers were responsible for some of the key ideas we now take for granted in computer programming. Wilkes continued to be involved in computer languages, helping to develop the language CPL by modifying ALGOL 60. The language was not a great success[5] but formed the seed for a later language called BCPL, which then helped inspire a language called B, and subsequently C. To this day, C (and its many variants, including C++, C#, Objective C) is perhaps one of the most widely used computer programming languages. Many of the familiar operating systems in use (such as UNIX, Linux, Mac OS X, and Windows) were written in C. Almost every computer today has a C compiler allowing you to write code in this language. Here's an example Quicksort function (the same Quicksort we met in the second chapter) written in C:[p]

```c
void quicksort(int arr[], int low, int high)
{   int i = low;
    int j = high;
    /* compare value */
    int z = arr[(low + high)/2];
    /* partition */
    do
    {    while(arr[i] < z) i + +;/* find member above */
         while(arr[j] > z) j--;/* find element below */
         if (i < = j)
         {swap(arr[i],arr[j]);/* swap two elements */
         i + +; j--;
```

```
        }
    } while(i < = j);
    /* recurse */
    if (low < j) quicksort(arr, low, j);
    if (i < high) quicksort(arr, i, high);
}
```

Maurice Wilkes (Figure 5) continued making achievements in computer science throughout his life. He was elected a fellow of the Royal Society in 1956; he helped found the British Computer Society (BCS) and was its first president from 1957 to 1960. He received the Turing Award in 1967 for his work on the EDSAC. In 2000, he was knighted by the Queen. Wilkes died peacefully in his home in November 2010 at the age of 97.

Figure 5. Sir Maurice Wilkes in front of the oldest working electronic computer (originally built for the Atomic Energy Research Establishment in Harwell in 1951) at the National Museum of Computing, Bletchley Park, 2009.

'The person who built the first operational stored-program computer was Maurice Wilkes. He and the people he worked with came up with a lot of ideas, software and hardware. I would say Wilkes was very influential,' says David Patterson.[12]

Computer historian Professor Simon Lavington agrees about the significance of Wilkes. 'If any person deserves the title of the father of British computing, it is surely Professor Sir Maurice Wilkes.'[13]

Bases for data

As programming languages grew in their capabilities, computers became faster and storage became larger and more reliable.[q] Soon computer scientists realized that computers could do more than calculate the results for equations. They could store large amounts of data and process that data quickly.

It is one thing to store a list of numbers. But how do you store a list of patient records for a hospital? Or the accounts of a company? The computer may need to find specific items of information rapidly—an attribute within a specific patient record, or the record of a payment made on a specific date. How do you arrange the data so that it can be found?

These are not new problems—we've needed to have quick access to a lot of information since the first dictionaries were written. The solution in a dictionary is to order the words alphabetically. Each word will either be later than or earlier than another, so we can start with any word and know whether to look backwards or forwards in the book until we find the one we're after.

The first databases were organized along very similar principles. First constructed in the 1960s, these are known as navigational database management systems.[r] When the database is first opened, it automatically provides a pointer to the first record stored (like starting at 'aardvark' in the dictionary). Records were arranged as linked lists or networks with each record pointing to its neighbouring records. To retrieve information, the computer needed to step through each record, following the links to the next record, until the desired information was found. If anyone wanted to retrieve all the records for patients suffering from heart disease in a large database, then every record would need to be examined. It's clearly a very slow and inefficient way to retrieve information, but in those days computers and storage devices were so slow that it was inconceivable to make such a request anyway. As strange as it sounds today, you didn't *search* for information in the first databases.

But the limitations of the navigational approach became more apparent as computers and storage improved. By the 1970s, a British researcher at IBM, Edgar 'Ted' Codd, decided a better approach was needed. Working with some of the same people responsible for creating the new hard-disk storage systems, Codd designed what he called a relational model for databases.[14] His method was clever. Instead of storing long lists of records, like entries in a dictionary, he arranged data in a series of tables linked by keys.

If you were to create a dictionary that looked like a relational database, you'd have a series of books, each containing different meanings for the same key words. You might have a book of verbs, a book of nouns, a book of adverbs, and so on. Then if you needed to look up a specific word—say it's the verb 'bow' you would only need to look in the verb book under that key word. If you wanted to find the meaning of a noun for the same word, you could look in the noun book. It's much faster than having one big dictionary, starting at 'aardvark' and flicking through every word until you reach the word you wanted.

Relational databases use keys to link records together in this way. So a database for employees might have a unique payroll number as the key. This key can be used to find the salary information stored in one table, or the home address stored in another, or the computer login details in another table. The values in each table could also be used as keys, so the job description for the person could be used as the key to find the security clearance in another table.[15]

By the late 1970s, a special language had been developed from relational algebra and calculus to enable users to access information in databases in complex queries. Known as SEQUEL (Structured English Query Language), this was soon shortened to SQL.[s,16] The language supports queries, expressions, clauses, and many other elements which enable users to ask for highly complex information from their databases. For example, if your company had a database of customers and wanted to know which customers had not ordered anything in the year 2004, you could use an SQL query looking like this:[17]

```
SELECT customers.* FROM customers WHERE customers.customer_id
NOT IN (SELECT customer_id FROM orders WHERE year
(orders.order_date) = 2004)
```

The underlying database management system is responsible for taking the SQL expression and interpreting it, returning the results in (hopefully) as short a time as possible. Subsets of SQL known as the data manipulation language (DML) and data definition language (DDL) allow users to modify or add data to their databases using similarly friendly expressions.

Databases continued to be developed, becoming object-oriented and further optimized. The idea of indexing was introduced, where frequently queried information is stored in a fast temporary database which then links to the main database. Like the index in a book, it allows users to find commonly needed information much faster. Today, databases are designed to be highly modular and accessible. Web-based languages such as XML and PHP are able to use SQL and connect to databases online. (The computer serving you the Web pages and your Web browser interprets these languages when you visit Web pages containing these clever commands.) The future of databases looks likely to be increasingly distributed across more computers, becoming more accessible, and faster to access.

We are already familiar with the results of these remarkable advances. Just a few years ago, we all had drawers full of old photos and shelves full of books, paperwork, videos, and CDs. But today almost all the information we find, create, or buy is stored digitally. Most photos are now digital, and electronic books are becoming mainstream. Most companies now prefer to send you bills electronically instead of on paper. Videos and music are already mostly digital. Our money has been nothing more than numbers in the memory of computers in banks for many years. Governments provide information digitally; hospitals store your medical history on computers. More and more of our shops trade online. We can purchase food, cars, and almost everything else, with just a few clicks of a mouse.

All these vast amounts of data are stored in databases. Their interface may look like a pretty Web page from which you view photos, or a gorgeous music-playing program, an online shop from which you choose products, or even an accounting application that you use to view spending. But underneath the interface, the clever machinery of the database makes everything work.

Software crisis

Everything works so well today that it may seem as though progress in software has always been smooth and without problems. But just as the electronics industry had their 'tyranny of numbers' which led to the development of the integrated circuit, the new software industry had their own crisis, which led to a whole new discipline.

The problems for programmers had been clear from the start. While the new high-level programming languages were extremely helpful in enabling developers to write code, significant new problems were emerging. By the 1960s, the invention of the integrated circuit and the result of Moore's Law meant that computers were becoming massively faster each year. Software applications were growing at a similar rate. But programmers were discovering that their programs were becoming unmanageable. There were too many bugs, the software didn't solve the problem it was commissioned to solve, and it seemed to be taking unexpectedly long to develop the systems.

Things came to a head in 1968. At the first ever conference on software engineering, computer scientists from around the world met to discuss their concerns. They were worried, as can be seen from their discussions:[18]

Robert Graham (from MIT): 'Today we tend to go on for years, with tremendous investments to find that the system, which was not well understood to start with, does not work as anticipated. We build systems like the Wright brothers built airplanes—build the whole thing, push it off the cliff, let it crash, and start over again.'

Bernard Galler (from the University of Michigan Computing Center): 'Let me mention some bad experiences with IBM. One example concerns a request to allow user extensions of the PL/1 language. After a week of internal discussion at IBM it was decided that this could not be done because the language designers were not to tell the implementers how to implement the desired extensions. Another example: the OS/360 job control language was developed without any users having the chance to see the options beforehand, at the design stage. Why do these things happen?'

Peter Naur (A/S Regnecentralen, Denmark): '... software designers are in a similar position to architects and civil engineers, particularly those concerned with the design of large heterogeneous constructions, such as towns and industrial plants. It therefore seems natural that we should turn to these subjects for ideas about how to attack the design problem.'

The conference was quickly followed by another conference to discuss technical and managerial ideas.[19] From this starting point, the field of software engineering was born. According to modern software engineer Professor Ian Sommerville at St. Andrews University (who is the author of many of the major textbooks in the area[20]) the name was intended to represent the adoption of an organized and systematic approach to the construction of software. However, the organizers of the conference, 'said that they introduced the term rather mischievously and it stuck'.[21] Indeed the name was intended to be 'deliberately provocative'[22] in order to stir the researchers into action.

It worked. Before long many key innovations were being made specifically to improve our ability to write effective software.[t] New programming languages were developed with these goals in mind. Researchers such as David Parnas introduced the notion of information hiding—a key concept in modular and object-oriented programming which ensures that data and related functions are encapsulated within objects and separated from other data and functions. The idea is much the same as building a car using standardized modules—the stereo can be exchanged for another without affecting any other component. It means that if a design decision in your program is later changed (perhaps a new function or data structure is needed to replace an existing one), all the other functions and data in the program will be unaffected.

Integrated development environments (IDEs) were produced in order to make programming easier. These resemble word processors for programmers—they allow code to be written in different windows, allow it to be compiled and debugged. Instead of the spelling or grammar checkers of a word processor, the IDE tells the programmer about errors in the program and provides a large array of clever tools to correct them. Modern IDEs may include simulators of hand-held devices, tools to design graphical user-interfaces, and extensive help systems to enable the programmer to find the right function to use in the libraries available (the application programming interface).

In addition to the tools for programmers, it was quickly realized that a better way was needed to design software. You can't just build a car as you go along—you need to plan exactly what it will be used for and who will use it, figure out costs, break the problem into smaller components. Which engine? Which transmission? Which steering, brakes, wheels, seats? How many people will it take? How long do they need to build it? A large software project may be much more complex than a car, so how should it be designed?

Researchers soon realized that there needed to be a clear software development lifecycle. First you must understand the requirements for the product and plan appropriately. You need to design, implement, and test the software, making sure its workings are documented clearly. You need to deploy the software, perhaps train users how to use it, and maintain the software for as long as it is needed.

These may seem like perfectly obvious things to do, but that does not make them easy. Requirements elicitation is not straightforward when the clients may not have a clear idea of their true needs, they may desire contradictory things, and they may change their minds. Often they are not able to express their needs in a form that can be easily translated into software or they have little understanding about what can and cannot be achieved technically. Sometimes it is not even clear who the users may be, so the right people are never given the opportunity to give their requirements.[20]

It's also not clear how the different design stages should be carried out. Should each stage simply follow each other like water flowing downhill (the 'waterfall model')?[u] Or should the stages be repeated, and a series of prototypes be developed in order to minimize risk (the 'spiral model'). Should software be developed iteratively and incrementally or should it be developed in an 'agile' manner, responding to change quickly? And even if you know which order to do things, how best to do each stage? Which design methods and tools should be used? How should the software be tested to ensure it actually works? How can software be maintained so that it continues to work in the future?

By explicitly focusing on these topics, software engineering has enabled software projects to keep up with the demands of evolving hardware and the complex requirements of users. The field focuses on every conceivable aspect of software development, from modelling and visualizing the architecture of software and corresponding businesses, to the use of formal methods to verify the correctness and reliability of software.[20]

Ian Sommerville believes there have been many important advances in software engineering that have impacted real software development in practice. 'Different types of software development require different software technologies and methods,' he explains. 'One obvious, cross-cutting development that is incredibly important is configuration management. Information hiding, proposed by Parnas in 1972 and developed through abstract data types has influenced most modern programming languages. In the area of critical systems, methods of safety and dependability analysis and fault tolerance have allowed us to build very safe and reliable systems that, for example, control aircraft or chemical plants. The Unified Modelling Language brought together modelling notations and is now the standard way of modelling software systems. The idea of programming environments, proposed in the 1970s and developed in the 1980s has now been universally adopted in the software engineering community.'[21]

Anthony Finkelstein, Professor of Software Engineering and Dean of the School of Engineering at UCL, feels that the discipline ensures programmers make effective use of their time. 'Without software engineering I think the gap between our hardware capability and our software capability would have broadened still further. It's still the case that the principal limitation of the development of software is the availability of skilled labour. If we were not able to deploy that labour in an appropriate engineering fashion we would not be able to make the progress that we have.'[23]

But despite the best efforts of software engineering, there are still problems remaining. One example is obvious every time we use our computers. For some reason, our software seems to become slower and slower each time we upgrade it. The effect was described by computer scientist (and creator of many programming languages[v]) Niklaus Wirth, and became known as Wirth's Law: '*Software is getting slower more rapidly than hardware becomes faster.*'[24] Similar comments have been made by other computer scientists, including former Intel researcher Randall Kennedy, who wrote that, 'Microsoft Office 2007, when deployed on Windows Vista, consumes more than 12 times as much memory and nearly three times as much processing power as the version that graced PCs just seven short years ago, Office 2000.'[25] The effect is caused by software bloat—new generations of the software are often not rewritten, they simply have new code added to the old. Also known as 'The Great Moore's Law Compensator', it means that despite having astonishingly fast computers, our software can still run slower than similar software we were running (on slower computers) ten years ago.

Computer scientists are hard at work to solve this problem. Sommerville knows that it's not the only challenge faced by software engineering. 'The major challenge faced by software projects is increasing complexity as we create systems by integrating systems and services from different providers. The assumption that underlies much of software engineering is that the developer of the software is in control of the system and can therefore make rational decisions about how to develop and change the system. When this assumption is no longer true, methods such as software testing have to evolve to take this into account.'[21]

Some computer scientists take this idea literally. Professor Mark Harman at UCL performs research into search-based software engineering. Often using genetic algorithms, which evolve solutions to problems,[w] he uses computers to search for the best tests for a given piece of software.

'Testing is one of the key ways to assess how good software is and to highlight ways in which it can be improved. One such task is trying to find an input that will force a program to execute a specific part of its code,' Harman explains. 'Searching for a test that reaches a particular part of the program code can be tiresome and painstaking for a human. It's like looking for a person whose phone number you don't know, by searching all the telephone numbers in an address book. However, for a computer, armed with a measure of how close a test case comes to the desired part of the program, we can easily automate this.'[26]

Clever testing is not always enough. We may no longer talk of a software crisis as it was described in the late 1960s, but the software industry has something of an image problem. Major software development projects still commonly fail, despite the best efforts of software engineers. Sometimes the problems are simply cost and time—we are not very good at figuring out how much it will take to build a new software system. 'We are very poor at software estimation,' says Finkelstein. 'If you say to me, "build a Web Fronted service that sells second hand text books" then I couldn't tell you off the top of my head how long it would take. If I was lucky I may have done one before, but that would be about the only discipline I really had.'[23]

But the major failures (and there is a long list of extraordinary and costly failures[x,27]) may be caused by something more subtle. Finkelstein believes the problem is not that analysts and developers don't understand what to do. 'My own opinion is that these systems fail for very well known reasons: making basic flaws in specification, or in the conduct of projects,' he explains. 'You have to ask yourself, why do those flaws reoccur, given that they are very well-known? Are people stupid? Haven't they read *Sommerville*?[20] It's in the first ten pages—they don't have to read that far! My feeling is that it is because of mismatches between business structures, governing policy-making structures, and the technical processes that make up software. So these systems fail not because of engineering failures, they're governance failures.'[23]

Other challenges include the need for security for our information and how to engineer software that scales rapidly to Internet scales.[y] There also may be an increasing need to look at so-called 'non-functional requirements' such as energy or battery life. Harman takes a practical view: 'If my laptop battery goes flat halfway through a transatlantic flight then the computer is useless even if the software residing on it is perfectly correct. How I would be happy for an extra four hours battery life at that moment, even if it meant using "buggy software".'[26] Finkelstein agrees: 'In software engineering we engineer for a series of attributes, but we've never engineered to minimize energy—unless you're designing spacecraft. But now it's critical. Suddenly new attributes are coming into the front.'[23]

And what of Patterson's Hail Mary ball from the previous chapter? Finkelstein is sure that it will result in significant change. 'The other big challenge for software engineering is multicore. It's no use having multiple cores on your machine if your software doesn't take advantage of it. Having one core for all your applications and the other fifteen running virus checkers is not where we want to be. It's not just a programming breakthrough that is required—it's a whole set of engineering disciplines that need to change to take that into account. It's a game-changer for certain.'[23]

Virtual futures

Software has never been more important. The original pioneers sitting in their classroom listening to Mauchly and Eckert never dreamed that the machines they were learning about would create a virtual industry. An industry of computer instructions. Growing from microcode, through machine code, assembly language, high-level languages, the many layers of software including databases, the software development process, right up to business structures. The thoughts of our ubiquitous computers rule the world. Software is so important that it should not be surprising that several of the richest people on the planet achieved their wealth through software companies.

Professor Mark Harman is passionate about the topic. 'Software underpins everything from social interactions, through transport, finance, business and health, to government, critical infrastructure and defence. The correct functioning of a nation state depends critically on software for everything it does.

'Improving software means improving everything.'[26]

Monkeys with World-Spanning Voices

The howler monkey is one of the loudest animals in the world. Its haunting calls can be heard several miles away in dense forest.[1] Today, with the help of the computer, even the quietest human voice can be heard anywhere on the planet.

Computers are social machines. They constantly talk to each other in a network that crosses oceans, mountains, and continents. They speak a common universal language, independent of country. Their pulsing, error-correcting messages comprise the industry, knowledge, culture, thoughts, and dreams of the human species.

The virtual Web of knowledge now connects humans together in ways never before possible. But with this freedom comes problems. Should we trust everyone who communicates with us? Do we need new ways to protect our privacy?

Claude Shannon took his hand from the chess piece and looked up. His sharp eyes fixed on his young opponent. 'Check!'

Shannon was visiting from Bell Labs in 1955. It was only natural that he should spend an occasional evening at the Palo Alto Chess Club, for he had a keen interest in chess. Five or six years previously he had published several papers about how computers could be programmed to play chess and he was increasingly becoming interested in how machines could be made to perform intelligent tasks.[a] His opponent, Peter Kirstein, a twenty-two-year-old PhD student of Stanford University, was enjoying the game. He had been playing chess since school and was no pushover. Kirstein didn't really know Shannon, but found the thirty-nine-year-old scientist to be an impressive person, very thin, with piercing eyes.[2]

Although the two players didn't realize it, this was a chance meeting of an established pioneer and a future pioneer who would build on Shannon's work in ways neither could have dreamed.

In 1955, the work that would become so important to Kirstein in the future was already in Shannon's past. It had originated because of crackling telephone lines. The research and development group in Bell Labs had been struggling with the issue of long-distance communications. At the time, telephone communication was analogue. The microphone in the telephone handset would turn sound into an electrical signal, so a high-pitched sound became a high-frequency electrical signal (more peaks and troughs per second), a low-pitched sound became a low-frequency signal (fewer peaks and troughs per second), a loud sound became a signal with a big amplitude (higher peaks and lower troughs), and a quiet sound became a signal with a smaller amplitude (flatter waves). If you transmit an analogue electrical signal such as this down a long wire, the signal shrinks in size because longer wires have more resistance to the electricity. The solution was to add amplifiers that took a small analogue signal and amplified it before passing it further down the wire. Unfortunately, the longer the wire, the more those precise frequencies and amplitudes of the signal are distorted and messed up, and the more crackle and hiss is introduced. That is then amplified, which makes the noise louder (and adds even more noise), transmitted further, which adds yet more noise, amplified again, which makes the noise even worse, transmitted further, which introduces more noise, and so on. Make the wire very long with several amplifiers along the way and the original signal is lost in a mess of hiss and crackle.

In 1948, Shannon decided to apply his ideas of Boolean logic to the telephone network. Instead of transmitting an analogue signal, which could not be distinguished from additional noise that might be introduced later, he suggested that just two types of signal were needed: a 1 and a 0. It's the simplest possible kind of information (any less than two states and you just have one possible value all the time, which is not much use for representing anything). Shannon called this two-state unit of information the binary digit, or bit.[b] He argued that simplifying all analogue information into bits would make it much easier to detect from the background noise. It's like being at a noisy party— you can't hear what your friend is saying to you above the background noise, but if he just shouts then you can tell when he's making a sound and when he is quiet. The result was digital communication technology—the audio signal is turned into binary numbers (lists of bits) that describe the shape of the audio waveform. The audio is digitized at one end, transmitted in an electronic shout of ones and zeros that is audible above the background noise, and turned back into an analogue audio signal at the other end, without any of the noise affecting the information in the signal along the way. Clever.

It took him another few months to work everything out, but Shannon went on to describe all the useful things that could be achieved with binary communication. He showed how many different frequencies could be used to transmit bits, so multiple bits could be transmitted at the same time down the same wire (like people with different pitched voices shouting at the party). He described the limits of transmission possible using this idea. He showed how error correction could be added into the binary numbers, so that even if some of the signal could not be heard over the background noise, the original could still be reconstructed without loss. He described compression: a method to use fewer binary numbers in order to describe more information. He explained how the rate of information, the capacity of a channel for handling information, and the average amount of information in a message could be precisely calculated.[c,3] The results were so important that his paper on the topic: 'A Mathematical Theory of Communication',[4] laid the foundations for an entirely new field of research, known as information theory.

It was to have a big impact. As you may have noticed, our computers, phones, televisions, radios, MP3 players (and every information processing device you're likely to use) are all digital. They speak binary, the language of 0s and 1s. Today, our information is almost exclusively transmitted (and stored and manipulated) in its digital form rather than the analogue original, whether that original was text, images, photographs, audio, or video. 'It is clear that most of the past fifty years of making communication faster is down to playing clever tricks with a better understanding of Shannon's work, all the way from modem links up to 100 Gbps fibre,' says Jon Crowcroft, Professor of Communications. 'It's all about information theory, coding and modulation.'[5] Shannon's work helped lead to the digital revolution.

Shannon married Betty, a co-worker at Bell labs in 1949. They had three children together. A year after playing chess with Kirstein, he moved to MIT and spent the rest of his working life there. Despite his astonishing breakthroughs, Shannon was a modest and quiet family man with a surprising range of interests and a good sense of humour.

He created more than thirty unicycles by hand, some motorized, some with weird off-centre hubs making the rider bob up and down like a duck, some too small to ride. He created a computer that processed Roman numerals, robots that juggled balls, and began some of the earliest ideas in artificial intelligence with his chess-playing computers.[6]

Claude Shannon developed Alzheimer's disease in his final few years. Sadly, he was never fully aware of the information revolution that his work helped to create. He died in a nursing home in 2001, aged eighty-four.

Diverse connections

At the time of their chess game, Peter Kirstein knew little of Shannon's work. He was halfway through his PhD on microwaves at Stanford, and had had no contact with researchers working on telephone networks. This was to change.

Kirstein had been born in 1933 in Germany. It was about five months after Hitler came to power and things were becoming unpleasant for the Jewish family. By 1935, Jews were becoming openly persecuted, so his parents decided to emigrate to England. His mother was able to obtain a visa without problems because, by chance, she had been born in England while her parents were working there for a few months. She moved to England in 1936. Peter and his father followed a year later. It was a move that no doubt saved all their lives.

Not long after arriving, his parents told their small son that little boys who sucked their thumbs in Britain would have their thumbs cut off by the police. Little Peter was shortly after discovered standing in front of a large English policeman with his thumb in his mouth, asking (in German), 'Where are the scissors?' He had decided to be an experimentalist quite early.[2]

Kirstein was evacuated three times during the war, but from age eight he attended the Highgate School in London. He loved chess, stamp-collecting, mathematics, and the classics. He received excellent grades in the topics he enjoyed, but did poorly in everything else. He was also active, enjoying tennis. By Sixth Form, he decided he preferred mathematics and started to focus on the topic. He was bright—completing his O-levels and A-levels two years early (although he took A-levels a second time in order to obtain a scholarship at Cambridge). After completing school, it was normal for students to spend several months in National Service, but with the assistance of his uncle he managed to escape and go to the University of California, LA (UCLA) for a semester, followed by a summer job for the US army. He returned the following year to continue the summer job. He was working as a human computer, calculating the rain runoff area for airports.

Kirstein then studied mathematics at Cambridge. In his second year he was able to choose which area to specialize in. He considered joining the Mathematics Lab and talked to Maurice Wilkes—the EDSAC 2 was now up and running—but decided instead to study electrical engineering for his third year. After graduating, Kirstein was awarded a fellowship to study his MSc and PhD at Stanford. His PhD did not go smoothly—there were a couple of false starts with different supervisors. But once everything had been resolved, Kirstein completed his doctorate in an astonishing six months, then spent another year lecturing. To recover from the hard work and have some fun skiing, Kirstein then chose to go to the newly opened CERN[d] in Switzerland. He stayed for four years, becoming familiar with some of the newest and fastest computers.

After finishing at CERN, Kirstein was offered a couple of places in universities, but he chose instead to stay in Switzerland (partly for the skiing) and work for the US company General Electric. It was a move that helped set the future course of his life. The job was to keep track of scientific developments relevant for the company. This role gave Kirstein an amazing opportunity to visit universities all over the world and make contacts. In addition to English and German, he became proficient in languages such as French and Russian. His 'GE-ing' work (as he likes to refer to it) was a role he held in parallel to his later jobs for the next thirty years and gave him a uniquely broad perspective across the whole of computer science.

On one of his visits to London in 1965, he expressed an interest in joining the University of London Institute of Computer Science. He had decided that it was useful to set up a remote link from the fastest computer at the time in the UK (an IBM 360–75 at Rutherford) to another computer elsewhere in the UK which could generate graphics (an IBM 2250 Graphics Display Unit). The Institute had no funds available to support this project, so Kirstein applied for and received funding, and began work as a reader at the Institute in 1967. Kirstein hired a student for the project—Steve Wilbur—who was able to help make the research a great success.

The idea of linking computers together into 'networks' was becoming a very hot topic for research. Already, in the early 1960s, American computer scientists such as Joseph Licklider (usually known as JCR or 'Lick') had proposed global networks that might one day take the place of libraries.[7] In 1965, a British computer scientist, Donald Davies of the UK's National Physical Laboratory (NPL), had proposed a national data network based on packet-switching (a method for chopping up data into small 'packets' which were then routed independently to the destination).[8]

Kirstein was right in the middle of this new field of networking. During a visit to UCLA at around the same time, he met with a friend[e] who introduced him to a graduate student called Vint Cerf.[f] It seemed there was a new project they were becoming involved with, to link several computers together. Kirstein found the ideas very interesting. It turned out that Licklider had convinced a colleague, Bob Taylor at the Advanced Research Projects Agency (ARPA), that the development of a network was a worthwhile project. Taylor hired a graduate from MIT called Larry Roberts to look after the project and ARPA had soon commissioned a company called BBN Technologies to make the new computers necessary to pass information over the network. ARPANET was born in late 1969—initially just a network between UCLA, the Stanford Research Institute, the University of Utah, and the University of California, Santa Barbara. The network was seen as an experiment, and indeed the project might have even ended there, were it not for the growing interest from researchers nationally and internationally. Soon the number of connected computers, both in universities and the US government, was slowly growing month by month.

In late 1970, Larry Roberts in ARPA, USA, proposed to Donald Davies at NPL, UK (which already had its own internal packet switching network), that their two networks could be linked together. They realized that the US Nuclear Monitoring Research Office had links to three seismic arrays in Alaska, Montana, and Norway. To make them work, the link went through undersea cable to London, to Goonhilly Satellite Earth Station, then by satellite to Washington, DC, where it could link into the ARPANET. So Roberts proposed they should exploit this connection and link NPL to the ARPANET. But the political situation in Europe at the time did not favour such close ties with America from UK government laboratories. Davies couldn't accept the offer. He could only help someone else with as much financial support as he could muster—£5000. That left only one person who could take up the offer—Peter Kirstein.[9]

Kirstein had his own vision of an international network (in 1968 he had chaired a meeting at NPL to discuss networking—he was to chair an anniversary event forty years later). He suggested that they used the existing London Institute link to Rutherford and thus have the largest computer in the UK act as a remote ARPANET host. He also suggested that other UK universities should be able to use the network. Politics were still against him, and even Cambridge decided not to support the project—a decision taken by Maurice Wilkes for financial reasons.[8]

But Kirstein was not a man to give up. He was perhaps the most well-connected researcher in the world, and he had contacts in many places—including several directors in the UK's Post Office, which maintained the telephone lines. Soon he had arranged for a free link for a year. Despite major difficulties in importing the necessary equipment from BBN in America, by 25 July 1973 London was linked to the ARPANET. It still linked only about thirty computers in total, but now this had become a truly international network.

Inter-networking

Although ARPANET now stretched across the Atlantic, there was still no consensus on how computers should talk to each other over a network. More and more computers were being linked together in diverse

networks being developed in different countries. In effect the computers on each network spoke different languages[h] to each other, making
the separate networks incompatible. To connect the networks in Europe
with ARPANET, Kirstein had to develop automatic translators. 'I had no
choice but to connect in very inhomogeneous networks,' he says.[2]

By this time Maurice Wilkes was working on his own networking
solution, the Cambridge Ring. Wilkes said to Kirstein, 'One of the big
differences between us is that I can do what I like, but you have to
worry about other people's standards and protocols!'

'That was also a problem,' says Kirstein. 'While the Cambridge Ring
was technically quite advanced, the result was that he never tried to
get it standardized and therefore it never took off.'[2]

The proliferation of completely different networks could not continue forever. In 1972, Robert Kahn started working for the Information Processing Techniques Office (IPTO) within ARPA. He recognized
that ARPANET needed an improved method to minimize errors in
transmission. He hired Vint Cerf to help. By 1974, they had published
a new 'connection language' or internetworking protocol for computers to speak.[10] Their method is known today as the Internet protocol suite, often referred to as simply TCP/IP (the Transmission Control
Protocol and the Internet Protocol). The name is something of a simplification however, because there are more commonly at least four
different layers of communication going on.

You can think of the internetworking protocol as being like two
important presidents of large companies who want to share some
information. The boss of the first company decides he wants to talk to
the boss of the second company and send her a file. Of course, he is too
important and busy to handle it himself, so he passes his order to his
director of communications to handle the details. This employee is

extremely thorough. First, he makes contact with his opposite number in the appropriate company, who acknowledges she is ready to accept the message. Then, he carefully divides the message into parts and writes a little cover note for each chunk to explain what it contains and whom it's for. He passes each separate part of the message, complete with the cover notes, to the mailroom of the company, where they are neatly wrapped up in packets, with the address written on the outside, ready for the mailman. The mailman then collects together several of the packets, puts them into a frame for safekeeping, and chooses the best route to deliver them to the mailroom of the appropriate company. If he damages some, or notices some look a bit dodgy, he may go back and ask for replacements. The mailroom of the second company then unwraps the packets and gives them to this company's director of communications. Using the cover notes, the chunks are then carefully reassembled into a whole message. If this director spots that a chunk is missing or has been damaged on the way over, she will send a request back to the first company that she needs that chunk sent again. She keeps waiting until all the chunks have arrived and the message is perfect. Then she hands it to her boss.

This is more or less how two computers talk over the Internet. The bosses are applications such as your Web browser and a Web server. The directors of communications are the TCP (transmission control protocol) layer. The mailrooms are the IP (Internet Protocol) layer. The mailman is the link layer (the low-level method of transmission, for example, local area network protocols such as Ethernet and IEEE 802, and framing protocols such as Point-to-Point Protocol).

It's a clever system of encapsulation or abstraction that ensures that information is transmitted accurately over phone lines, satellite links, or fibre optic cables, without the applications or the TCP/IP data ever needing to worry about how the transmissions are made. It's commonly said that TCP/IP will work between two cans and a piece of string, for that reason.

Bob Kahn and Vint Cerf's creation was an important advance that had the potential to make computer communication over networks more reliable and easier to achieve. But it was one thing to create a new standard protocol. It was quite another to make everyone use it. For many years, more and more new types of network just kept on coming. In the UK, new protocols were developed (with Kirstein doing his best to encourage the adoption of compatible approaches) following the so-called 'coloured book' protocols.[i,11] These managed to be different even in the way machines were addressed: instead of 'peter@cs.ucl.ac.uk' the coloured book protocols reversed the address to 'peter@uk.ac.ucl.cs'.

Kirstein kept finding ways to connect all the networks together, despite their incompatibilities. It was a service that insulated the users of the networks from the underlying clash of protocols, something he later questioned. 'I still can't decide if what I was doing was good or bad. What I was doing was let the British do what they liked and still be able to interconnect.'[2]

Kirstein and Cerf published the first ever paper on connecting incompatible networks in 1978.[12] (By this time Cerf was Kirstein's project officer in DARPA.) It was a paper of contrasting opinions. Cerf believed only one protocol was needed for everyone. But Kirstein's broad perspective gave him a unique awareness of the diversity of different networks spreading across the world. 'I didn't really believe that a single protocol would sweep the world,' says Kirstein. 'On the other hand, Vint was always a visionary. Vint believed TCP/IP networks *would* sweep the world. That's why we wrote the paper together because our views were not the same. Both were needed depending on how things developed.'[2]

The London Institute closed in 1973 and Kirstein's group joined the Department of Statistics and Computer Science at University College London. They moved physically in 1975 (and surprised the mathematicians with the amount of equipment). By 1976, he had contracts with many ministries in the UK government. Kirstein then achieved a contract with the UK Defence to develop networks between the UK and USA further. He also collaborated with international research on communications with satellite and radio. Increasingly new places all over the UK were connected.

Kirstein somewhat reluctantly took the role of Head of Department when a new Department of Computer Science was created in 1980, a position he held for the next fifteen years until his old student Steve Wilbur took over. His group was to host several important researchers in networking including Jon Crowcroft and Mark Handley.

Kirstein continued his role of connecting incompatible networks and now ensuring that they could support TCP/IP. 'Whenever there was a new network technology we made sure that it was deployed in a reasonable way and that the Internet was integrated in it from the beginning. Many of the networking people neither knew nor cared about the existence of the Internet.'[2]

With some considerable effort, Vint Cerf's vision was becoming a reality. By 1981, TCP/IP had become the new standard protocol for ARPANET. A year later and Kirstein migrated UCL's transatlantic satellite links to TCP/IP. CERN created its own network based on TCP/IP and countries such as Australia followed. Network research accelerated in America, with the National Aeronautics and Space Agency (NASA), the National Science Foundation (NSF), and the Department of Energy (DOE) all creating TCP/IP networks. ARPANET was finally decommissioned in 1990. The British academic network JANET started supporting IP traffic from 1991. New networks continued to migrate to TCP/IP over the following decade. The many networks of the world were at last speaking the same language: the language of the Internet.

Soon something resembling the Internet as we know it had emerged—an astonishing network of networks. It continued to expand every year, and is still growing today. As it grows, computer scientists study it, much as biologists study biological networks in the brain. One such researcher is Shi Zhou. He believes the Internet has some very important properties that make it efficient. 'It exhibits a property called disassortative mixing,' says Shou, 'which means peripheral, lesser-connected nodes tend to connect with well-connected nodes, or rich nodes. It also shows a so-called rich-club phenomenon,[13] where a small number of rich nodes are tightly interconnected with themselves forming a club. The rich club collectively functions as a hub for the Internet by providing a large selection of shortcuts. So a typical path between two nodes on the Internet consists of three hops:[14] the first is from the source node to a member of the rich club, the second is between two club members, and the final hop is to the destination node.'[15] These remarkable properties emerge without any planning or design as new networks in different countries are connected and the Internet grows.

It is very significant that this cohesive global network arose as much from political negotiations and persuasion as it did from the technical inventions of the equipment. Jon Crowcroft (now Marconi Professor of Communications at the Computing Laboratory of Cambridge) argues that Kirstein played a hugely significant role in the creation of the Internet—with the stress on the 'inter'. 'It is not an exaggeration to say that Peter Kirstein effectively created the *Internet*,' says Crowcroft, 'in the sense that he made the Internet a network of networks in the broadest sense.'[16]

'That is certainly true,' Kirstein says with a smile. 'Unlike the vision of Vint, which is that the whole world could be converted, I didn't have that vision. I felt we had to work. He could do that from the USA where there was some chance of converting the world. There was no chance of converting the world from the UK. So therefore one had to inter-work between the various things that were happening. One had to stay—not only technically but also politically—somehow at the pace of the countries or regions we were working with.'[2]

Because of Kirstein's uniquely global perspective and unrivalled contacts, he was able to forge collaborations between Europe, America, and many other countries around the world. Indeed when asked about his biggest achievement, Kirstein replies, 'Consistent forging of international relations.' It is perhaps not surprising, given its global reach, that the creation of the Internet today was as much a political effort as a technical one. 'I think it was,' Kirstein says. 'It couldn't have happened without the excellent technology. But it also needed to have the examples that it could work. And I played my bit!'[2]

Cerf has known and worked with Peter Kirstein for over forty years. 'UCL has had a central role in the evolution of the Internet,' he says.[17]

Kirstein (Figure 6) continues his work at UCL to this day, helping developing countries in Central Asia and Africa create and improve their networking capabilities and join the Internet. The networking research group is still world-leading at UCL. He also helps lead the future shape of the Internet—a task that is becoming of vital importance as this global network matures.

Figure 6. Peter Kirstein in front of racks of modern computer servers in the machine room of Computer Science, UCL, 2011.

Addressing for success

From the beginning of the development of networks, it was clear that computers needed to know where to send their information. Computers needed to have addresses. One approach could have been to allocate numbers for them (just as telephone companies allocate phone numbers for us) and store them in a central directory. But there are many problems with this idea: numbers are hard for us to remember, so it would be more natural to use English words. If all the numbers are stored in a single directory, then there may be so many requests to look up the numbers that it might become very slow. Even worse, if the computer that stored the directory failed, then the whole network would fail.

For most networks including the ARPANET, it was decided to use two types of address. There would be a collection of English letters or names, and also a set of numbers. People would write the address using the more memorable method, and this would be mapped to the number system, which would then tell the computer exactly where to send its message. The approach was inherited by the Internet, and is used to this day. It's the reason why Web addresses look the way that they do.

Professor of networking at UCL, Mark Handley, is a member of the Internet Engineering Task Force, which produces many of the standards used in the Internet.[j,18] He traces the steps taken by the computers if he wants to go to the address 'bbc.co.uk'. 'Suppose I type bbc.co.uk into the address part of my Internet browser,' he explains. 'First we have to figure out the address of bbc.co.uk. It's just a name. We want to map that name onto an address.

'My computer will be preconfigured with the Internet address of a domain name server (DNS). It's a computer on the Internet that I can ask to do the name mapping for me. So my computer sends out a request to that server to say, "what's the IP address for bbc.co.uk?"

'That server probably won't know the answer. But it knows the IP addresses of the thirteen root servers of the Internet. So it will next send off its requests to one of those servers saying "I would like to know what bbc.co.uk is."

'The route servers don't know what bbc.co.uk is either, but they know what uk is. So they will respond with, "Here are the servers for uk."

'So now my DNS can go to one of the servers for uk and say, "where is bbc.co.uk?" and it responds, "I don't know where bbc is, but I know where co is. These servers will respond to co."

'The server then goes to one of those and finds the servers for bbc. Finally it will go to bbc's named servers and say, "where is bbc.co.uk" and bbc will reply, "it's at these IP addresses." The DNS now can tell my computer the IP address of the web server for bbc.co.uk.

'So my web browser will make a connection to that bbc server. It will send a request saying, "I would like to set up a TCP connection with you." The bbc server will say, "yes that is ok." Once both servers have set up the connection, my computer can ask for a file, and the server can send it straight to my browser.'[19]

It may seem like a terribly overcomplicated way of finding the address of a computer, but this approach makes the network extremely robust against failure. No single computer knows all the addresses, but many computers know parts of the addresses. So even if major sections of the Internet fail, it will not affect anyone else on the Internet. There will always be other computers that can help figure out each address.

Handley observed this directly after the tragic events of March 2011, which resulted in over 10,000 lives lost and devastation to major parts of Japan. 'After the huge earthquake, the Internet barely blipped,' he says. 'The Internet traffic in and out of Asia dropped only fractionally. It was down about five per cent for a very short amount of time. The Internet had enough redundancy—enough robustness. It just routed around the problems.'[19]

For the ARPANET, the role of allocating domain names and IP addresses was performed by the Internet Assigned Numbers Authority (IANA), which was mainly the efforts of a single person, Jon Postel. Today IANA is managed by the Internet Corporation for Assigned Names and Numbers (ICANN). The rights to allocate domain names were distributed to registrars and companies, which is why you can buy names today. However, IP addresses were distributed from this central authority.

At the beginning of 2011, no more IP addresses could be allocated. We had run out. The problem was caused because the IP version 4 address system (which is the one used by the whole Internet) is just thirty-two bits of information long, separated into four numbers. (If you've ever set up your computer on a network you'll know that its IPv4 address is four numbers, each with a value of 0 to 255, separated by dots.) That means there are only 4,294,967,296 unique addresses available, and many of these are reserved for special purposes—4.3 billion may sound like a lot, but it is not nearly enough. It's a major threat to the future of the Internet.

One commonly used solution is the Network Address Translator (NAT)—a clever trick that hides a whole subnetwork of computers behind a single IP address, mapping their internal IP addresses to this external one when they wish to talk to the Internet. This works and is used extensively worldwide, but it means that 'NATted' computers cannot be addressed directly, which causes problems for many applications.

Handley knew we would run out of addresses many years ago. 'It was fairly obvious as early as the early 90s that problems were going to happen. So we came up with a bunch of different proposals for what might be an alternative. The one that was standardized by the IETF was called IP version 6. So whereas IPv4 has 32-bit addresses, IPv6 has 128-bit addresses. It should be enough to address pretty much every atom in the universe.'[19]

It may seem very strange that in spite of the solution to this significant problem having already been found, the entire Internet continues to use IPv4. Handley likens it to a similar problem. 'In 1967 Sweden switched from driving on the left to driving on the right. They had to plan it for years. They designed all the road junctions so they worked both ways. Eventually they had some kind of flag-day when they switched from driving on one side to driving on the other. Switching the Internet from IPv4 to IPv6 is just as big a deal.'[19]

The last time the Internet was changed was in 1981, when TCP/IP was formally adopted in the ARPANET. About two hundred computers needed to change over. Today there are several billion, and thousands more every day, as Internet-enabled phones and tablet computers are increasingly popular. It is no longer feasible to change the addressing system of the whole Internet overnight. There is also little desire to make the effort. Again it is down to a combination of engineering and politics to push for the change. Perhaps unsurprisingly, both Vint Cerf and Peter Kirstein are at the forefront of campaigns for IPv6.

'I think as the addresses run out, more and more people will pay attention to the problem,' says Cerf. 'The trouble is they will do it in a crisis and I think engineering in a crisis is a very bad idea. So I continue to preach sermons about implementing IPv6 in parallel with IPv4 as soon as possible.'[20]

'It's not just a question of persuading an Internet Service Provider to adopt IPv6,' says Kirstein. 'You've also got to do something about industries and their processes and their thinking. I think you've got to look at the whole business processes and how to inter-work across them.'[2]

Spinning webs over networks

While the Internet comprises the networks and a 'communication language' that enables our computers to talk to each other, increasingly what they have to say has become dominated by something new. We call it the World Wide Web. This simple, but world-changing, innovation was the brainchild of a single person.

Tim Berners-Lee was born in London in 1955. His parents were mathematicians and had met while working on the Ferranti Mark I computer. Tim was perhaps one of the first children ever to grow up surrounded by computer outputs (five hole paper tape). Unsurprisingly he took up electronics as a hobby and enjoyed mathematics. He chose to study physics at university, building his own computer in his spare time, and took a job in a telecommunications company.

By 1980, Berners-Lee was a twenty-five-year-old contract researcher at CERN. The large research centre had the biggest computer network in Europe at the time, and its scientists frequently needed to exchange information and files. Berners-Lee proposed a new kind of program that could help people to find information. It was built around a concept known as hypertext. The Englishman had not been aware of previous work on the topic,[k,21] and built a program that could display pages of information from a database, where many of the words were 'linked' to other pages in the database. If a user selected a word, then the program would retrieve the appropriate page. In this way, large amounts of information could be accessed quickly and intuitively. He called his program ENQUIRE.

The program remained in use as Berners-Lee returned to CERN as a fellow in 1984. But he realized that although it was a useful tool, the centralized database was a nuisance to maintain. 'There was clearly a need for something like ENQUIRE but accessible to everyone,' he says. 'I wanted it to scale so that if two people started to use it independently, and later started to work together, they could start linking together their information without making any other changes. This was the concept of the Web.'[22]

By 1989, Berners-Lee and colleagues at CERN had created a simple Web system for telephone numbers. One computer would be the 'server'—it would run a program that provided information when requested to do so. Other computers would run 'browsers'—they would ask the server for information and then display it in an easy-to-read form. Two years later he made the server and browser software available to everyone on the Internet, and let a few people know about it online. 'From then on,' says Berners-Lee, 'interested people on the Internet provided the feedback, the stimulation, the ideas, source code contributions, and the moral support which it would have been hard to find locally. The people of the Internet built the Web.'[22]

At the request of Berners-Lee, soon different people around the world were writing browsers to access the early Web pages. *Erwise* (created by students at Helsinki University of Technology) ran on X-Windows, as did *ViolaWWW* from Berkeley. *Cello* from Cornell was the first browser for an early Microsoft Windows. *Mosaic* (from the National Center for Supercomputing Applications at the University of Illinois at Urbana Champain) soon became a multi-platform browser.[1]

Images and point-and-click mouse interfaces became common, and the number of Web servers grew exponentially. The amount of Web traffic on the Internet was suddenly becoming significant. 'Rising from 0.1 per cent of the total traffic in March 1993 to 1.0 per cent in September and 2.5 per cent in December, the Web was growing at a rate unprecedented even in Internet circles,' says Berners-Lee. By 2010, at least seventy-five per cent of all Internet traffic was from the Web. Around a quarter of the traffic was from Web pages, with new developments such as Web video using another thirty-seven per cent during normal television viewing hours. (Around thirty-five hours of new video was being uploaded every minute.)[23]

The World Wide Web was made possible because Berners-Lee had created three important concepts. The first important idea was that every document or image should have its own identifier, just as every computer on the Internet had its identifier. Working with the IETF, he decided to create a standard that was similar to the UNIX directory structure, which uses forward slashes to separate files and directories. So if a Web file was called 'welcome.html' and it was within the directory (or folder) called 'news' of the computer that was running Web server software, and that computer resided at 'bbc.co.uk', then the Universal Resource Locator would be 'www.bbc.co.uk/news/welcome.html'.

This is why we talk of URLs today when we want to visit a specific Web page. The URL provides the exact location of the file, directory, and computer address. Everything you see on a Web page has been loaded by the browser via a URL—and it's quite possible that the images may come from one place in the world, the text from another, adverts from yet another. All have their own URLs and so your browser knows where to go in order to download and display them for you.

A second important idea is the special language used in Web pages to enable them to show such complex contents. Berners-Lee created a high-level language that could be written easily by people who wished to design their own Web pages. It would be fast and easy to transmit by Web servers to any other kind of computer. It would then be interpreted by Web browsers in order to display text, graphics, hyperlinks, and everything else you might want in a document. He called it the hypertext markup language, or HTML. To make it easy to use, HTML was simply text and a series of codes (or tags). For example, a Web page can be as simple as the following:

```
<html>
<head>
  <title> My Webpage about the Internet </title>
</head>
<body>
  <h1>The Origins of the Internet</h1>
  <p>Here's a diagram of the first four nodes of the ARPANET:</p>
  <img src = 'http://www.peterjbentley.com/1969ARPANETimage.gif'
  width = '520' height = '421'>
  <p>This a hyperlink to <a href = 'http://www.example.com'> the
  website www.example.com </a>.</p>
</body>
</html>
```

which if interpreted by a Web browser would result in the following Webpage being displayed:

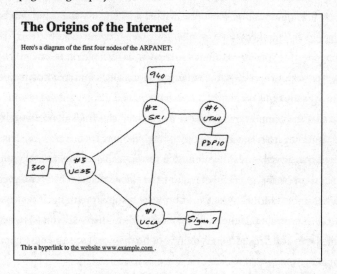

The title of the page appears in the title bar of the browser window. It should not be too difficult to figure out how the other content of this simple page is defined in the HTML file. Text with a hyperlink is shown underlined and often in a different colour. Today we are on the fourth version of HTML, and anyone who uses a computer today can see just how useful, intricate, and beautiful Web pages can be.

The third important thing that Berners-Lee created was a new language that the computers would use to communicate Web pages to each other. He called it the Hypertext Transfer Protocol, or HTTP. The language is not a replacement for TCP/IP—it uses TCP/IP to transmit its messages (it's an application layer protocol that sits on top of TCP/IP). If TCP/IP works like two company presidents sending messages, then HTTP is the agreed set of orders in a special language used by our presidents as they demand things of each other. Because they are in the business of the World Wide

Web, they generally demand text, images, and videos. Their messages are chopped up and sent exactly as before, using the layers of TCP/IP.

HTTP assumes one computer will be a client, and the other will be the server. The client (for example, your Web browser) asks in the HTTP language for specific resources such as an HTML file or an image. The server responds in the same language with a set of specific information (such as the time, the size of the resource, and details about the resource so that the client knows whether its cached[m] version is good enough). If the client hasn't cached a copy of the resource from a previous visit then the server sends the requested resource. There are several commands or 'verbs' in HTTP that allow the client and server to send each other information.[24] When your browser wants something, it may use a GET command. If the Web page contains a form and you have just filled it in and clicked 'Send', then your browser will send a POST command to the server, with the data you have entered.

The modern World Wide Web allows extremely advanced forms of communication between server and client. Programs can be run, databases searched. Users are able to create and edit content in special pages, collectively called a wiki.[n] Innovations such as social networking sites (such as Facebook and LinkedIn) and blogs[o] are now massively popular and are creating wholly new ways for us to connect with each other.[p] Video over the Web is the new television. Yet despite the cleverness of their designs, all rely on the simple foundations of URLs, HTML, and HTTP.

Berners-Lee moved to MIT and founded the World Wide Web Consortium (W3C) in 1994, which oversees the future development of the Web. Sir Tim Berners-Lee was knighted in 2004. He took a professorship at Southampton University to work on a new project: the Semantic Web.[q,25] In 2009, he became an advisor to the British government. He also founded the World Wide Web Foundation, which aims to advance the Web socially and technically, with an emphasis on keeping it free and open for all.

'The web is like paper. It doesn't constrain what you use it for: you have to be able to use it for all of the information flow of normal life. My priority is to see it develop and evolve in a way which will hold us in good stead for a long future,' says Tim Berners-Lee.[26]

Weaving tangled webs

Today the Internet is used for much more than entertainment. It is used for the transfer of important information, for commerce, and even for elections.[27] None of these applications could be possible if the Web was not secure. Another significant innovation was needed to make this possible. The origins of that breakthrough date back to the work by pioneers such as Claude Shannon and Alan Turing.

Shannon and Turing's work on encryption was designed to help governments transmit information more securely, both during and after the war. While most such work was classified and never published, Shannon was able to publish his work.

Nicolas Courtois is a computer scientist at UCL who specializes in encryption. He believes Shannon's work was hugely significant. 'In addition to being the father of Communications and Information Theory, Shannon is the father of Cryptography. His two papers on communications[4] and cryptography[28] in the 1940s were almost the only papers published on the subject until the 1970s. He brought cryptography from an art and made it into a science. His work contains the seed for all further development in cryptography.'[29]

There are three main methods to make the Web secure. These can be thought of as stages—each more secure than the last.[30] The first is simply to design your software to be so complicated that nobody understands how it works—and to keep its internal algorithms completely secret. It's the most basic, and also the most commonly used approach, says Courtois. 'You do something but nobody knows what it is. It works because nobody knows how you do it. It's total secrecy. Some people call it security by obscurity. It's typically what people do even today in the commercial sector. But it has been compromised a long time ago. It's a very bad thing to do because this kind of protection is usually broken by hackers. Just give them enough coffee and they will penetrate it.'

Security by obscurity was not good enough during the Second World War. Governments quickly realized that they needed secure methods of communication that could not be broken. For this reason, the second stage of security was created by the code-makers and code-breakers such as Turing and Shannon during the war. It uses the analogy of a key to secure information. The sender encrypts their message using a secret key, like locking a box with the message inside. The box (encrypted message) is sent to the recipient, and can only be unlocked (decrypted) if an identical key is used. Even if you know how the lock works (the method of encryption is known) you still cannot unlock the box without the right key. Compared to the first stage, there is much less to keep secret. 'You can make everything public: the encryption algorithm, the source code and how it works, and everything,' says Courtois, 'and all you need to do is keep the key secret—a short quantity of information.'[29]

Today we're all very familiar with this symmetrical key encryption method. It's the reason why we use passwords for accessing our computers or our bank accounts. The password is our key. We 'lock' them with the password, and we need to type in the identical password to 'unlock' them again. But the problem with this method is that you have to share the key with anyone you want to be able to unlock your message. Clearly you can't transfer your key over the Internet in case somebody monitored your transmission and intercepted it. (If you wanted to encrypt that key, you'd need to share yet another key to decrypt it.) So keys for the most important communications might have to be transferred physically by courier, or face to face. We also have the problem of needing ever more keys.

Many of us already have too many passwords to remember. When a security audit of a company is performed it's common for the experts to find sticky patches around monitors and computers. That's where the notes with all the passwords are usually stuck. Kirstein laughs about the problem. 'It's all very well insisting on secure passwords that are changed frequently—but people cannot remember such things so they write them down, and completely defeat the purpose!'

If you can find the password, or intercept the key when it is being shared, or crack the encryption and figure out the key, then you can unlock everything encrypted with that key. If you use the same key (or password) for many things, that means you're in trouble. This is a real problem. 'Many companies around the world have very poor security using smart cards,' says Courtois. 'They use the same key on all of them. Break one and you have broken them all.'[29]

Courtois knows only too well how susceptible this form of encryption is to hackers, for he specializes in breaking it for his research. 'I have become a code breaker. I break things,' he says. 'It's also an area of mathematical and cryptographic engineering, but it's on the evil side! I have managed to break quite a few encryption systems including things proposed to be international standards for governments or for international commercial standards.'[29] The systems broken by

Courtois include the encryption on the Oyster smart card used for travel on the London underground and various access cards used all around the world. His methods were directly inspired by the work of Shannon, after attending a talk describing the theories of this pioneer. 'Shannon wrote something that was almost overlooked for 50 years. He wrote in his paper that breaking a large cypher should involve solving a system of algebraic equations. This is how he defines how secure it should be. For almost 50 years it did not work. Nobody found an attack of this kind. I was one of the first to show that you could break real cryptographic systems with this type of algebraic mathematical approach.'[29,31]

Symmetric key encryption is clearly not perfect, but it was all we had. This might have been the end of encryption. Our encryption methods might have become better and the keys more secure (which they have), but we would always have relied on sharing a key to communicate secure information. But quite unexpectedly, a third method of encryption was discovered. It was first found by researchers in the Government Communications Headquarters (GCHQ) in the UK in 1973.[32] However their work was kept top secret. It was not until three years later that American researchers Whitfield Diffie and Martin Hellman published their identical method,[33] followed two years later by MIT researchers Rivest, Shamir, and Adleman[34] (who named their method RSA).

The idea is known as asymmetric key encryption (or public key encryption). It relies on some extremely clever, but simple mathematics that allow us to use two keys—one for encrypting, and one for decrypting. You make your public key visible to everyone. They use that key to encrypt their message and send it to you. But the message can only be unlocked by your private key, which you never need to share with anyone. It's like giving someone a self-locking box. They can make the message secure and send it back to you, but only you have the secret key to unlock that box. No longer do you need to share your key with the world; no longer do you need a different key for every new secure communication.

The new form of encryption was a marvel of mathematics, and a great surprise to everyone. Courtois is animated when he describes the concept. 'Nobody thought before that it was possible to do such a thing. It was a disruptive technology. It was not obvious at all that it could exist and to this day it's not possible to prove mathematically that public key cryptography could exist. It's a big discovery—a big singularity in the history of science.'[29]

It was also a revolution for the World Wide Web. While banks had had their own secure networks for communications and financial transactions for some time, there was nothing like this possible for the general public. But in 1994, the Netscape browser introduced HTTPS—a secure version of HTTP, which used the concept of public key encryption to encrypt the HTTP data. By 2000, this had evolved into a standard which became adopted worldwide. You can confirm for yourself whether a Web page is using secure HTTP by simply looking at the URL in the browser. If it starts with 'https' then it is.

Today we have electronic commerce because of this encryption method. It's the reason we can have online shopping, banking, trading, auctions, marketing, all on the Web. It's why companies can operate online, even selling virtual products and making millions. Nicolas Courtois has no doubts about the importance of this clever mathematical security. 'The whole of the digital economy is underpinned by cryptography. Secure networks cannot exist at all without cryptography.'[29]

Webs of deceit

While encryption is a very important tool to have, if you're sending a secure message to the wrong computer, then you're still in deep trouble. For example a computer could 'pretend' to belong to a bank, and fool you and your Web browser into sending all your details to them. (Because you are using their public key to encrypt your message, they will be able to decrypt it.)

It's a common saying in the field of computer security that encryption without authentication is like meeting a stranger in a dark alley: whatever happens, there won't be any witnesses. In his role as a code breaker, Courtois understands this only too well. 'Authenticity is by far bigger and more important than confidentiality, which is almost impossible to achieve. It's very hard to keep secrets. But it's always possible to have authenticity, even to fix it if it goes wrong.'[29]

There are many ways to perform authentication. Passwords, fingerprint scanners, or software that checks to see if your computer is the right computer are all used. They can also all be broken. Another common approach is for 'certificates' to be signed by a trusted third party, to confirm that the Web site is the one it is supposed to be. Luckily the same kinds of encryption algorithms can be used for these purposes. There are also more advanced methods of mutual authentication that confirm both your computer and the computer you are connecting to are to be trusted.

Sadly, humans are often the weak links in the system. Criminals are highly adept at 'social engineering'. They send emails that appear identical to those from your bank. Click on a link in the email and you will see a Web page identical to the bank's—except for the URL which will be different. Type in your details, and you have just given your account and password information to a fraudster who will quickly withdraw all your funds. Or you may receive a message asking you to confirm a payment that you never made.[r] Or join a non-existent social networking group. Or help a poor injured or terminally ill person in Africa. Or you might get a message saying your password and details need updating. It could even be a nice email with the subject 'I love you'—which turns out to be an email virus that infects everyone in your address book.[35]

It's not a new problem, says Handley. 'You can't expect people will be any more robust to scamming online than they are to scamming offline. People get scammed regularly.'[19]

However it's a problem that needs careful consideration, Kirstein believes. 'We thought security was just a matter of technology. We thought that public keys were strong—you only had to develop the software and deploy it. In fact that's the tip of the iceberg on what you have to do. Now we realize it is just as much about the people as it is about the technology.'[2]

There is also an increasing risk that computer systems can be hacked and disabled—not only by lone hackers, but also by hostile states. China actively censors the Internet available to its citizens. In Eastern Europe, there was a 'coordinated cyber attack' against Georgia in 2008, which coincided with the conflict with Russia.[36] In 2010, Iranian nuclear plants were targeted by hackers, with techniques that were said to be 'almost certainly the work of a national government agency'.[37] In 2011, a report described inadequate security practices of NASA which left their satellites open to attack. '. . . Network servers revealed encryption keys, encrypted passwords, and user account information to potential attackers.'[38]

Kirstein has sometimes found himself at the centre of these events as one of his projects supported the introduction of the Academic

Internet in the Caucasus and Central Asia under a NATO Science for Peace initiative. 'The massive cyber attack on Georgia took down all their Web servers. One of our Web servers provided under that project was the first to recover after the attack on Georgia, and was used to help bring all the other servers back online. Sections of the real NATO realized that what we were doing as academics for science was starting to be important there!'[2]

It remains to be seen how governments will choose to handle this new form of electronic warfare. In the meantime, we have to decide how much privacy we are willing to give up in order to be protected. It's a difficult balance. More effective authentication means more details about us—perhaps our fingerprints, retinas, even DNA—need to be stored. Yet the more information about us online, the more it could be misused. We may not want insurance companies trawling through our DNA data to figure out whether we have a high chance of heart disease, and removing that cover from the policy or charging a higher premium. Yet we may be very happy for a medical centre to store the same information. We may not want our likes and dislikes used by marketing companies to sell us more products, yet we are happy to store them on social networking sites for friends to share. 'You are trading privacy for security,' says Handley. 'It's a difficult trade-off. Privacy is a really big deal. It's not something people rate nearly highly enough.'[19]

Internet companies are doing their best to protect us from the fraudsters. Some, like the Internet search engine Google, are able to visit so much of the Internet that they can warn us that a Web page may contain 'malware' that could be harmful to our computer. However, the more we rely on outside protection, the more we give up our privacy, for we have to tell these companies which sites we'd like to visit before they can tell us if they are harmful or not. Imagine if all the information about you from every Web page you visited was collated together. Just think what could be done with that information. 'It's very clear that every one of these technologies can be abused in a terribly dangerous way,' says Kirstein.[2]

Digital lives

The Internet and the World Wide Web are redefining many aspects of our lives. From the mid-1990s it seemed that Internet companies would be the new way to make money. Just adding an 'e' to the start of your company name (e.Digital), or a 'com' to the end (boo.com) was enough to increase the value of the stocks. Large numbers of Internet companies were created, with very unrealistic sales predictions and hugely inflated valuations. This 'dot-com bubble' burst in the year 2000, when we learned that the so-called 'dot-com' Internet companies were not invulnerable to failure. Many went bankrupt.[39]

Yet today the Internet dominates business, and Internet companies can be very big business indeed. In 2010, Facebook's market capital was estimated at around $25 billion. At the beginning of 2011, Google's market capital was valued at a staggering $190 billion. Apple's market capital was $313 billion,[s] largely because of its recent Internet-enabled mobile computing devices and Internet-based marketplace for music and applications.

The ability to browse the World Wide Web and access social networking sites is now integrated into new operating systems, and Internet connectivity is a major requirement for all new computers, whether they are desktop, laptop, tablet, or mobile phone. Games consoles use the Internet for multi-player games. Most major shops allow customers to buy their products online.

The Internet began as just one network out of many. Today everything is turning into the Internet. Mark Handley describes how the technology is evolving. 'Phone networks are disappearing. They're all becoming part of the Internet. Cellular networks will just become another part of it.'[19]

In 2011, in the UK, BT was in the process of commissioning their twenty-first-century network—an Internet-based network—and turning off the circuit switched phone system. Your phone service doesn't change; you still have a phone that plugs into the wall socket. But on the other end of the wire everything is different—your voice is transmitted as data over the Internet.[40] 'It is all Internet technology behind the scenes,' says Handley. 'It's all packets not circuits any more.'[19] Indeed, most international phone calls are already routed at least partly through the Internet at some point.

This freedom of access to information is already changing us. We can already store our data on the Web and work whenever or wherever we like. We can be directed to almost any location, and even look at photos or videos of the place before we arrive. We can keep track of friends and communicate in a variety of different ways. Entertainment is becoming on-demand. Handley describes his personal experience. 'I've got a 10-year-old son and he doesn't watch broadcast TV anymore. He watches iPlayer. He has lost the concept that there is a set time at which things are broadcast.'[19]

As the number of portable Internet-enabled devices increases seemingly without limit, the future of the Internet seems to be wireless.[1] 'The Internet will have a steady growth in every way. Wireless will play a huge role in everything. Whether we want all of it is another matter. It's not what technically could happen, it's also about the side effects of what would happen if it was allowed,'[2] warns Kirstein.

But that does not mean the underlying technical concepts will change. The experts still believe TCP/IP is here to stay. 'My expectation is that the power of the legacy system will overwhelm any potential advantages we might have had by coming up with a different design. We will have to talk to machines already on the Internet,'[19] says Handley.

But the future is very hard to predict. 'I recognize that there are things I can foresee and things I cannot. I've been blindsided so often,' says Handley. 'The one thing I am fairly sure is that I cannot foresee what the applications will be. Every time some new killer application comes along I haven't seen it coming. They'll come from odd places. They don't come from the mainstream. They come from people who are thinking differently.'[19]

It is extraordinary how a simple computer networking experiment, combined with software that can share information, has changed the world. We have created an Earth-sized society of computers talking to each other at high speed, day and night. This amazing network is independent of country and culture, robust against failure, and is now central to the world's economic, social, and political landscape. The Internet is one of the crowning achievements of the twentieth and twenty-first centuries. Rupert Murdoch, the media mogul, has had to reinvent much of his media empire because of this electronic revolution. 'The Internet has been the most fundamental change during my lifetime and for hundreds of years. Someone the other day said, "It's the biggest thing since the printing of the Gutenberg Bible." Someone else said, "No, it's the biggest thing since the invention of writing."'[41]

My Computer Made Me Cry

When a tool can be used for everything, how do we design that tool so that we can use it most effectively? The cleverest machine in the world will do nothing for us if we cannot interact with it. We need interfaces to the digital minds we create. Physical interfaces that turn our movements into input. Visual interfaces that enable us to interrelate, turning images into two-way communication.

When those interfaces are good enough, we may become immersed into the digital universes of our machines, giving us amazing new experiences. Or they may allow computers to become seamlessly integrated into our lives, as ordinary as a pair of glasses. When the interface is emotional, perhaps they will give us joy, motivate us when we are fearful, or comfort us when we are sad.

But how far do we want our integration with technology to go? We are already becoming cyborgs – fusions of human and machine. If computers know our every secret, how can we protect ourselves from being influenced in ways we do not want?

A black and white face fades into view on the screen. A slim middle-aged man with neatly combed-back hair is talking with a stiff 1960s Oregon accent. Hooked over his right ear he wears a modern-looking

earpiece with microphone attached. He is speaking about his programme of research at Stanford. 'If in your office you, as an intellectual, were supplied with a computer display, backed up with a computer
that was alive all day and was instantly responsible…' He pauses, looks
up and smiles. 'Responsive. Instantly responsive to every reaction that
you have—how much value could you derive from that?'

You can tell he is excited and nervous to be speaking in front of a
thousand people, but the years of lecturing has given his voice the
tone of a practised speaker. 'Well this basically characterizes what
we've been pursuing for many years in what we call the Augmented
Human Intellect Research Centre at Stanford's Research Institute.

'Fortunately the products of this programme, the technology of it,
lends itself well to an interesting way to portray it for you. So we're
going to try our best to show you rather than tell you about this. A
very essential part of what we have developed technologically is what
does come through this display to us,' he points to the camera. 'I'm
going to start out without telling you very much. I'm going to run
through the action that this [display] provides us.'[1]

His amplified voice echoes around the Convention Center in San
Francisco. His presentation is the star event of the Fall Joint Computer Conference. It is December 1968 and Douglas Engelbart is dem-
onstrating more innovations at one time than had ever been seen
before.

Engelbart was an Oregon boy. Born in Portland in 1925, he was the
middle child of three children. His mother was artistic, and his father
owned a radio repair shop. This did not exactly encourage him in electronics. 'When you're little, it has a mystique; it is intimidating,' he
says.[2] His life was turned upside down by the death of his father when
he was nine, resulting in the family moving to a country home in

Johnson Creek. Nevertheless his school studies were successful (although he studied more to understand how things worked than for the grades) and he developed an interest in the secret technology of radar. He graduated from Franklin High School in Portland at the age of seventeen and entered Oregon State College (later to become Oregon State University) to study electrical engineering. He found it difficult to choose the focus of his work. 'I'd become quite disappointed midway through the first semester, in one professor or another, and finally started realizing I would like them to be the father I didn't have, instead of being a professor.'[2] He was only halfway through his course when he was drafted into service of the US Navy as a radar technician. After his training, he was stationed in the Philippines.

While on the way to his station, he stopped off at the island of Laiti. There he found a little bamboo hut on stilts that was the local library maintained by the Red Cross. Browsing the books and magazines, Engelbart discovered a magazine article by Vannevar Bush, entitled 'As We May Think'.[3] The article described a vision of the future where machines could help us to store and access all scientific knowledge. It was to have a major influence on Engelbart's thinking.

Engelbart completed his service in the Navy and returned to finish his degree. In 1948, he was recruited to work at the NASA Ames Research Center as an electrical engineer to build and maintain electronics for various projects. He began to visit the library at Stanford to broaden his general knowledge. He also took up dancing and started to lose his natural shyness, eventually meeting a girl and becoming engaged. But a day after he had proposed he suddenly realized he had no goals in life. He decided to figure out a plan for his life—earn enough money to get by, and do something that might benefit society. But what could that be? 'I just had this flash that, hey, the complexity of a lot of the problems and the means for solving them are just getting to be too much,' says Engelbart. 'The time available for solving a lot of the problems is getting shorter and shorter. So the urgency goes up. So then I put it together that the product of these two factors, complexity and urgency, are the measure for human organizations or institutions. The complexity/urgency factor had transcended what humans can cope with. It suddenly flashed that if you could do something to improve human capability to deal with that, then you'd really contribute something basic. That just resonated.

'Then it unfolded rapidly. I think it was just within an hour that I had the image of sitting at a big CRT screen with all kinds of symbols, new and different symbols, not restricted to our old ones. The computer could be manipulating, and you could be operating all kinds of things to drive the computer. The engineering was easy to do; you could harness any kind of a lever or knob, or buttons, or switches, you wanted to, and the computer could sense them, and do something with it.'[2]

Engelbart was no mathematician. He was not even an expert in computing. But he had realized that if a computer could make calculations, then it could become more than a giant calculating machine that did nothing but examine large and complicated problems. Engelbart realized that if everyone had access to a computer, with a screen and clever input devices on their own desks, then they would be able to work in ways never possible before. He even imagined collaborative working. 'I really got a clear picture that one's colleagues could be sitting in other rooms with similar work stations, tied to the same computer complex, and could be sharing and working and collaborating very closely. And also the assumption that there'd be a lot of new skills, new ways of thinking that would evolve.'[2]

To pursue his new vision, Engelbart decided to go back to university and study. He chose Berkeley, since it had a fledgling computer programme up and running. There he learned about computers, and completed a PhD in electronics by 1956. After teaching for a year, he decided to exploit some of his inventions by patenting them and forming a company. The company didn't last long, and Engelbart decided instead to join the Stanford Research Institute. He began well by achieving more patents for inventions. He also still had his vision, but it was tough for him to gain any support. By 1962, he had written up his ideas in a formal document: 'Augmenting Human Intellect: A Conceptual Framework'.[4] With the help of some support by a friend at NASA named Robert Taylor[a] he finally received funding to start his visionary programme.

Support from ARPA followed with the help of ARPA researchers Licklider[b] and Ivan Sutherland, the latter also a pioneer of computer interaction. While Sutherland had been at MIT performing his doctoral research, he had created SketchPad, an amazing program for designers. Users could use a light pen and a set of buttons to draw lines and arcs on the screen, which the program could then automatically adjust. The user could zoom in on their designs and the computer would 'clip' the edges of the image to the sides of the viewing window. They could rotate, copy, move, and resize parts of their designs by dragging lines or points. Today these concepts are all standard features in every art package or computer-aided-design system. With this background, Sutherland was the perfect ally for Engelbart's vision.

Soon Engelbart was hiring talented new staff. The new Augmentation Research Center (ARC) was up and running. In the following few years, Engelbart invented the computer mouse, and tested it against other available devices.[c] He also created an astonishing array of ideas that were ahead of their time. In December of 1968, he and his team, with the help of several collaborators, demonstrated the outputs from his programme of research. It was to become known as 'The Mother of All Demos'—and for good reason.

The birth of friendly computing

Back in the convention center, Engelbart sits with something that looks like a big tray in front of him. In the middle is a computer keyboard. On the right is a clearly recognizable mouse—albeit rather chunky—which controls a familiar looking pointer on the screen, which Engelbart likes to call a 'bug.' On the left is a 'chord keyset'—something that looks like five piano keys that he can press in different combinations. Each key or combination of keys is equivalent to pressing one key of the normal keyboard—perhaps rather hard to learn, which is why it didn't stand the test of time.

Over the next hour Engelbart demonstrates a word processor, writing with a computer keyboard, and cutting and pasting text with a mouse. He shows auto numbering of headings, replacing words, hiding parts of documents from view, categories of items, sorting, selectively showing items in a list. He shows simple cross-references (hyperlinks), clicking on words and jumping to different information. He illustrates moving to different pages of information by clicking on different links and viewing pictures. He shows a simple image with live hyperlinks—click on a word in the image and a new page of text is shown. He starts a video-conferencing call with researchers several miles away. Via this video link, with the video appearing as a window on his innovative cathode ray screen, his colleagues demonstrate their programming languages and programming environment. They show

how they can format documents for printing, share files for collaborative working, even share each others' screens. They show how the mouse can be used to draw images on the screen. Nobody had seen anything like this before. In 1968, the demonstration was like watching miracle after miracle.[d,5]

Engelbart ended by mentioning a new project—an experimental network being set up by ARPA. 'In that network we're going to try to develop a special service to provide relevant network information for people. The kind of information that it takes to operate such a network. Who's got what services, what protocol do I use to get there, who's up today, where's the user's guide, where can I find the paper that describes this system.'[1]

Engelbart's group did indeed provide a simple information service on the ARPANET, and was influential in shaping the early Internet. Had progress continued at the same rate, perhaps Engelbart might have created the World Wide Web, or something very similar to it. But sadly things were to take a turn for the worse in the following decade as management reshuffles and sponsor problems caused confusion and dissent at the Stanford Research Institute. By 1977, Engelbart had been fired.

Engelbart tried to continue his work in a new company called Tymshare, which aimed to commercialize the outputs from ARC, but soon found himself marginalized and unable to innovate. But what was bad for Engelbart was good news for another research centre. Xerox Palo Alto Research Center (PARC) inherited many of the staff from Engelbart's ARC, and soon it became the new centre of excellence for research in the area.

Staff at PARC had already invented the laser printer in 1969. With the ARC researchers, and the new manager Bob Taylor,[e] developments in computer interfaces soon flourished. The concept of 'windows' was refined, where one program could have several windows, one for each document, and later separate programs could each have their own windows. Menus were invented—drop down lists of options that only appear when you click on a keyword. Icons were created—little images that could represent files, folders, programs, or 'minimized' windows. Radio buttons (a list of options, only one of which can be selected) and check boxes (an option that can be on or off) provided yet more visually intuitive ways for the user to interact with their computers. All these ideas were combined with a pointing device—the mouse. The new style of interface became known as WIMP (windows, icons, menus, and pointing device). It was a world away from the traditional 'command line' interface, where users could only interact by typing obscure commands into the computer.

Before long, operating systems had graphical user interfaces (GUIs) based on these concepts. Xerox introduced their Star Workstation (the Xerox 8010 Information System) in 1981, which was the first commercial machine to exploit the new ideas. It exploited the idea of WYSI-WYG (pronounced wizzy-wig), standing for What You See Is What You Get. The user saw documents on the screen as they would appear on paper, providing an intuitive and simple way to perform work. The machine also incorporated networking, email, and enabled objects from one document to be inserted into another (for example a chart created in a spreadsheet could be inserted into a word processing document).[6]

Steve Jobs, one of the founders of a new computer company called Apple, was extremely excited at the user interface of this new machine. He led the development of a new personal computer called the Apple Lisa, which went on sale in 1983, soon followed by the Apple Macintosh in 1984.[7] Other universities and computer companies copied these ideas, with X-Windows for UNIX computers in 1984, and the Atari ST and Commodore Amiga in 1985. By now, the IBM PC was a standard piece of office equipment, but the clunky command-line MS-DOS[f] interface was showing its age. By 1985, a primitive new graphical user interface for MS-DOS had been introduced, known as Windows. This was iteratively improved, and by 1990 Windows 3.0 (and version 3.1 in 1992) was released, which became a massive success for PCs worldwide.[8]

The face of computers had changed forever. As competition between the personal computer companies intensified, innovation and imitation ensured that the best ideas were constantly improved. Today our modern operating systems are all windows-based. Underlying complex functions can still be executed using a command-line interface, but the standard is now a gorgeous, graphical experience for users. With the advent of mobile computing on phones and tablets,[g] post-WIMP interfaces were developed. Apple was one of the first adopters of the trackpad on their PowerBook laptop computers. The company still leads the way in many of the newer innovations, for example, the use of multi-touch-sensitive displays and intuitive interaction methods such as finger swipes to move between pages, a two-finger pinch to zoom in or out, a two finger rotation or scroll.[h]

Engelbart never again achieved the same influence over the future of computer science. But he was still active even in 2010. He founded the Doug Engelbart Institute, which ironically is now part of the Stanford Research Institute. It aims to 'boost mankind's capability for coping with complex, urgent problems'.[9] He retains his vision, first glimpsed in the 1950s. 'The way you portray your thoughts to people, I just think the computer has so much more flexibility. It would be hugely important if we could understand all the complexity that's charging down on us. People keep saying we're here, and I keep saying, "No we're not here yet".'[10]

Seeing with new eyes

The 1960s had been a busy time. In some respects, Engelbart had been lucky with three consecutive heads of ARPA's Information Processing Techniques Office (IPTO). Licklider was a visionary, not just on the topic of networking, but on the subject of how people should interact better with computers.[11] This grand perspective made it easier for him to believe in Engelbart's goals and provide funding. Sutherland, who replaced Licklider in 1964, was a pioneer in interactive graphics. Taylor, who replaced Sutherland in 1966, was also greatly interested in the ideas of networking and graphics, and in addition to helping start the ARPANET project, went on to manage the computer science lab at Xerox Parc.[12]

Of these pioneers, Sutherland's contribution was to become one the most remarkable. His brief time at ARPA was little more than a distraction from his real love of computer graphics. He had already pioneered SketchPad. Now he set his sights on something much more radical.

Ivan Sutherland was born in 1934, in Hastings, NE, USA. He and his brother Bert shared a love of computers from an early age, and were building machines from relays through childhood. They were also influenced by their father, who was a civil engineer. By the time Ivan was in his teens, the family was living in Scarsdale, on the outskirts of New York, and both brothers were able to take part-time jobs with computer pioneer Edmund Berkeley (a co-founder of the

Association of Computing Machinery). For a minimal wage, Ivan wrote programs for Berkeley's personal computer (the first of its kind) called Simon.[13] 'I wrote the very first program for it to do division so that it divided numbers up to 15 by numbers up to 3,' says Sutherland. 'Berkeley was very helpful and taught me quite a lot about computing.'[14]

At around the same time, Berkeley introduced the Sutherland brothers to Claude Shannon, who was still based in Bell Labs. 'Bert and I went down to visit Shannon and spent a very pleasant day with him.'[15] It was to be a useful contact later in life. The brothers went on to create a maze-solving robot mouse,[h] inspired by Shannon's work, for Berkeley.[16]

Ivan completed school and went on to gain a BSc in electrical engineering from Carnegie Institute of Technology (now Carnegie Mellon University), and an MSc in the same area at the California Institute of Technology, as well as a summer job at IBM. But with his growing interest in computers he realized that MIT had a better computing programme. So Sutherland contacted Shannon who had joined the faculty there. 'He remembered our visit and invited me to come out to his house,' says Sutherland.[15] 'He made an enormous difference as to what my stay at MIT was like.'[16] Ivan's PhD was on Sketchpad, the amazing interactive design program.[17] His thesis committee (the people who advised him during his work and judged its quality) included Marvin Minsky—a pioneer of artificial intelligence—and Shannon as the chairman.

Following his doctoral research, Ivan entered the ROTC (Reserve Officers' Training Corps), a compulsory duty required of students by many major US universities at the time. After a year of serving in the army as technical eyes and ears for a Colonel, and building computer display systems for America's National Security Agency (NSA), he was transferred to ARPA and given the role as the director of ARPA's Information Processing Techniques Office (IPTO) as a first lieutenant. He stayed for two years making valuable contacts in the developing field of computer science, such as David Evans, another computer scientist specializing in graphics. But this was not where Sutherland wanted to remain. 'I said I would stay about two years. I had a career to get on with. It was time to go do something else.'[16] Sutherland handed over the IPTO to Bob Taylor and accepted a tenured position at Harvard. It was there he decided to embark on his radical new research idea.

Two-dimensional graphics were already possible on the new cathode ray tube displays, although they were nothing more than wireframe images (outlines made from straight lines). But if you could make two-dimensional images, then what about three dimensions? Why not create one image for each eye and produce the illusion of a three-dimensional image? And if you could see a 3D image, then why not detect the movement of your head, and alter your view of the image in response? 'The image presented by the three-dimensional display must change in exactly the way that the image of a real object would change for similar motions of the user's head,' says Sutherland.[18]

The result would be a 'virtual reality' for the users of the system. They would see only the virtual world created by the computer, and by moving around, they would move in the virtual world.

It was an extraordinary idea, and it took Sutherland and his team several years of effort to make a working system. But in 1968, the same year of Engelbart's demonstration, Sutherland published the details of his head-mounted three-dimensional display.[19] Although the display was indeed head-mounted, it was so heavy that it needed to be suspended by cables from a frame on the ceiling. The graphics were very crude, the most complex image being a 'room' with a door and three windows (a wireframe cube with one rectangle and three squares on its sides). The ultrasonic head position sensors were also prone to cumulative errors which made the system unusable for more than a few minutes at a time. But despite all this, it worked. 'An observer fairly quickly accommodates to the idea of being inside the displayed room and can view whatever portion of the room he wishes by turning his head,' says Sutherland.[19]

Much of the work was performed at Harvard, but Sutherland moved to the University of Utah in 1968, as his friend David Evans had created the computer science department there. Sutherland's impact on the world of computer graphics (and computer science as a whole) was soon remarkable. One of his students, Danny Cohen, created a flight simulator for training pilots, which ran on general-purpose computers. Their work led to the Cohen–Sutherland three-dimensional line-clipping algorithm—a method used for automatically 'clipping' images to the edges of the screen or viewing window. Evans joined forces with Sutherland to found the company 'Evans and Sutherland', leading to significant work in hardware for real-time graphics, 3D graphics, and languages for printers. Some of their former employees went on to create highly successful companies such as Silicon Graphics (Jim Clark) and Adobe (John Warnock).[19]

While at the University of Utah, Sutherland's students also became extremely well known. Henri Gouraud developed a realistic method of rendering graphics with shading, which became known as Gouraud shading. Frank Crow created anti-aliasing—the method of 'smoothing' jagged edges of lines with shades of grey (and used universally on every computer and television today). Edwin Catmull became co-founder of Pixar and President of Walt Disney and Pixar Animation Studios.[20]

Sutherland stopped working in graphics and in 1976 moved to Caltech where he was the founder and head of the computing department, encouraging the topic of integrated circuit design as a topic in computer science.[20] In 1980, he created another company Sutherland, Sproull and Associates, which was to be purchased by Sun Microsystems and become Sun Labs, and eventually Oracle Labs. Sutherland became a fellow and Vice President at Sun Microsystems, before moving to Portland State University and performing research into asynchronous systems[21] in 2008.

Photos and chicken wire

Computer graphics matured rapidly from Sutherland's early pioneering days. As demand for computer games grew, the software algorithms and computer hardware became more powerful. Today (as we saw in Chapter 010) the fastest supercomputers in the world are based around processors originally designed for graphics. New advances in display technologies mean that 3D televisions and computer displays are becoming mainstream.

Despite the extraordinary advances, in general all computer graphics still use two simple ideas: bitmaps and vectors. The bitmap image (or raster image) is simply what you create with your digital camera—it's an image at a fixed resolution, made up of millions of little differently coloured dots (called pixels, or picture elements). If you enlarge a bitmap image, then eventually things look 'blocky' because that's what the image is made from. It's why a digital zoom in a camera is worse than an optical zoom. The digital zoom just enlarges the size of those pixels without giving any more details. The optical zoom uses lenses to magnify the image, resulting in more detail.

In contrast, vector graphics are images calculated by a computer and carefully drawn afresh each time for you. It's much as you might remember from your maths classes at school: you plot points on your graph paper and use a ruler to draw lines between them. In vector graphics, all images are made up from points and lines[i]—even the text. This has the advantage that if you enlarge or zoom into a vector image, the computer will just recalculate all the lines and redraw everything with the same perfect clarity. You never lose detail with vector graphics. (Ivan Sutherland's SketchPad was perhaps the first ever use of vector graphics on a computer.)

Many tricks can be performed using vector graphics. To build a complex three-dimensional form, a 'wire mesh' can be created. Looking rather like a model made from chicken wire, the form is built from thousands of polygons (shapes with straight sides such as triangles, rectangles, or pentagons). These can be filled with colours by the computer, and shaders (such as the Gouraud shading algorithm) can make them look solid by figuring out how the light should change their surfaces and cause shadows. Make the polygons small enough, use many of them, and add some clever shading methods, and you can produce the illusion of curved surfaces. Shapes can be made to look more three-dimensional by the simple rule that things look smaller the further away they are—so points and lines further from the viewer should be reduced in size. Add some clever algorithms to detect when a closer object is in front of a more distant object, and you can make the computer hide objects behind each other. There is an extraordinary array of methods in computer graphics that allow astonishing images to be rendered, and complex lighting effects, mist, water, fur, and fabric to be simulated. If you've got enough time then you can even use a method called ray-tracing—for every pixel on your display, the computer figures out where each ray of light has come from. Did it reflect off the virtual water? Refract through some glass? Should the movement of an object cause a visible blur in this split-second?[22] Highly advanced methods such as these are used in modern computer-generated movies such as *Avatar* or *Shrek*.[23]

But ray-tracing can be slow. For fast graphics that are being produced in real time—such as in computer games—a key trick is to combine bitmaps with vector graphics. It is often extremely challenging to design vector graphics that are sufficiently messy; all too often they look clean and perfect. Obviously artificial. But bitmaps can be photos (or drawings created on the computer) that are very messy. They can provide all the glorious details of grainy wooden surfaces, or pores on skin, or rugged landscapes. The only problem is that bitmaps are two-dimensional and shaped in perfect rectangles. We often want three dimensions, or images that have curved or distorted surfaces. So the solution is to 'stretch' the two-dimensional bitmaps over the vector graphic wire mesh. It's a process called texture mapping.[j,20] We colour the polygons using the bitmaps, and then apply all the clever shading methods on top.[k]

The result is an illusion of reality so convincing that it is no longer possible for the human eye to distinguish between a filmed scene and a computer-rendered scene. Graphics processors are now so cheap and powerful that even a phone can render photo-realistic imagery. We are limited only by our imaginations, and because computers have no bias towards our reality, they are able render images in any style we choose. If we want a movie or game to appear as though it is drawn and shaded like a comic book, the computer can do it. If we want it to look like a moving Monet painting, the computer can do that too. If we want a movie to appear as a bumblebee might perceive it—the computer can do that.

There are also no limits on what the computer can show us. We can watch long extinct dinosaurs walking in ancient forests. We can view cities as they might have looked before video cameras existed to film them. We can see the tiniest of particles or the largest galaxies in the universe. We can even see within our own bodies and watch our brains watching themselves.

Waking dreams

We may have extraordinary computer graphics today, but virtual reality is still not an everyday experience for us. After Sutherland's pioneering work in 1968, research in head-mounted displays stagnated until the mid-1980s.[24] Then the quirky computer scientist and artist Jaron Lanier co-founded VPL Research, Inc. It was the first company to sell head-mounted displays and 'datagloves'—gloves that allowed the user to interact inside the virtual world. Lanier also introduced the term virtual reality to computer science.[25] (Lanier remains influential—he was a consultant for Linden Lab's Second Life,[l] and helped design Microsoft's body movement sensing Kinect device for Xbox 360.[m])

Head-mounted display technology has now improved, but it is not ready for everyday use. The best head-mounted displays are still expensive and heavy. To overcome these problems, many virtual reality researchers use 'caves'—special rooms with three-dimensional images shown on the walls, floor, and ceiling to give the illusion (often with the help of special glasses) that you are completely immersed in the virtual computer-generated world. Your movements are tracked so that the perspective is correctly shown: when you lean over a preci-pice you see further down, when you jump up you can see further, or when you walk (or use a control to 'fly') you can travel through the virtual landscape. The illusion of the virtual reality is now so good that users quickly feel completely immersed. They may be surrounded by walls, but they no longer perceive those walls. In virtual reality, you only experience the virtual world.

Mel Slater is a research professor of Virtual Reality at the Univer-sity of Barcelona (and Professor of Virtual Environments at UCL). He runs the EVENT Lab (Experimental Virtual Environments for Neuro-science and Technology), which hosts an astonishing array of research into the applications of virtual reality. Slater believes there are two important reasons why this computer interface is so appealing. 'One is that somehow in virtual reality we have the realisation in technical form of the age-old dreams,' he says. 'People have always dreamed themselves to be in other places. To be in different places where fan-tastic events happen. What virtual reality makes possible is a techno-logical realisation where one can create in principle any world that you can dream. And then you can go into it.'[26]

But while he may be motivated by such dreams, Slater's research is about practical benefits. 'The other aspect of virtual reality is that your reactions, your behaviours, are really quite different. Imagine you are interacting with a virtual human. It's really quite different when you only see through a screen and the virtual human is the size of your finger, compared with one that's your height, stares you in the eye and in principle could hit you—or kiss you.'[27]

The difference is noticeable when the behaviour of immersed users is studied. Amazingly, the graphics do not have to be very realistic for peo-ple to behave as they would in the real world. Any kind of simple illusion of standing on a tall building is enough to make people with vertigo extremely nervous. Even cartoon-like virtual people sitting as an audience are enough to give the shakes to someone scared of public speaking. Slater's group studies these responses, with the help of psychologists and neuroscientists. 'It's really easy to create a virtual environment where people can go on top of a tall building and look down', says Slater. 'People with a phobia of heights will do that in virtual reality and they'll have pretty bad anxiety symptoms. Which means that the psychologists can work with them on that. It's much faster, compared to spending months and months trying to persuade them to go near a high building.'[27]

It's not the only kind of human behaviour they have studied. 'More recently, with my PhD student Sylvia Xueni Pan, we looked at the interaction between shy men and virtual women,' says Slater with a smile. Astonishingly they discovered that even when a virtual girl leans towards a shy man, the man will move away. 'That was very successful,' explains Slater. 'The point is to show that this is useful for therapy—that they have similar responses to virtual as they do to real. The shy men get a bit freaked out for a while. But after a while they calm down.'[27]

The researchers have even studied how virtual reality may be used to help people with paranoid tendencies. The work grew out of the observation that all users tend to create stories about their experiences. 'They'll come out and they'll say, "That woman over there, whenever I looked at her she turned her head away. She doesn't like me." But the movement was purely chance. It was just random.' Following a suggestion from a psychologist, they began working with Professor Daniel Freeman, an expert on paranoia who was then at the Institute of Psychiatry at Kings College London. The initial study was to assess whether non-psychotic people with paranoid tendencies tend to have the same degree of paranoia in virtual reality as they do in every day life. 'The answer was yes,' says Slater. 'It was also quite amazing. We designed the environment; we knew what was in it. The subjects of the experiment just had to be in a library. It was silent. The ones with a greater tendency to paranoia in everyday life, they would come out and tell us, "whenever I turned my back on this one he started talking about me. I heard him whispering." Or, "there was a business man who didn't like me." These kinds of incredible stories.'[27]

'Virtual reality allows us to present many people with exactly the same neutral social situation,' says Freeman. 'What is very nicely illustrated is that a proportion will view it as a positive experience, a proportion will view it as a neutral experience, and some people will view it in a paranoid fashion.'[27] The work is continuing with more realistic scenarios. The group anticipates that studies such as these will enable breakthroughs to be made in therapy. Already there are companies offering virtual reality therapy for people with phobias of flying or fear of heights.

There is no shortage of other significant applications for virtual reality. Archaeological sites can be reconstructed to enable people to experience the buildings as they once were. Pilots and military personnel are routinely trained on virtual reality simulators. Increasingly virtual reality is being employed for training surgeons (it's better to make mistakes on a virtual patient than a real one). It is also being used for remote surgery—surgeons operating through robots while experiencing feedback from their instruments as if they were present in the operating theatre.

The related area of augmented reality is also becoming popular, where virtual objects or people are overlaid on top of the real world.

It can be much easier to produce augmented reality technology. For example, a tablet computer or smart phone, which has built-in accelerometers and cameras, can be transformed into a 'window' onto an augmented reality. You might be in a museum, and moving your device in front of an object might overlay new details around the object, perhaps showing you how the object would have looked in its original environment. Or you might be walking outside and your augmented reality window could use geological and palaeontology data to reveal the layers of rocks and fossils lying beneath your feet.

Perhaps one of the most startling uses of virtual reality is to investigate a phenomenon known as the body transfer illusion. 'One thing that virtual reality is uniquely able to do is give you a new body,' explains Slater. 'The way this works is very simple. You put on a head mounted display, so you see the virtual world. You can move your head around, so you see more of the virtual world as you look around. But one obvious thing you can do is look down at yourself. What you can do is program a virtual body to be where your real body is. To substitute your real body.'[27]

When researchers give users brand new virtual bodies, the people have the powerful sensation that this is now their body. 'It makes sense,' says Slater. 'Through the history of life, whenever you look down you see your body. So in some sense the brain has no alternative than to say when I look down and I see my body—it's my body. It results in a very strong illusion.'[27]

The illusion is enhanced by three-dimensional motion-tracking sensors. Move your real body and the virtual body moves in the same way. It can be further enhanced by adding haptics (touch). If you see a virtual ball touch your stomach and feel a ball touch your real stomach simultaneously, then your brain is fooled into thinking the virtual is real—even if it may look different from the real. It's an enormously useful tool for studying how we perceive ourselves and our world, increasingly being exploited by cognitive neuroscientists.

It may also have some fascinating applications. For example, if you participate in a situation as someone else, how does this transformation of your self-image affect your attitudes? 'Suppose it's a very small person and they go into virtual reality and suddenly they're now towering over everybody. How does this change their stance in a negotiation?' says Slater. 'Or suppose you are someone with a prejudice against a certain group. You go into virtual reality, you look down at yourself or look in a virtual mirror, and you are a member of that group. How does it change your attitude and behaviour?'[27]

The researchers are still investigating the answer to this question. Whatever it may be, there can be no doubt that through virtual reality we are learning more about ourselves than we can safely do in our everyday reality. Many of us are already becoming used to immersive computer games with 3D displays and body-sensing technologies. Perhaps in the future we may become used to virtual training and therapy to keep our minds active and healthy.

The computer scientists who work on virtual reality have their own vision. 'If you ask anybody who is working in virtual reality for their vision of the future, they would always give you the same answer,' Professor Mel Slater says with a smile. 'The vision has already been published. It's the holodeck in Star Trek. It's to make virtual reality...real. You enter into a room and you know it's not real, but nevertheless it seems to be.'[27]

It's not what you do but the way that you do it

The miracles of interactive computer interfaces, whether virtual reality or more everyday graphical user interfaces, are realizations of the dreams of computer scientists. They enable us to control computers in diverse and intuitive ways. They allow us to experience the diversity of output produced by computers in imaginative and enjoyable ways. And sometimes they don't.

It turns out that many of the miracles of human–computer interaction have their downsides as well. Sometimes computer peripherals can even result in injury. 'We used to joke that when Engelbart was coming and giving a talk a few years ago, that there should be demonstrations by all the RSI [repetitive strain injury] victims using mice, waving placards outside,' says Angela Sasse, Professor of Human-Centred Technology. 'When you look at what's causing RSI, the use of the mouse is much more significant than the use of the keyboard.'[28]

Similarly, when the new Wii games console became popular, with its innovative wireless input controller, a new injury developed: *Wii-itis*. Over-proficient youngsters learned to play Wii tennis with small flicks of their wrists instead of the intended large movements of the arm. Overplay the game in this way for several hours continuously, and you might end up in hospital with strained tendons.[n]

Indeed, every time a new input device is created, there may be repercussions for our health. This may result from the shape, weight, material, and movement of the devices. Some devices, such as the Xbox Kinect, sense the movement of players without them explicitly holding a peripheral, yet that does not stop them from affecting our behaviour. 'It's not only about the technology itself, it's shifted to the type of movement that is imposed on the user,' says Nadia Bianchi-Berthouze, an expert in affective interaction.[29]

Because of the complexity of the issues surrounding humans and how they interact with computer technology, a new breed of computer scientists have emerged. Some are cognitive scientists who are interested in how people think and interact with technology. Some are experts on human factors—they study all aspects of how we relate to our world in order to improve performance, safety, and the user experience with the technology. Some focus on how best to design new software interfaces or peripherals that are better suited to our needs. A new field called human–computer interaction (HCI) has grown up over the last thirty years to embrace all such research.[30]

It's an increasingly important area of research. Ann Blandford is professor of human–computer interaction at UCL. 'Early on in the history of computing, engineers did all the designing,' she says. 'Even today there is still a tension between technologists who build things and want to understand how things work, and the HCI people who like to understand how things could work better, or why they don't work. This clash persists to this day.'[31]

Sadly there is no shortage of examples of designs that do not meet our needs. Sometimes the problems are caused because old solutions are re-used for new and inappropriate problems. Angela Sasse has studied the increasing use of passwords as a method for authentication. 'When passwords were first deployed you'd have one password and you could easily remember it,' she says. 'But it became the de facto authentication system. We began to need passwords for everything. The password is just not suitable for that. The way human memory works: you can't just remember everything you want; unless you access it frequently you tend to forget it; unaided recall is very hard;

similar items seem to sit in the same partition of memory and compete; and when you don't need a password anymore you can't just wipe it, forget it—it's still there. So if we've got more than two or three passwords, or passwords you don't use very frequently—we can't cope.'[29]

Things are made even more difficult for us because the engineers who design the security systems have attempted to improve the quality of our passwords, without taking humans into account. They often introduce password policies to ensure we pick secure codes (more than a certain number of characters must be used, there must be a mixture of upper and lower case letters, numbers, and punctuation symbols, and the passwords must be changed every few weeks). 'We've done studies where people have sat there for twenty minutes trying to come up with a password that the policies would accept,' says Sasse. 'The costs are phenomenal, if you add them up.'[29]

Sasse has performed research with companies on this area. She monitors the minute-by-minute activity of employees as they use their computers at work. Sometimes there are so many different computer systems that employees spend a significant amount of time simply logging into each computer. 'It's not untypical for just the act of logging in to add up to about 30 minutes a day,' she says. 'That's three weeks a year! When I say to people in the company, "do you realize your employees spend three weeks a year just logging in to various systems?" they fall off their chairs! "No! That's not possible!" I show them the data. It is perfectly possible. It's utterly insane.'[29]

Problems are also caused by designers of computer systems who believe features are more important than functionality. While the early versions of the software may have had carefully designed interfaces with intuitive functions, later versions needed something new.

So more features are added. More options. More capabilities. All too often the result is a piece of software that is bloated and cluttered with so much complexity that it is too slow to be usable, and too complex to use without extensive training. 'We've got millions and millions of people sitting at work and muddling through all of the time,' says Sasse.[29]

'The problem is that the people who design the systems don't really think about what people are going to do with them,' says Blandford. 'Efficiency and effectiveness and happiness of staff should matter. How things are designed makes a big difference, particularly those things you have to use. When products are safety critical it can make the difference between life and death. Poor design of the interfaces can mean it takes people longer to use than they should. Mistakes are made. In hospitals, looking longer at devices than at patients is not good.'[32]

But times are changing. Companies no longer automatically upgrade their systems to the latest versions—if the current systems work, then why should they go to the expense of new technology, and retraining their staff? The HCI researchers have also shown the effectiveness of their approaches. One innovation is the living laboratory, where new technology is tried out by real people before its release. The principle is much the same as clinical trials in medicine—first the new drugs are carefully assessed under laboratory conditions to see if they function correctly and have no side effects. Only when enough trials have been performed can the drugs be released for use by everyone. The living lab allows us to do the same for computer systems.

Already some Internet companies use a similar principle to test out new versions of their Web pages. 'Big websites will often do A/B testing,' says Blandford. 'They put up an experimental version of their site and one in ten people will be routed through. Their behaviour is measured against the original. Big companies can either move forward to the new, or roll back to the old. You need to be big enough to have enough throughput to be statistically significant.'[32] Familiar companies such as Google, Microsoft, Facebook, and eBay all use this approach.

Another highly effective tool used by HCI researchers is eye-tracking technology. As people use computer interfaces, the exact parts of the screen that their eyes focus on can be detected. This allows researchers to discover whether interfaces are confusing, whether they attract our attention, or whether we simply ignore certain areas. 'Rich media can be an attention grabber, but can also be a distraction,' says Sasse. 'People in task-focus mode learn to ignore things. They skip over the stuff; develop blind spots.'[29]

Soon we may understand how to present information to users such that they need the minimum amount of time to find it on the screen, perhaps dynamically changing the display depending on what we are looking at. 'Combining intelligent interfaces with adaptive technologies allows us to work without being interrupted,' explains Sasse.[29]

Large companies such as Google are already investing heavily in intelligent interfaces to help us find information faster. 'Finding ways to detect introductory articles, so a straight search will give you good introductory texts. Exposing the first few lines of the article, or giving alternative search words. Google does many of these,' says Blandford.[32]

However, if novel technology such as eye-tracking becomes standard in every personal computer, there may be other problems. Advertisers are very excited by the possibilities of understanding us in more detail. Already companies build profiles of what we like to buy, and monitor where each of us clicks our mouse on Web pages in order to fine-tune the placement of adverts. If they knew where we are looking as well, they might be able to influence us in ways we do not want. It's one thing to understand us in order to improve our interaction with computers. It's quite another to understand us in order to exploit us. 'The problem is not that you are shown adverts that are relevant,' says Sasse. 'The problem is adverts that induce you to spend money that you don't have, or spend money that you don't want to spend. Better to have a system where you can declare up front how much you can afford and then after that it won't bother you. Don't show me anything more this month if I've got no cash left.'[29]

As intelligent interfaces improve, people are worried that the computer might discover their deep desires and make them an offer they can't refuse. Angela Sasse remembers one story she heard from a participant of a research study. 'What I worry about,' said the participant, 'is when you've got face recognition. You might just be wandering about. You have half an hour to kill so you go into a shop. You just kill time by browsing. You don't really need any clothes and shouldn't be spending any money. Suddenly your mobile phone goes off and it says, "Hello Suzi, nice to see you back in BigStore. We've noticed that you just lingered that little bit longer around these pants. From retail anthropology we know you're interested. If you buy two of them in the next five minutes we'll give you 20 per cent off." '[29]

There are no easy answers in human–computer interaction. Provide more information to a computer system and you may have a system that meets your needs better, and even improves your well being. But then you may have to face problems relating to privacy.

There can be no doubt that the most recent consumer-oriented computing devices are moving in the right direction, however. Their

designs are generally simpler, often with deliberately reduced functionality, and fewer but more intuitive controls. Instead of a phone full
of tiny buttons, many are now nothing more than a screen, responsive
to touches and swipes of our fingers. 'Often great design is about taking things away, simplifying it,' says Sasse. 'It's also often about ignor-
ing or not thinking about things. When do humans actually want
control and when do we want things done automatically?'[29]

My pet computer

One problem faced by HCI researchers is that people are always very
subjective about what they like and dislike. In fact, it is claimed by neuroscientists such as Antonio Damasio that much of our ability to make
decisions comes from our emotions. In one famous example cited by
Damasio,[32] an accident caused a large rod of iron to be driven through
the skull of a railworker Phineas Gage, destroying the left frontal lobe
of his brain. Astonishingly Gage survived, but showed a large change
in his personality. He no longer felt emotions, and as a result, could no
longer make rational decisions. From examples such as this, Damasio
proposed a model of emotion that suggests we use our emotions as a
kind of shortcut to decision-making. If a decision in the past resulted
in us being happier, then we are more likely to make a similar decision
in similar circumstances in the future. If a decision made us unhappy,
then we are more likely to choose differently in similar circumstances.
So rather than laboriously analysing the pros and cons of every decision (and becoming paralysed with indecision) our emotions enable
us to decide instantly. 'Emotions add flexibility, the ability to learn, to
take decisions in a more flexible way by mapping previous experience to the current environment,' says Nadia Berthouze. 'Emotions are

fundamental to the way we make decisions, the way we direct our attention. Without emotions our behaviour is not that smart.'[30]

A new branch of HCI known as affective computing takes models such as these very seriously. In this very new field of computer science, the aim is to create better technology that can sense our emotional state and use emotional processing to facilitate its performance. Ideally the technology would also respond to humans on an emotional level, perhaps by expressing emotion.[33]

Affective computing researchers study our emotions as we interact with new interfaces and devices—are they enjoyable to use? Can they improve our psychological well being? The researchers also use machine learning methods[o] to enable computers to understand our facial expressions, body language, and tone of voice in order to judge our moods. They also work with robots and artificial intelligence researchers[p] to create emotional devices—computers and robots that have a 'personality' and 'moods'.

Beyond the obvious applications in toys, these technologies address some real needs of people. 'We are working on technology to support patients suffering from chronic pain, in self-directed physiotherapy programs,' says Berthouze. 'The aim is to motivate them to do physical activity. It's about keeping them active. Normally as soon as they finish a programme at the hospital—often just a month of physiotherapy, they stop. Fear and anxiety influence the experience of chronic pain and often lead patients to avoid movement. But not moving is the worst thing they can do as it further exacerbates their physical condition.'[30]

Many of the patients may continue to experience their chronic pain, even when the injury has healed. Now the negative emotions associated with the pain keep the feeling of pain real. Berthouze's research aims to support the patients physically and give them feedback on progress, but significantly, also addresses their psychological state and uses that information to provide feedback and encouragement, or help them to relax before doing the exercise. Their computer algorithms analyse the movements and facial expressions of patients in order to figure out how they are feeling. 'Depression, anxiety, fear can all accompany pain,' says Berthouze. 'So we look at whether the emotional state affects the way they make movements. We can see a lot of guarding movements to avoid feeling pain. But if they're not afraid then the movement is different. The way you recruit muscles is different depending on whether you are anxious or not.'[30]

Fascinatingly, people will also respond quite differently to technology depending on whether it seems to have a personality or not. If you have a computer or robot monitoring patients in a hospital, or children with special needs, or elderly in a care home, then people are far more accepting of the technology if it can communicate on an emotional level, or even behave like a pet. 'A few years ago it was unthinkable to have a robot companion,' says Berthouze. 'Today it is considered something that is possible—robot pets are being taken to nursing homes to see how the elderly react.'[30] Surprisingly, focus groups and other studies have shown that there is a strong acceptance from the participants. 'I think society is ready,' says Berthouze. 'Industry is listening; there is a market. So I think this will speed up.'[30]

Human–computer integration

Computers are not traditionally thought of as emotional devices, yet of course as they interact with us, they provoke many emotions in us. Perhaps a common emotion may be frustration or irritation when we are learning how to use badly designed applications. But think back to all the other times computers affect you. Thanks to pioneers such as Engelbart, we can increasingly gain pleasure from the gorgeous design and interfaces of modern tablet computers and other consumer electronics. Because of the work of pioneers such as Sutherland and his students, entire movies have been made using nothing but computer graphics, and like all movies they can stimulate anything from excitement to tears in the viewer. But that's not all. Computer games may provoke anger, frustration, pleasure, and pain. Software that enables us to communicate with friends and family gives us great comfort, and some robots are already being used to provide companionship or support for autistic children or isolated elderly people.

Perhaps surprisingly the science of computers now also includes social sciences, where people are studied in order to understand how they interact with technology and how best to create interfaces to meet their needs. Virtual reality and computer graphics are not just used to create amazing images, movies, and visualizations, they are used to provide therapy for people with phobias or to help train people to cope with new situations. User interfaces are designed to be as natural and intuitive as possible, helping us to enjoy using technology and actually address our needs. As we have already seen, the commercial world has begun to exploit such knowledge, tracking our behaviours and ensuring that suitable advertisements are placed exactly where you will notice them.

It is hard to predict what the computer interfaces of tomorrow will look like. Will we just wave our hands around, or use a brain–computer interface and just think what we want? Will we have virtual or augmented reality headsets that are indistinguishable from today's prescription glasses? Will we have robot pets that have their own moods and interact with us just as living creatures do? Will computers become so integrated with our lives that even the word 'interface' becomes redundant?

Or will your next computer be more frustrated and angry at your inability to understand it, rather than the other way around?

Building Bionic Brains

Since the birth of computer science, researchers have secretly thought of themselves as brain-builders. After all, our thoughts are made from billions of little electrical impulses fired by neurons. Why can't computers be made to think in similar ways to us, using the electrical impulses in their electronic circuits? Why can't we make intelligent computers that can perform tasks that require intelligence? We could have learning, predicting, walking, talking, seeing, speaking computers. We might also have computers that can diagnose our illnesses, drive our cars, or explore distant planets for us.

But how do you make intelligence? Through logic and reasoning? Or through lessons learned in life? How do intelligent minds think about their environments and themselves? Could we ever create a conscious artificial brain?

Cheerful music plays in the background. The grainy colour film shows a tall, slightly gaunt American man wearing a dark suit. As he speaks, he holds up something in his right hand. 'This is Theseus.'

The film switches to a close-up of a little white mouse in a maze, moving forwards, flicking right, left, and forwards again. 'Theseus is an electrically controlled mouse. He has the ability to solve a certain class of problems by trial and error, and then remember the solution. In other words, he can learn from experience.'[1]

Once again, the work of Claude Shannon was attracting the attention of the public and academics alike.[a,2] When he demonstrated his amazing machine at the Eighth Cybernetics Conference[3] it created nothing but fascination and admiration from the other scientists. Perhaps to sound a little more serious, he usually called the mouse a 'finger' at the scientific conference.

'You see the finger now exploring the maze, hunting for the goal,' says Shannon, as he demonstrates the device live at the conference. 'When it reaches the centre of a square the machine makes a new decision as to the direction to try. If the finger hits a partition, the motors reverse, taking the finger back to the center of the square, where a new direction is chosen. The choices are based on previous knowledge and according to a certain strategy, which is a bit complicated.'

'It is a fixed strategy?' asks a scientist called Pitts. 'It is not a randomization?'

'There is no random element present,' explains Shannon. 'I first considered using a probability element, but decided it was easier to do it with a fixed strategy.' He returns to his demonstration. 'The sensing finger in its exploration has now reached the goal, and this stops the motors, lights a lamp on the finger, and rings a bell. The machine has solved the maze.'

'If it knows how to get from the origin to the target,' asks a scientist called Bigelow, 'does it not always know how to get back to the origin?'

'No. You see this vector field, if you like, is unique in going in the direction of the vectors, but going backward, there are branch points, so it does not know where it came from,' says Shannon.

'Like a man who knows the town, so he can go from any place to any other place, but doesn't always remember how he went,' muses a scientist called McCulloch.

Another scientist, Van Foerster, asks, 'What happens if there are no goals?'

'If there is no goal, the machine gradually works out a path which goes through every square and tries every barrier, and if it doesn't find the goal, the path is repeated again and again. The machine just keeps looking for the goal throughout every square, making sure that it looks at every square.'

'It is all too human,' exclaims Frank.

'George Orwell, the late author of 1984, should have seen this,' says Brosin.[3]

Teaching computers how to play

Shannon's maze-solving machine was made from telephone switching relays and motorized magnets to move the little mouse (or 'finger') around the maze. Although this simple robot had rudimentary decision-making abilities and memory, its controller was not a general-purpose computer. Nevertheless its relays were more than enough to let it explore a maze and remember the path it took to find the goal.[b] Several versions of Shannon's robot mouse were created and demonstrated up to the 1970s. It was a remarkable and perhaps unlikely achievement from this pioneer of Boolean logic, information, and communications theory. It had been inspired by something equally remarkable and unlikely: a computer that played chess.

In 1950, just a year after publishing his extraordinary work on communication theory and a year before creating his maze-solving

Figure 7. Claude Shannon and 'Theseus' the Maze-Solving Mouse, moved magnetically by his maze-solving machine, 1952.

computer, Shannon (Figure 7) had published a paper about a machine that could play chess.[4,c] Shannon thought about the game of chess in a clever way. Influenced by a 1946 book written by John von Neumann and economist Oskar Morgenstern on the theory of games and economics,[d,5,6] Shannon imagined the game of chess was like a mouse finding its way in a maze. Every time it is your turn to make a move in chess, you would think about the labyrinth of different moves you could make from the current point in the game until you reach your goal, when you have checkmated your opponent. Like a mouse trapped in a maze, there are some moves that you can make, and some that you cannot. Instead of walls blocking your path, it might be a rule of chess that forbids you from moving your pieces in a particular direction. So moving a knight this turn might open up the board and allow you to move a castle the next turn. But move a pawn this turn and you might not be able to move the castle next turn. Each turn there are many choices you might take, and depending on which choice you take now, different new choices may become available to you in the future. Instead of moving to a new position in a physical maze, by moving a chess piece, you are moving to a new configuration or state of the chess board.

But unlike a mouse that is trying to find its way in a static maze, in chess the moves you make in the future also depend on the moves of your opponent. So if you're searching for the best sequence of moves to enable you to win, you have to assume that your opponent is doing exactly the same. It's as if the mouse in its maze has to cope with an opponent who keeps moving the walls in order to stop the mouse reaching its goal.

Von Neumann had already anticipated this problem, although he was studying economics and game theory at the time. He had proven a theorem that shows that in this kind of game[e] there exists a strategy for the player that will maximize the chances of them winning, while at the same time minimizing the chances of the other player winning. Shannon used von Neumann's 'minimax' idea in his chess-playing computer. When it was the computer's turn to move, it would look at the next couple of moves that both it and its opponent might make. Each board configuration was analysed by an evaluation function—a set of 'rules of thumb' (or *heuristics*) that try to quantify exactly who is winning and by how much.[f]

After any four moves (two by each player) the result would be a new board configuration which might mean one player is doing better than the other in the game. So the aim for the computer is to find the best two moves such that it will maximize its chances of winning and minimize its opponent's chances—while assuming that each time it moves, its opponent will try to do exactly the opposite. Once it has identified which sequence of moves looks like the best, it plays the first and waits to see what the real opponent does. In the worst case the human opponent may make the best move available to them, as anticipated by the computer. In the best case the human may make a mistake and the computer might do even better than it predicted. Then to decide its next move, it looks ahead another couple of moves, and so on.

Shannon's plans for a chess-playing computer would by no means make a perfect chess player, but his 'minimax algorithm' laid the foundations for countless other game-playing computers in the future. All would use search algorithms to find good moves each turn, from the vast number of different choices. Shannon's work was groundbreaking also because he had identified two different ways in which a computer could play the game. It could use a brute-force approach and just examine every possible move by every piece for each player each turn, in order to find the best. Or it could use heuristics to examine only those moves that somehow looked more likely to result in better results for the player. Shannon favoured the latter approach, because if you look at fewer options each turn, you can potentially look ahead more turns in the game.

In the late 1940s and early 1950s, Shannon was not alone in thinking about intelligent chess-playing computers. Around the same time, Alan Turing wrote the first computer program (on paper) to play a full game of chess. It worked using the same principle of using search to find the best move from a range of possibilities. There was not a general-purpose computer in existence capable of running Turing's program, so he acted as the computer himself, following his own program (and taking half an hour per move) against a colleague. (His program lost.)[7]

Perhaps because of these early pioneering attempts, chess and similar games such as draughts (checkers[g]) and Go became established as benchmark problems for computer intelligence. For decades to come, many researchers studied the problem of how to make a computer play games better. In chess, the landmark event came in 1997 when a computer built at IBM called Deep Blue was able to beat a Grand master in chess. It was the first time a computer had been able to beat a world champion playing under the standard chess tournament rules. Although a remarkable piece of engineering which showed some astonishingly human-like abilities in its game-playing, it worked in a very non-human way. Its beginning and end games were played by using large databases of previous games played by humans, and most of its 'intelligence' came from brute force search: considering billions of possible moves each second. Deep Blue (and most other chess-playing machines before and since) was nothing more than a massive chess-move searching machine, with no ability to learn or improve its game play.[8]

The birth of intelligence

Back in 1950, both Shannon and Turing used the idea of a chess-playing computer as an example of intelligence. Shannon thought that if a computer could play chess, then perhaps it could make logical deductions, translate one language into another, or even compose music.[4] Turing also believed that a chess-playing computer might be capable of other feats of intelligence.

Turing was not as skilled as Shannon in constructing devices; building mechanical mice was not his style. Turing's approach was perhaps more ingenious. He had just published his own views on machine intelligence in a paper, 'Computing Machinery and Intelligence',[9] that was to become another foundation of computer science. Turing's first words in the paper were, 'I propose to consider the question, "Can machines think?"'.

To address this deep and very difficult question, Turing had invented the idea of an 'imitation game,' which today we call the Turing Test. It was, he believed, a scientific way to understand whether a computer was intelligent or not. It didn't rely on the ability of the computer to play chess, solve a maze, or to perform a job that is normally performed by a human. It relied on the ability of the computer to hold a conversation.

Turing described the game like this. Imagine there are three rooms, one containing a person, one containing a computer, and one containing you, a human interrogator. As the interrogator, you can ask questions and hold a conversation (by typing and reading text) with the individual in each room, but you don't know whether you are talking to a person or a machine. After about five minutes of conversation, if you can't correctly figure out which room contains the computer, then the computer passes the Turing Test.

In the same paper, Turing says, 'I believe that in about fifty years' time it will be possible to programme computers, with a storage capacity of about $10,^9$ to make them play the imitation game so well that an average interrogator will not have more than 70 per cent chance of making the right identification after five minutes of questioning....I believe that at the end of the century the use of words and general educated opinion will have altered so much that one will be able to speak of machines thinking without expecting to be contradicted.'[9,h]

Turing was not alone in the UK in exploring ideas of intelligent computers. He was a member of the Ratio Club—a recently formed group of young researchers in the UK.[i] The club was formed specifically to discuss behaviour-generating mechanisms and information processing in brains and machines[j,10] and hosted American researchers such as McCulloch.[11]

But while the British were exploring such ideas in the 1950s, researchers in America were creating a new field of research specifically on the topic. Stimulated by the cybernetics conferences (such as the one in which Shannon demonstrated his maze-solving mouse) there were now several scientists in the USA actively working towards the goal of making computers more intelligent.[k,12] In 1956, they came together for a month-long brainstorming conference in Dartmouth College, New Hampshire. The organizers were Claude Shannon, John McCarthy, Marvin Minsky, and Nathaniel Rochester. Attendees included Ray Solomonoff, Oliver Selfridge, Trenchard More, Arthur Samuel, Herbert Simon, and Allen Newell. All were to become pioneers in the new field of artificial intelligence (AI), a name they agreed upon during the conference.

It was a groundbreaking event, which identified many of the key problems they believed should be addressed. Even today, their questions remain important areas of research. Could computers be programmed to use a natural language such as English? Could a program that simulated the neurons in the human brain be produced? Could computers improve themselves by learning? How should a computer represent information? Can creativity be produced by adding randomness?[13]

Rather like the Moore School lectures nearly a decade previously which helped trigger the building of computers worldwide, the Dartmouth conference helped launch the new field of AI. It would become a field that transformed the whole of computer science, for AI researchers frequently invented techniques that became mainstream in other fields of computing. 'The artificial intelligence people, I think, pioneered many of the advanced computing techniques: non-numeric programming; dealing with compiler languages; describing languages and so on,' says Sutherland, whose PhD thesis committee comprised both Shannon and

Minsky. 'I think that the whole effort has now reached a point where it is taught to undergraduates as computer science.'[14]

However, progress in AI was far from smooth. From the early days, opinions differed on how best to make a computer intelligent. Some, like McCarthy, believed that reasoning through logic was the route to intelligence. Others, like McCulloch and Pitts, believed models of neurons might be the way to go. Some, like Minsky, believed that it was important to add real-world knowledge into the computer to make it intelligent. The debate was to lead to hype, public failures, and nearly the death of a major part of the field. Minsky was at the heart of the controversy.

The seasons of AI

Marvin Minsky was born in New York City, in 1927, a middle child with two sisters. His father was an eye surgeon, but Minsky was more interested in chemistry and the emerging field of electronics as a child. He attended private schools and excelled, his intelligence clearly evident. Even as a child of five when he was given an intelligence test, his answer was unusual. When asked how one should look for a ball if it is lost in a field of tall grass, his tutors were nonplussed when the young Marvin contradicted their answer of starting in the middle of the field and spiraling outwards. Minsky had instantly realized that to start in the middle you must cross the field—it is more efficient to spiral inwards from the outside. It was an event that stayed with him. 'Everybody remembers the disillusion he experienced as a child on first discovering that an adult isn't perfect,' he says.[15]

He spent a year in the US Navy after graduating high school, before entering Harvard. He began with a major in physics, but soon became interested in genetics, mathematics, music, and the nature of intelligence, although he did not agree with the prevailing theories. As an undergraduate Minsky was performing experiments in the laboratories, both in the department of psychology and in the department of biology (dissecting crayfish and examining their neurons)—even as he switched his major to mathematics and wrote a thesis on topology.[15]

During these years of education and exploration, Minksy became fascinated by the work of neurophysiologist Warren S. McCulloch, and mathematician Walter Pitts. They had written a paper in 1943 on an abstract model of neurons.[16] It was a huge simplification of the way real neurons work: each artificial neuron had several inputs (binary values of either 1 or 0) whose values were weighted (multiplied by either a 1 or a −1) and summed. The result inside the neuron was then compared with a threshold. If the sum was above the threshold, the neuron would produce a 1 on its single output, otherwise it would produce a 0. Connect several of the neurons together in the right way, with outputs of earlier neurons feeding forward into inputs of later neurons, and even neurons this simple were good enough to behave like simple logical circuits.

Minsky had his own ideas about how a model of neurons could be designed. 'I imagined the brain was made of little relays—the neurons—and each of them had a probability attached to it that would govern whether the neuron would conduct an electric pulse; this scheme is now known technically as a stochastic neural network.'[15] Minsky's idea could allow neurons to learn by adjusting the input weights of the neurons. It's the same idea that Donald Hebb published shortly afterwards, and became known as Hebbian learning—often summarized as 'cells that fire together, wire together'.[17]

He then moved to Princeton for his PhD. Before long he became interested in the idea of actually building an artificial neural network. With the help of a colleague at Harvard, they obtained funding and built a prototype in 1951. It was a monster with 300 vacuum tubes that could learn like a brain. They tested it by giving it similar problems to Shannon's mouse in a maze.[1] To their surprise it could not only learn good routes for a single mouse (the correct choices being reinforced by making it easier for the machine to make the same choice again) but it could even handle two mice at once. Minsky continued the work for his PhD, examining how the addition of another memory might allow the neural network to make predictions. 'If a machine or animal is confronted with a new situation, it can search its memory to see what would happen if it reacted in certain ways,' says Minsky. 'If, say, there was an unpleasant association with a certain stimulus, then the machine could choose a different response.'[15]

Minsky did not make use of the computers being built at the time. 'On one hand I was afraid of the complexity of these machines,' says Minsky. 'On the other hand I thought they weren't big enough to do anything interesting in the way of learning. In any case, I did my thesis on ideas about how the nervous system might learn.'[15] Minsky occasionally talked about his work with von Neumann, who was on Minsky's thesis committee. Minsky's head of department, Tucker, was nervous about the ideas. 'Later Tucker told me that he had gone to von Neumann and said, "This seems very interesting but I can't evaluate it. I don't know whether it should really be called mathematics." Von Neumann replied, "Well if it isn't now, it will be someday—so let's encourage it." So I got my Ph.D.'[15,m]

After he achieved his PhD in 1954, von Neumann, Shannon, and Weiner supported Minsky's nomination to be a fellow at Harvard. For two years he developed his ideas about intelligence in men and machines, until 1956 when he helped organize the Dartmouth conference. Even during the conference Minsky was developing new ideas, such as an automatic theorem-proving program that could discover some of Euclid's theorems. Two years later he joined Shannon (and other researchers such as McCulloch and McCarthy) at MIT.

It was a time of great innovation. Hugely important ideas such as time-sharing[n] were invented by these pioneers. Ideas of artificial intelligence were refined, with AI researchers approaching the problems in many different ways. 'How could we build a machine that thinks and does all the sorts of things that you would say is thinking if a person did them? So that's one question,' says Minsky. 'Another question is: is there a theory for this? Could we understand principles of intelligence or something like that? But the third one and the one that's really the most effective definition is very weak, namely the AI labs are the places where young people go if they want to make machines do things that they don't do yet and that are hard to do with the currently existing methods. So in that sense, AI is just the more forward looking part of computer science.'[15]

By the early 1960s, there were some clear AI design philosophies, which did not seem entirely compatible with each other, but that all showed great promise. John McCarthy, Minsky's colleague at MIT, was the advocate of mathematical logic. Inspired by the work of researchers such as Chomsky who had shown that the structure (syntax) of human language is different from its meaning (semantics), McCarthy showed how logic and logical computer languages could be used to enable computers to reason about statements. His work resulted in the development of computer languages designed to support these ideas, such as LISP (and later PROLOG[o]), and was to have a significant impact on AI research until the present day. 'It's the idea of getting computers to do some of the reasoning that humans can do,' says Robin Hirsch, 'and if that's what you want to do then you have to devise the right kind of logic to express it.'[18]

The approach led to some amazing success stories. A new kind of program called an expert system emerged from McCarthy's work, which stored information and corresponding logical rules about a topic, extracted from human experts. These programs could then ask a series of questions and produce logical answers (perhaps diagnoses of illnesses or recommendations of suitable financial products, depending on the specialization of the expert system). Researchers learned they could use computers to perform natural language processing—automatically finding and processing the different parts of sentences. 'Chatterbot' programs emerged such as ELIZA and PARRY, which combined many of the ideas to enable the computer to process the input from a user and produce relatively convincing responses—in some cases good enough to fool people for a short time that the computer was actually a real person.

By 1963, McCarthy had moved to Stanford to create his own AI lab. Minsky had formed the Artificial Intelligence Group with Seymour Papert (which eventually became the Artificial Intelligence Laboratory at MIT), part of a larger Project on Mathematics and Computation. It was the beginning of a divergence of approaches in AI. Researchers on the West Coast of USA, led by McCarthy's example, became known as the 'Neats' because of their focus on logic and proofs. Those on the East coast, led by Minsky's example, became known as the 'Scruffies'.

Minsky's approach was not based on mathematical logic. He believed logic alone was not sufficient to create artificial intelligence. Instead he introduced the idea of 'frames'[19]—data structures that could hold real-world information that might not always be logical, but which nevertheless were truths about the world. Based on the idea of semantic networks,[p] information in a frame comprised slots, values, and types. So to represent knowledge about an elephant, the frame might look like this:

Slot	Value	Type
Elephant	–	(This Frame)
ISA	Mammal	(Parent Frame)
NUM_LEGS	Default = 4	(Default, inherited from Mammal Frame)
SEX	OneOf (Male, Female)	(Procedural attachment)
EARSIZE	Large	(Instance value)

Because the frames could link to each other and inherit information from each other, it was possible to create programs that could search and reason about the information in a seemingly intelligent way. Another of Minsky's innovations was the creation of 'micro-worlds'— highly simplified toy environments or scenarios that could be used as test-beds for the AI approaches. For example, in the 'blocks world' there was nothing but a set of blocks that needed to piled one on top of the other in a specific order. The simplification enabled researchers to create and test new AI methods of many types (for example, a natural language understanding program was created to interpret commands typed by a user for the blocks world[20]).

The successes by both the Neats and the Scruffies led the pioneers to make some ambitious predictions. In 1965, Simon claimed that, 'machines will be capable, within twenty years, of doing any work a man can do.'[21] In 1970, Minsky said, 'Within a generation...the problem of creating 'artificial intelligence' will substantially be solved.'[22]

After McCarthy left MIT, Minsky and Papert spent the following few years examining a wide diversity of topics relating to AI. One topic that increasingly drew their attention was the neural network. In

1957, an old classmate of Minsky called Frank Rosenblatt had created a more advanced model of neurons. He called it the perceptron.[23] It was almost identical to the simple neuron proposed by McCulloch and Pitts, except that the weights of the inputs could vary between −1 and 1, and the threshold could also be adjusted. Rosenblatt also proposed a certain topology or connections between neurons: an input layer, which is connected to an internal hidden layer, which is then connected to an output layer of neurons. The work had caused a flurry of researchers to experiment with neural networks in the 1960s. But because of his earlier work in the area of neural networks, Minsky was not convinced. After a series of heated debates between Minsky and Rosenblatt, Minsky decided to write down all his objections in a carefully produced book, *Perceptrons: An Introduction to Computational Geometry* which was published in 1969.[24] The book was to have a devastating effect on neural network research.

'There had been several thousand papers published on Perceptrons up to 1969,' says Minsky, 'but our book put a stop to those. I now believe the book was overkill. What we showed came down to the fact that a Perceptron can't put things together that are visually nonlocal.' Minsky picks up a spoon and places it behind a bowl. 'This looks like a spoon to you, even though you don't see the whole thing—just the handle and a little part of the other end. The Peceptron is not able to put things together like that.'[15]

John Shawe-Taylor is Professor of Machine Learning and author of some key texts on the topic, who works on neural networks and related methods to make computers learn. 'It was a wonderful, beautifully written book. It's got a lot of interesting results in it. But you started believing his propaganda. Everything in the book was correct. He wasn't making false statements . . . but they were made in a way that left very little option for development of the ideas. I think it was very damaging for research funding at that time.'[25]

Despite Minsky later saying how much he admired the simplicity and capabilities of the perceptron,[15] the damage was done. What followed in the early 1970s became known as the first AI winter. It was also fuelled by failures of early natural language processing to provide good translations from one language into another. In 1973, a report for the British Science Research Council[26] was deeply critical of the achievements in AI, which seemed to be so different from the predictions of the pioneers such as Minsky and Simon. Support was withdrawn for AI research in all but three UK universities (Essex, Sussex, and Edinburgh). Across the world, funding for AI dried up. Careers were lost.

Research into AI continued slowly, and eventually some of the methods began to be used in the real world. By the 1980s, fuzzy logic controllers enabled smoother and more intelligent control of devices from lifts to washing machines. Expert systems became widespread, and major new parallel computing projects were started, with logic-based languages such as LISP at their heart. Major projects such as CYC[q] began, which had the ambitious aim of creating a massive knowledge base of all common-sense knowledge. In the world of neural networking, new types of neuron were invented (the Hopfield net) and new learning methods such as back-propagation seemed to offer the solution to all the previous problems. Funding in all areas returned. Summer had returned to AI.

But for a second time came public failures. The expert systems were found to require too much time to elicit knowledge from people, and they simply gave silly answers if confused by any information outside their domain of expertise. Several of the major AI computing efforts failed.[r] Many companies based on the technologies also failed, and research funding was quickly withdrawn. Even the new neural network approaches suffered from problems—they were slow, not guaranteed to converge on optimal solutions, and did not scale to larger problems.[27]

There were also eloquent new critiques of the foundations of most of artificial intelligence—symbolic processing. Both Scruffies and Neats used computers to manipulate symbols, such as 'chair' or 'under.'[s] The philosopher Searle likened the computers to a person in a Chinese room.[28] The person is handed a piece of information written in Chinese that he cannot understand, he looks up the appropriate response in his filing cabinet, and returns a new piece of information in Chinese that he does not understand. To somebody outside the room, it might appear that the room contains a native Chinese speaker, when in fact the person understood no Chinese at all. Searle argued that by performing symbolic processing, computers could never be intelligent no matter what they did.[t] Even if a chatterbot passed the Turing Test, it would not understand the words it used, any more than a mail-sorting machine understands the concept of a love letter.

Once again AI fell into disrepute, and a second AI winter froze the field in the late 1980s. The remaining researchers were now fearful of even using the name artificial intelligence. Alternatives such as intelligent systems, computational intelligence, and machine learning began to be adopted. AI research continued quietly, with nobody daring to make any bold predictions. Slowly, behind the scenes, AI began to mature into something new.

Intelligence from feet to head

By the early 1990s, influence from philosophers and robotics engineers was changing the way researchers thought about intelligence. The new

MIT professor Rodney Brooks captured the change of thinking in his aptly titled paper *Elephants Don't Play Chess.*[29] He argued that compared to any kind of robot or computer program, a mammal such an elephant is hugely intelligent. It can move around in its world, communicate with other elephants, indeed it can even mourn the dead. But elephants don't play chess. They don't have logical thoughts. They don't reason or manipulate symbols.

The AI programs of the day might be able to reason logically. They might be able to play a decent game of chess. But they couldn't control a robot in the real world. They couldn't figure out where anything was in the real world, or what it was. They couldn't cope with the variety, diversity, and inconsistency of the real world. Reality is messy and 'Good Old Fashioned AI' (GOFAI) as it became known, simply couldn't cope with it.

Brooks argued that AI had things upside down. Instead of creating a model of the brain and then trying to program that into a computer, researchers should take a more behaviour-based approach. Intelligence could be built from the bottom up, not the top down. 'I realized that I had to invert the whole thing,' says Brooks. 'Instead of having top-down decomposition into pieces that had sensing going into a world model, then the planner looks at that world model and builds a plan, then a task execution module takes steps of the plan one by one and almost blindly executes them, what must be happening in biological systems is that sensing is connected to action very quickly.'[30]

Using this insight into biology, Brooks built his 'subsumption architecture' for robots. Intelligence was built from layers of instinctive behaviours, some of which could override others. So a low-level (most important) behaviour might be the instinct to avoid walking into an object. A higher-level (less important) behaviour might be to walk about randomly. An even higher-level behaviour might be to explore the environment. Sensors directly affect all behaviours, but lower-level behaviours take priority—they can interrupt higher-level ones. 'This idea came out of thinking of having sensors and actuators and having very quick connections between them, but lots of them,' says Brooks. 'As a very approximate hand waving model of evolution, things get built up and accreted over time, and maybe new accretions interfere with the lower levels. That's how I came to this approach of using very low small amounts of computation in the systems that I build to operate in the real world.'[30]

The result was a complex set of behaviours that dynamically switch and combine in response to any environment, giving a more natural intelligence. Significantly, there was no processing of symbols, no internal lists of facts about the world. To Brooks, the world was its own model, and the robot's behaviour simply fitted that world.[31] When they created their first robot that worked in this way, the result was amazing. 'At the time there were just a very few mobile robots in the world; they all assumed a static environment, they would do some sensing, they would compute for 15 minutes, move a couple of feet, do some sensing, compute for 15 minutes, and so on, and that on a mainframe computer,' says Brooks. 'Our system ran on a tiny processor on board. The first day we switched it on the robot wandered around without hitting anything, people walked up to it, it avoided them, so immediately it was in a dynamic environment. We got all that for free, and this system was operating fantastically better than the conventional systems.'[30,32]

Phil Husbands is a professor at Sussex University who specializes in AI and robotics. 'Brooks' slogan that the world is its own best model doesn't make any sense on one level. What does it mean for the world to model itself?' he says. 'But it is a nice phrase that refers to the fact that many adaptive real-world behaviours do not require the behaving agent to hold an internal model of the external world. A central assumption of traditional AI was that behaviour was generated through building and reasoning with such internal models. Brooks demonstrated that this was not necessary and indeed his method produced impressive real-time behaviour, something that was beyond traditional AI at the time.'

The idea was not entirely new. Ross Ashby, a British pioneer and member of the Ratio Club with Turing, had created a device in 1948 that worked using similar principles.[u,33] The Homeostat was a strange machine that maintained its own internal stable behaviour (comprising interacting pivoted magnets), even when disturbed. It may have just looked like a bunch of boxes on a table, but its self-regulating behaviour was interesting enough for Ashby to claim in a *Time* magazine article that it was 'the closest thing to a synthetic brain so far designed by man.'[34] At around the same time, another member of the Ratio Club, Grey Walter, had demonstrated robot 'tortoises' which moved autonomously using simple sensors and motors that produced remarkably complex behaviours. Walter was a significant inspiration to Brooks and many other pioneers in autonomous robotics. When describing his robots, Walter wrote, 'Not in looks, but in action, the model must resemble an animal. Therefore, it must have these or some measure of these attributes: exploration, curiosity, free will in the sense of unpredictability, goal-seeking, self-regulation, avoidance of dilemmas, foresight, memory, learning, forgetting, association of ideas, form recognition, and the elements of social accommodation. Such is life.'[35]

But Brooks' clearly articulated ideas in the early 1990s were a turning point in AI research. Suddenly researchers could dare to explore non-symbolic approaches to intelligence. Another researcher, Stewart Wilson, helped trigger similar research into what he called 'animats' at around the same time, in his own seminal paper, 'The Animat Path to AI'.[36] He believed (and extensively referenced Turing's ideas) that researchers should simulate artificial animals in progressively more complex environments. Like Brooks, he believed that intelligence should be built from the bottom up. 'The basic strategy of the animat approach is to work toward higher levels of intelligence 'from below'—using minimal ad hoc machinery,' says Wilson.[36] He proposed that researchers should begin with simple artificial creatures in simple environments, and slowly increase the complexity of the environment or tasks to be formed in the environment. Then the complexity of the animat should be increased only enough to make it cope in that new environment. Ideally adaptive solutions should be used where possible. In this way intelligence would arise if and when it was needed, just as it had evolved in nature. This would enable researchers to understand how each element of a brain might emerge and work together with other elements. The many problems relating to perception, locomotion, prediction, and survival, would eventually lead to greater understanding of the higher-level problems such as communication, planning, and reasoning. It was a radically different view from the top-down ideas that had dominated the field for decades. AI had changed forever.

Soon there were major new conferences on the simulation of adaptive behaviour and artificial life. Researchers were not just exploring the mathematician's view of intelligence any more. Computer scientists now worked hand-in-hand with biologists and philosophers to explore the origins of intelligence, and of life itself.[v,37]

Adaptation by natural selection

We see something swimming. It appears to be made just from blocks, but somehow it resembles a little turtle as it paddles its way through water. Another strange swimming creature comes into view, this time using three pairs of paddles in a row on its blocky body. 'This demonstration shows virtual creatures that were evolved to perform specific tasks in simulated physical environments,' says an American voice.

We now see something that moves just like a snake or eel, swimming by undulating its body in waves. 'Swimming speed was used to determine survival,' continues the voice. 'Most of the creatures are the results from independent evolutions. Some developed strategies similar to those in real life.'

We see more beautiful swimming snakes made from a chain of square blocks. Three elegantly swimming tadpole-like creatures swim into view and brush against the sea floor. 'Once they're evolved, multiple copies of these creatures can be made and simulated together in the same environment.'

We switch to a view of land. A small worm-like creature undulates its way across the ground. 'This was a creature first evolved for its ability to swim in water then later put on land and evolved further. A successful side winding ability resulted.'

We see a swimming turtle with four paddles, which seems to have an amazing manoeuvrability in the water. It is attracted towards a red light, changing direction to follow the light when it moves. 'This group was evolved for their ability to adaptively follow a red light source,' says the calm American voice. 'The resulting creatures are now being interacted with. A user is moving the light source around as the creature behaves.'

There is more to the video, but here we must stop. This is Karl Sims's Virtual Creatures, first shown in 1994.[38,39] If the new approach to artificial intelligence was the idea of a slow, incremental, evolutionary increase in complexity to the programs, then this was perhaps the pinnacle of the new bottom-up approach. But Sims's work was also one of the most impressive demonstrations of a related branch of computer science interested in evolution.[w] His work was an early triumph in the field of evolutionary computation and the simulation of adaptive behaviour, showing the astonishing power of evolution in a computer. With nothing but a requirement to swim or walk better, a realistic model of physics, and a model of evolution, Sims showed that virtual creatures would evolve that looked and moved in astonishingly familiar ways.

Karl's work was not the first demonstration of evolution. In fact the first studies of the topic dated back to the birth of computer science itself. One of the first people ever to achieve a PhD in computer science also founded the field of evolutionary computation.

John Holland was born in Fort Wayne, IN, USA in 1929. He grew up in the small towns of neighbouring Ohio (or 'Ohiah' as he would pronounce it then). He was an intelligent child, encouraged by his parents with chemistry sets and games of checkers with his mother from an early age. He was also interested in building mechanisms, such as a toy submarine. Unlike other pioneers such as Minsky, Holland never had the opportunity to attend specialist schools. Instead he grew up in small local schools that had no specialist teachers. This was to cause problems as he grew older and thought about college. 'In high school I had to get a tutor who worked in the sewage system to teach me trigonometry because my school did not teach trigonometry and I needed that as an entry requirement for MIT,' says Holland.[40] He had been interested in mathematics from an early age. Indeed it was the lack of a mathematic foundation in biology that was to make him lose interest in that topic. 'In high school I was very interested in biology but I couldn't see how to do any mathematics in biology. I probably would have gone on in biology if there'd been a clear road to do something more formal.'[40]

Despite the lack of any privileged education, Holland came third in a state-wide test for physics, which resulted in him winning a scholarship for MIT. He began his studies there in 1946, and chose to focus on physics. In his final year he was able to work on the newly finished Whirlwind computer for his dissertation. This valuable early experience in computing enabled him to get a job at IBM in the planning group for IBM's very first commercial computer, the 701. Holland soon discovered that he was one of the only people with experience of computer programming. 'I actually taught a simple course on programming to the people who were working in the laboratory putting the machine together,' he remembers.[40]

While at IBM there were several visitors, allowing him to meet McCarthy (who taught him to play Go) and other pioneers such as J. C. R. Licklider and John von Neumann.[x,41] Holland also worked with his boss Rochester on models of neural networks, implementing one of the very first Hebbian neural networks[41] (and visiting Hebb at McGill University several times during the process). After eighteen months, he decided to study for a PhD. IBM allowed him to work in the summer and study in the winter. He chose the University of Michigan because of its excellent department of mathematics.

Holland focused on mathematics and had even begun writing a dissertation on cylindrical algebras (an extension of Boolean algebra), when he met Arthur Burks. Burks was starting a new programme on

Communication Sciences at the university and suggested Holland might be interested. Burks knew more than most about computers, having been the senior engineer of the ENIAC, a consultant in the design for the EDVAC, the supervisor of Eckert, roommate of Mauchly, and later a colleague of von Neumann at the IAS in Princeton. He had also given nine of the Moore School lectures.[42]

Holland decided to take more courses in psychology and language, and eventually completed his thesis on a study of an abstract logical network created by Burks, similar to the neural networks of McCulloch and Pitts. As he finished, in 1959, a new department was created: the Department of Communication and Computer Science. 'My degree which was in 1959 was the first Ph.D. labelled in that general area,' says Holland.[40] It was the first doctorate in the brand new field of computer science.

He decided to stay at the University of Michigan as a member of staff (and there he stayed for his whole career). It was not long before the idea of adaptation through natural selection became attractive. He had discovered a mathematical book by the well-known British mathematical statistician, R. A. Fisher: *The Genetical Theory of Natural Selection*,[43] which introduced important concepts into the understanding of natural evolution, including the fact that fitness improvements in evolving organisms seem to correspond to changes in the variance of their genes. Holland was attracted by the mathematics but immediately saw something that seemed to need explanation. Fisher seemed to suggest that genes acted independently of one another. Holland knew this was not the case. Through his extensive reading he knew that groups of genes could act together and together create a useful element of a living organism. These groups were like building blocks—they would be used over and over again in everything from a carrot to an elephant. 'Even then I understood that alle-les[y] didn't work independently of one another—they interacted,' says Holland, talking about Fisher's work. 'That was a challenge for me to go from his assumptions of additive effects on alleles to something where clusters of alleles could interact.'[40]

Holland's solution was to create a computer model, which he called a genetic algorithm. It was a model of evolution, with a population of individuals, each comprising a set of genes. The genes were represented by binary numbers. To mimic natural selection, a 'fitness function' (representing the problem that needed to be solved) would evaluate the effects of each set of binary numbers (alleles). Those that solved the problem would be given higher fitness scores and those individuals with better fitness scores would become parents, producing a new population of offspring. The offspring would inherit some genes from one parent and some genes from the other,[z] with some random mutations. This new generation of individuals would then be evaluated by the fitness function, the better individuals would have children again, and so on. The result was evolution in a computer program. Holland could watch and analyse the changes in frequencies of clusters of alleles as evolution progressed.

'This notion of co-adapted sets of genes (or whatever you want to call them) is important so I started wanting to do for them what Fisher did for single alleles. I said to myself, what if I try to treat these as sort of a super-allele. What could I do mathematically?'[aa,40] The work led to his building block hypothesis—the idea that evolution is not trying to build good solutions through tweaking one gene at a time. Instead evolution finds good clusters of alleles, which are then preserved together and inherited like building blocks. Holland still believes this idea is a fundamental concept that can be seen everywhere around us. 'I think that recombination of standard building blocks is a phenomenon that we can see very broadly in all sorts of things. If I take something like the internal combustion engine, every single piece of that has been well known for over a hundred years. It was the unique combination that was important, not the parts.'[40]

Holland refined his ideas in the 1960s.[44] He introduced the idea of a classifier system—something looking like a cross between an expert system and a genetic algorithm—which was able to learn its own rules. Holland published the work in a book called *Adaptation in Natural and Artificial Systems* in 1975.[45] However perhaps because of the dominance of GOFAI, it was not until his student David Goldberg published a new book in 1989 on genetic algorithms[46] that the field of evolutionary computation suddenly took off.[bb,47,48] Before long, evolutionary algorithms were being used for optimization, to discover new mathematical functions, or provide the basis for adaptation in machine learning software, across the whole of computer science. It turned out that evolution was particularly good at finding solutions to very difficult problems that other methods struggled to tackle.

Other nature-inspired algorithms followed, some based on the movement of swarms of ants in an ant colony.[49] Another of Holland's students, Stephanie Forrest, invented algorithms based on the immune system.[50] Yet another of his students, Chris Langton, became one of the founders of the field of artificial life.[51] The latest research in evolutionary computation examines how the process of growth (embryogenesis or development) can be incorporated into evolutionary algorithms and enable the evolution of more complex solutions.[cc,52] Today evolution forms an integral part of research in artificial life and robotics. It is also exploited by many companies, for diverse applications that include the evolution of antenna designs for mobile phones and the testing of memory chips.

Holland continues his work in evolution and learning to this day. His philosophy was always grounded in the idea of a bottom-up learning system, even before it became fashionable. 'I very much agree with Rod Brooks. First of all, things have to be situated,' says Holland. 'There have to be environments where they can cause interactions with the environment and, so to speak, ask their own questions. I've believed that from square one. I just don't think you can do this without learning and adaptation.'[40]

Learning to learn, predicting the predictors

Artificial intelligence has taught us many lessons in recent years. Perhaps the biggest lesson we've been forced to learn is that intelligence is complicated. Whether the method is top-down logic programming, or bottom-up evolutionary and adaptive, we still haven't solved all the problems. There are no programs that can pass the Turing Test.[dd,53] We still struggle to create intelligent machines that can control robots in unpredictable environments—indeed it's exceedingly difficult even making a two-legged robot walk in a natural way.

But when we break the problem of intelligence into easier chunks, and focus on each chunk separately, we can make progress. One of the most significant areas of improvement in recent years has been in creating computer programs that learn, an area of research now known as machine learning. We may not be at the level of teaching computers in the same way that we teach our children. But in machine learning we can teach computers how to tell the difference between one set of data and another (a problem known as classification) or to learn the structure of a stream of data and make predictions about what may come next. Both are enormously useful for real-world applications. If you can differentiate between different classes of data then you have the ability to make decisions: is this an image of a car or a bus? Does this sequence of genes indicate a greater likelihood of one genetic disorder or another? If you can make predictions then you can potentially predict whether a certain trading strategy in the stock exchange will make money, or whether a drug will have the desired effect, or whether a pattern of network traffic data looks abnormal, indicating an intrusion by a hacker.

Evolutionary computation provides one notable method for machine learning, known as genetic programming (GP).[54] Instead of evolving genes made from strings of binary digits, GP evolves mathematical functions and operators as its genes. Given a set of inputs, and some examples of correct outputs, GP evolves a program or mathematical function that produces the right result from the inputs. The advantage of this method is that the learned equation or model can then be examined to see how it works. Bill Langdon is a leading GP researcher. 'GP has the advantage that it produces models that people can actually understand,' he says. 'While I was working for GSK [GlaxoSmithKline] we did some work on modelling drugs. In a two-day workshop we turned up in the last afternoon. There had been lots of lectures by machine learning experts. My presentation had a slide with the model on it. No one else had such a slide. The meeting erupted at this point. There were shouts from the audience: 'Look John, I told you that term was important two years ago—you didn't take any notice!' The point was that they could relate to what was in the model. It was intelligible for them. It was in the units they were familiar with.'[55]

Neural networks provide another important way computers can be used to learn. Since the troubled days of the perceptron and limitations of back-propagation (a method of automatically adjusting input weights of neurons), many new types of neural network have been created, along with many clever ways of adjusting their input weights and connectivity to make them learn.[ee,56] Those investigating neural networks are often motivated both by a desire to enable artificial intelligence and to understand the brain. Geoff Hinton, the scientist who first used back-propagation with a neural network, and the creator of another method called the Boltzman Machine,[57] has clear ambitions in these areas. 'I'm interested in how the mind works and how the brain computes,' he says. 'I see that as essentially the same question. I've been interested in that since I was at school.'[58]

More recent developments in machine learning have less to do with biology and more to do with mathematics. A new breed of statistical-based machine learning had emerged with the creation of the support vector machine (SVM). Although it resembles a simple neuron, researchers have developed a deeper theoretical understanding of learning.[59] Professor John Shawe-Taylor is a leading computer scientist in the area. He explains how an SVM learns, imagining a problem where the computer needs to decide what a newspaper article is about, perhaps to help a user who is looking for something. 'You want to make a decision about whether an article is about a specific topic,' he says. 'Say is it about sport. Based on certain words being present, you weight more strongly the likelihood that this is an article about sport. So if you see the word 'football' then obviously that makes you quite confident. The article still might not be about sport, it might be about the politics of football, but it points you in that favour. The idea of making a decision (using a classifier) based on a weighting of characteristics

of an object (in this case an article but it could be any object) is fundamental and is used in support vector machines.'[25]

An SVM makes a decision based on a weighted combination of
characteristics of a situation. The idea is not unlike the way a simple
perceptron neuron fires depending on the weighted sum of its inputs.
But one of the key ideas behind SVMs that makes them powerful is
that we don't actually have to explicitly state all of these characteristics. Instead 'similarity functions' are defined between objects. For
example, one newspaper article might be similar to another if it shares
many common words. The similarity function is then used by the
SVM to learn how to separate one group of data from another, for
example, to decide which set of articles is about sport and which are
not. 'It's to some extent a heuristic,' says Shawe-Taylor. 'But it's backed
up by some reasonably solid theoretical statistical analyses that show
you that the thing you optimize in the algorithm corresponds to
something predictive.'[25]

There are now many varieties of SVM and other statistical-based
machine learning methods. Some can enable computers to calculate
the probabilities of different things being related (such as Bayesian
leaning). This 'softer' approach can make it possible for computers to
learn surprisingly complicated relationships. 'It seems to me that adding probabilities into things and making a 'soft' (if you like) AI—a
probabilistic AI—actually gives you the edge that enables you to do
things that appear much harder,' says Shawe-Taylor. 'Sometimes sof-
tening the problem makes it easier. Although it looks harder and is
more complex in a sense it is actually easier to solve.'[25]

These remarkable advances mean that our computers are finally
able to achieve many of the marvels that pioneers such as Shannon,
Turing, and von Neumann had dreamed about. Computers can now

read car number plates because of clever image-processing software. They can identify fingerprints, retinas, and even faces. They can learn the sounds of our voices and allow us to dictate instead of type. Even cheap digital cameras now have computers which can recognize and follow faces, automatically correct flaws in the picture, and recognize the kind of scene they are being pointed at. Computers learn our preferences based on our patterns of shopping and predict other products we might enjoy. They alert us when unusual patterns of transactions are detected in case our credit card has been stolen. They adjust car engines, washing machines, and a thousand other devices to make them more efficient and suit our needs better. The first robot vacuum cleaners and autonomous robot toys are now emerging. Artificial intelligence is all around us, and although it may not be as intelligent as we'd hoped, and we still struggle to scale up the complexity of the problems it can tackle, it's clever enough to help us every day.

Complex futures

Artificial intelligence and its many related fields such as heuristic-based search, artificial life, evolutionary computation, and machine learning, continue to inform and challenge us in many deep and fundamental ways. They allow us to take a fresh perspective on questions posed by philosophers for centuries. Why are we here? How did life first begin on the planet and how did the myriad forms of complex life emerge? What is intelligence? What is consciousness?

Today agent-based models are used extensively to help answer all of these questions. This new form of AI creates models of individuals (*agents*), their behaviours, and their interactions between themselves and their environments.[60] The agents may comprise genes and evolve, as in evolutionary computation. They may have neural network brains, or they may learn using another machine learning method. They may use logic and reasoning to plan their actions, or simulated emotions, or knowledge frames to represent the environments around them. They may be constructed using detailed models of artificial chemistries, or as patterns in a cellular automata universe. The agents may be physical robots, each with its own computer, able to communicate with their companions through light, sound, or touch. They may even be made from synthetic biology—artificial cells designed in collaboration between biologists and computer scientists. Through all such models, researchers aim to gain real insights into ourselves. 'My feeling is that this sort of agent based approach where the agents learn and adapt is critical if we are going to study those processes,' says John Holland.[40]

He should know, for he is one of many pioneering scientists who spend their time studying complex systems at the Sante Fe Institute, New Mexico, the first centre dedicated to the analysis of complexity. Today we increasingly recognize that many natural and artificial phenomena are mathematically unpredictable, despite often being composed of a collection of relatively simple individuals. Holland has been studying complex systems for several decades. 'I've always liked this notion of generating complex things with relatively simple rules,' he says.[40] It's easy to understand what he means. Our complex economies are made by countless simpler financial transactions. Ecosystems support and maintain their countless constituents through unthinkable numbers of interactions between plants, animals, birds, and fish. Our immune systems keep us alive through the interaction of cells and proteins. Our genes define how we develop from a single cell to a massively complicated organism, via countless interactions of genes, proteins, and cells. Our thoughts are created through interactions between billions of neurons. Through agent-based computer models we gain new understanding of all these processes.

The brain has long been an obsession for many, and computer scientists have developed their own hypotheses of how and why we think. Yet many deep philosophical questions remain. Even if a computer can be used to model a brain, will that mean it is really thinking? 'I think if we had a huge computer and let's say we managed to get the simulation right of all the spikes going on in your brain, and we managed to get all the chemicals levels bathing the synapses right, and so on, that thing would be thinking,' says Geoff Hinton. 'It may be a simulation of a real brain but if the real brain was thinking then the simulation would be thinking too. That's my view.'[58]

How could we ever know? Perhaps if a computer can pass the Turing Test, we will finally have created a digital intelligence to rival our own. Or will we always assume that if we chatted just a little longer about some new topic, or studied its behaviour a little longer, the computer would reveal itself to be an unthinking machine? 'How long is a piece of string?' says Bill Langdon. 'You've been studying this computer for five years and you're still not convinced. In the meantime it's gone on and graduated and maybe made a fortune on the stock market. But you're not convinced.'[55]

Robot pioneer Professor Owen Holland is one of an ambitious few aiming to go even further. 'I see building robots inspired by biology in terms of building tools for investigating the behaviour of biological systems, especially ourselves,' he says. 'We need a conscious robot to help us to understand consciousness PERIOD. There is no evidence that such a robot would be a better robot than one that had no trace of consciousness, or that merely behaved as if it were conscious (a so called zombie). In fact I could make a case for a conscious robot having the potential to be very much worse, like Marvin [the fictional depressed robot in *The Hitchhiker's Guide to the Galaxy*, by Douglas Adams]. However, it also seems likely to me that consciousness is an inevitable result of developing a model-based predictive way of dealing with the world, which may well be the best way of dealing with the world. The quest for an intelligent robot may well lead us as a side effect to a robot that is conscious.'[61]

John Shawe-Taylor is one of many people who remain uncomfortable with this idea. 'Maybe we will realize that actually intelligence isn't the important thing, the important thing is experience. We have experience and machines don't,' he says. 'I come out on the side of philosophers who say that machines can't experience in the way that we experience. That's consciousness if you like. Maybe it's just an illusion that we have experience. I am not averse to that argument. But I can't quite buy it. (Maybe that's because I'm quite a poor machine.) I can see the logic of it. But it doesn't quite fit with my sense of reality.'[25]

John Holland remains optimistic. 'When we start building conscious machines—and I think we will—and when most people think, "yeah it's conscious," I think, no matter what, they're going to be quite different from us,' he says. 'I do hope that we are going to learn more about things like consciousness. It seems to me that once we do, it is going to have an impact on how we teach people, how we treat people, on and on and on. I really think, with time and effort, it is achievable.'[40]

Perhaps Alan Turing most aptly summarizes the challenges that remain in AI: 'We can only see a short distance ahead, but we can see plenty there that needs to be done.'[9]

111

A Computer
Changed My Life

Our world is digitized. Thanks to pioneers such as Turing, Shannon, and von Neumann, we have the amazing technologies of today. We have strong mathematical foundations for remarkable silicon machines that run amazing software. We have connections to everyone in the world through easy-to-use interfaces. We even have intelligent machines that help us in ways we could never have dreamed.

The journey has only just begun. Every year new pioneers exploit the technologies of computer science for startling and imaginative applications. Artists and musicians use computers to entertain us, biologists use computers to understand us, doctors use computers to heal us. We even use computers to protect ourselves from crime. It's an exciting time.

The young artist enters the large room, rolls of drawings under his arm. There are twelve large cube-shaped computer monitors on desks surrounding him, apparently connected to mainframe computers on the floor below. Blinds cover all the windows, darkening the room, and allowing strange graphics on the screens to shine brightly.

The artist nervously unrolls his drawings on the floor of the computer lab, filling the space with his carefully drawn renderings. One large sheet looks like a strange abstract swirling piece of Hindu art with snakes or tentacles flowing outwards from the centre. Another looks like a weird bug-collector's display with a myriad differently shaped bugs placed randomly—except that similar bugs are always next to each other. Another looks like an evolutionary tree of abstract shapes, from Viking helmets to beehives, each morphing into another. The watching group of scientists and computer programmers have never seen anything quite like this.

The artist had struggled to gain acceptance for his ideas from his own community. The art world was not ready for his use of computers to help generate his art. Would this audience be any different? William Latham looks up at his audience of scientists, and begins to explain his work.

Computer creativity

Latham was no ordinary artist. Born in 1961, he grew up in Blewbury, England. It was a rural setting, but because of the nearby Harwell Atomic Energy Research Establishment, he came into contact with scientists throughout his childhood. His father worked as an industrial chemist, his mother was a composer and conductor. The dual influences of science and arts were to stay with Latham. He attended Stowe school—a grand boarding school in Buckinghamshire set in landscaped parkland designed by Lancelot 'Capability' Brown, and then attended Oxford University to study art. His early art had been figurative (clear representations of real sources such as human figures).[a] But he was soon being strongly influenced by Russian constructivism (a form of art based on abstract geometrical shapes), and by several artists[b] who were developing automatic methods to create art. 'It was a revelation to me that you could use systems to generate art,' says Latham. 'I started to attend classes at the University of Oxford Computing Lab. I learned Fortran and they had big Benson plotters which would draw things out.'[1] He learned the principles of programming but understood that he needed help. 'I could see the potential but I realized that I was never going to be a great coder myself.'[1]

By 1979, despite visiting the physics and computing labs in Oxford University for help, Latham was finding it difficult to produce his art using computers and plotters. 'There was always a lot of frustration because I could never quite get the results that I wanted,' he says. So he stopped using computers and instead made large sculptures that resembled giant spider's web structures made from balsa wood. In 1982, he moved to the Royal College of Art (RCA) to study fine art, but again his work went through a crisis point—how could he generate the art he wanted to produce? He started spending a lot of time in the Natural History Museum, London. He was drawing naturally occurring geometric shapes such as snake skeletons and antlers.

Latham's ideas continued to develop. He produced large evolutionary drawings where shapes would change according to very simple rules. 'At that time I was using my brain as a computer and drawing the results like a glorified graphics device,' says Latham. 'What was interesting is that the human mind can conceptualize distortions, surface deformation—things that are very hard to do technically.'[1] Having worked with computers before, he knew the limitations of what could and couldn't be done at the time. In 1983, he started writing programs again for the BBC Micro and Macintosh—not to produce the artwork, but to produce a list of instructions that he would follow in order to draw his art. It would choose from his set of rules, and list what to draw. 'The idea was that there would be no aesthetic boundaries,' says Latham. 'If you're an artist and you are drawing, there is always this envelope you never cross. So the idea was that by using an iterative approach—which is what it was—with no limit to the number of iterations, you start to get into visual areas which were unknown.'[1] The results were fascinating. They looked like Outsider Art—art by naïve or self-taught artists who were outside the mainstream and never institutionalized by the art establishment.

The RCA had no computers, so Latham started making use of the computers at the Middlesex and the City of London Polytechnics, and working with programmers there. Before long he heard that IBM had a research laboratory in Winchester[c] where researchers from different disciplines would collaborate using their new computers. He called them and explained what he did. They immediately invited him to come and give a talk. It was an exciting lab to visit, with scientists, programmers, molecular chemists, archaeologists, even surgeons modelling a pulsing heart for the first time. A stimulating environment for a young artist struggling to find his way.

Latham took his drawings to Winchester and gave a talk, explaining his ideas of using computers to generate art. The talk was well received by the scientists. 'They were quite captured by it,' says Latham. 'They said, "Sounds like you've got a lot of great ideas. Why don't you come along and do some interesting work with us?"' This was an opportunity that Latham couldn't turn down. 'It was a culmination, quite a key point in my career,' he recalls. 'At that point computers became pretty dominant in my life.'[1]

Three months later and Latham was an IBM research fellow at the centre. It was perfect timing, for the field of computer graphics was now able to create photo-realistic images, even beautiful images. One of the researchers, mathematician Stephen Todd, had been writing a modelling program called ESME (Extensible Solid Model Editor) that could be used to create three-dimensional models, but it was hard to edit and modify the forms. He became a collaborator with Latham and they developed new software that followed Latham's artistic rules, plus used random mutation, to evolve new artworks. They called the software Form Grow and Mutator—it was like a simple genetic algorithm. Latham's rules for how shapes should be iteratively combined and modified were embedded inside, and he acted as a breeder, judging which members of an evolving population were aesthetically pleasing enough to have children.[2,3] Over three or four hours of evolving, Latham and Mutator could generate hundreds of new surprising artworks. The art was virtual sculpture—three-dimensional shapes with textures and patterns that could be viewed from any angle, with any kind of virtual lighting. The pieces were exotic and convoluted. Twisted forms that defied the imagination. 'There were things like ammonites, alien structures from another planet. All had been evolved under an alternative evolutionary system,' says Latham. 'They looked like they were natural but they were also very synthetic. For me it was like Pandora's Box.'[1]

Jon McCormack is another artist who uses computers to generate his work. He understands the power of using evolution to generate art.[d] 'Evolution frees you from the limitations of your imagination,' he says. 'It can free you from prejudices, existing paradigms or conceptualisations. Through the use of evolutionary and generative processes, the artist can have a synergetic relationship with the machine, a kind of "creative amplifier" that allows us to generate things that we could not have imagined or created without the computer. I still think that is an amazing and stimulating proposition.'[4,e]

Latham's work was soon internationally famous. They were making films by animating the forms[f] and exhibiting the images in art shows. 'I could fly around the world. I had big exhibitions in Tokyo, Germany, Hong Kong, Australia, all sponsored by IBM,' says Latham. 'The IBM PR machine was getting my images everywhere.'[1]

His work was also being appreciated in unexpected places. 'What I didn't realize is that my films had been shown continuously during raves,' laughs Latham. 'I had this huge cult following. I had no idea!' Because of his popularity amongst ravers, a well-known band called the Shamen[g] approached Latham to make a video for them. So he set up a giant 'render farm' across several IBM labs in the UK and used their powerful computers to make the music video. 'The head of IBM PR found out about this. He came down from London and said, "Can I have a chat with you?" He said, "Well, you know, William, IBM can't be associated with the Shamen. Just finish the video, but don't do any more!"'[h]

But despite the popular success, Latham's work caused controversy in the art world. Could computer-generated images be considered as real art? 'The art world definitely hated my work,' says Latham. 'A lot of people said to me, "William you could have gone on to become a great artist." Going towards computers alienated me from the art world. Ultimately the art world always needs something to sell. With a computer you can produce a hundred million copies—how do you sell it?'[1]

Part of the problem was Latham's very different approach. He saw the computer as more than just a clever paintbrush; he saw it as a machine that could even be creative in its own right. 'The Form Grow and Mutator code that we'd implemented represented my ideas as an artist,' says Latham. 'Then all I was doing was making decisions about whether something was aesthetically pleasing or not. The skill of me as an artist was to create rules that generated an interesting space to explore.'[1] Latham even examined the idea that the computer could make the aesthetic decisions itself, an idea not liked by many artists. 'Intellectually that would be most interesting—if you could replace the artist with a machine,' he says. But if the computer can truly generate its own art,[i] then would that mean it is as creative as us? This is a harder question than it may seem. If you use Latham's Form Grow and Mutator software and evolve your own artwork, we might justifiably say that you are being creative and behaving like an artist as you use the system. So if a computer takes your place and evolves its own artwork that is just as good as yours, why shouldn't we call the computer creative as well?

Gordana Novakovic is an artist who specializes in collaborating with technologists and computer scientists.[j] She is convinced that true creativity is beyond the reach of computers. 'At this stage of technological development they can only mimic creativity,' she says, 'which is a complex process involving intention, emotion, reflexive and critical thinking and so on. I don't think this will change soon, and it probably never will'. Novakovic is pessimistic about the possibility of computers ever gaining the ability to create their own masterpieces and 'own' those pieces. 'To achieve this transition,' she says, 'computers would have to create a complex system of social interactions that would give rise to the philosophical, socio-political and economic conditions for art to emerge. They would then have to reach a consensus about what art is. And perhaps they might, one day, although I see no signs that it could happen in the foreseeable future.'[5]

But Latham thinks quite differently from many artists. He has no problem with the idea that computers could be creative. 'I personally think human creativity is overrated,' says Latham. He is also not impressed with talk of intentionality, emotional content, and other words commonly used by most artists to describe their work. 'That's all a form of self-aggrandizement,' says Latham with a smile. 'It's all rubbish. Artists like to build this myth about themselves. I've never shared that viewpoint at all. It's not some mystery. Some people are just a bit more visually articulate than others.'[1]

Latham is perhaps being modest about his own input to the software. McCormack knows the importance of Latham's work. 'In terms of evolutionary art, which uses evolutionary-inspired methods,' he says, 'the pioneers are William Latham and Karl Sims. Richard Dawkins—though not an artist—inspired the process.'[k]

McCormack is another computer artist[6] who shares Latham's views of creativity. 'I would argue, yes, a computer can be independently creative,' he says. 'Computers can already originate things that are new, as computational evolutionary systems clearly demonstrate. Much of our technology already makes creative decisions for us. Modern digital cameras have "Auto intelligent" modes that evaluate a scene and determine all the settings automatically, even down to when the actual picture should be taken! Previously the photographer would use his or her skill and creativity to do these things. The latest version of Adobe Photoshop has a mode called 'content aware filling' that can be used to automatically remove or change objects from complex scenes—for example to automatically remove rubbish or unwanted roads from a landscape image. These kinds of technology replace individual human aesthetic judgment with machine "creativity," and obviously, this is just the beginning. A more vexed question is: who determines the aesthetic criteria by which the machines make their aesthetic judgments? What will be the long-term effect of deferring our creative judgments to machines?'[l,4]

Latham spent six years at IBM, but his position was abruptly cut short when recession forced the company to cut much of its research.

He chose to move to industry, first creating a company called Computer Artworks[m] in 1993, then GamesAudit a decade later. As he expanded his second company Latham continued to be invited to conferences to speak about his old IBM work. Following one such talk, mathematician Professor Frederic Leymarie invited him to Goldsmiths College, London. It was the beginning of a whole new chapter for Latham. With the help of Leymarie who was excited by the potential of the work (and also realized it needed a research home), Latham took an academic position and in 2007 became Professor William Latham at Goldsmiths.

The move to academia has enabled him to return to research again. 'We restarted the Form Grow and Mutator project, which had been on ice for fifteen years,' he says. Working with his old IBM colleague Stephen Todd, his son Peter Todd, and new colleagues at Goldsmiths such as Leymarie, Latham began a collaborative project with bioinformatics researchers Lawrence Kelley and Ben Jefferys at Imperial College, London.[n] The work uses Latham's Form Grow language to visualize protein structures[o] as they evolved in our past, and as they might be designed in the future,[7] linking to bioinformatics data such the Worldwide Protein Data Bank (PDB).[p] With the ability to interact and modify the resulting forms and hence design novel protein structures, Latham is now able to think of the art of chemistry. 'The underlying idea is to explore whether an artist should be redesigning nature,' he says. 'It's the idea of Capability Brown. The parks are beautiful. Every tree is placed. It's nature, it's a hybrid of nature. Is that more beautiful than the original version of nature?'[1]

Latham may be an unusual artist, but he is perhaps one of the first of a new breed. He is a technical master who explores the world as an artist, discovering creative new solutions to every problem. His medium is very different from most. He paints his pictures, not just with physical tools like brushes, but with computer code and human expertise. His canvas comprises the sprawling, evolving, creative industries. To his surprise, Latham has become a specialist in the application of computers in games and art. 'One thing I've learned,' he says, 'is that you don't need to have the knowledge yourself. If you claim you do know it, you probably don't know it. The key thing is to know people you can bring on to work with you that will trust you to work with them.'[a,1]

William Latham's story is one of many pioneers who continue to transform our use of computers today. Whether in computer games, the music industry, the film or television industries, or just at home playing with an art package, computers have become everyday tools that make creativity easy. 'When I was at Art College in the late 1980s,' says Latham, 'artists were a special breed. But actually now everyone is pretty creative. They're all using Facebook in novel ways. They're all doing digital photography. Look at the number of people using Unity.[q] Or using Garageband. Everyone is being pretty creative. I think computers have democratized creativity.'[a,1]

Computational biology

At Goldsmiths, Latham's new work was the visualization of protein structures, a collaboration with bioinformatics researchers. The prediction of protein structures by computers is a good example of a particularly challenging problem tackled by researchers.[r] When our genes are expressed, strings of molecules called amino acids are produced. These then fold themselves up in complicated balls of strings, exposing some regions and hiding others. Each twisted ball of amino acids is a new protein, and proteins are used as the language of cells. Proteins control the expression of other genes and they control the fate of cells. It's the shape of these proteins that determines what they do, so predicting their shapes from the amino acid sequence is extremely useful. Correct predictions help tell us how genes help define us. They also enable us to design drugs or enzymes that have the desired effect.

Today bioinformatics researchers have developed many powerful computer techniques to try and predict protein structures. Some are based on calculations of which atoms in the large molecules like to glue themselves together more often; some use machine learning to learn from the structures of previously discovered proteins, some use search methods such as genetic algorithms and supercomputers to find likely shapes that minimize the free energy of the structure.[8]

The field of bioinformatics is much more than this, of course. In fact some might argue it's more than one field. Some of the earliest uses of computers in biological research date back to the birth of computers in the late 1940s. British pioneers Andrew Booth and his boss, the great crystallographer John 'Sage' Bernal, studied the arrangement of atoms in crystals at Birkbeck College, London. To do so, Booth pioneered some of the earliest computing equipment in the UK, including an electromechanical calculator in 1946, and designed a relay computer based on the von Neumann architecture in the following two years. He later redesigned the machine as an electronic device using valves,[s] which was built by student Norman Kitz[t] in 1951.[9]

'Before the use of modern computing in crystallography became commonplace, the usual way of carrying out the many thousands of calculations needed to determine the three dimensional structure of a biological molecule was to use various types of mechanical calculators,' says Professor of Bioinformatics, David Jones. 'Today it is impossible to do any work in crystallography at all without state-of-the-art computing.'[10]

The revolution of bioinformatics began when scientists first learned to sequence proteins and the DNA of living organisms. They were reading the molecular codes that defined life, evolved over millions of years, and the amount of information soon became impressively large. Even the very first DNA-based genome to be sequenced (a virus that infects bacteria, called Phi X 174)[u] had eleven genes in 5386 bases (nucleotides). Humans have about 23,000 genes and around three billion base pairs—that's about 725 megabytes of data if each base pair is stored as two bits. That may not sound too bad, until you think about searching it for specific strings of data, especially if you need to consider partial matches (and since our genes are always slightly different from our parents, this is important).[11]

Soon proteins from many organisms were being sequenced and it was realized that the relatedness of creatures could be determined by examining their similarity. But to handle this amount of information, new computer techniques were needed. 'The algorithmic breakthrough in the field was in 1970 when the first useful method for comparing sequences (as strings of letters) was developed by Needleman and Wunsch,'[12] says Jones. 'This quickly led to better and faster algorithms being developed.'[j]

The more similarities that could be found,[v] the more related the organisms, meaning that the evolutionary tree (pylogeny) can be calculated with great accuracy. American physical chemist Margaret Dayhoff led the way at Georgetown University Medical Center, Washington, DC. In the 1960s, she produced pioneering computer techniques to search for similar protein sequences (finding homologies),[13] enabling her to produce the first reconstruction of an evolutionary tree from such data.[14] She also developed the first probabilistic model of protein evolution[w] back in 1978,[15] which is still in use today.

Perhaps one of the most significant advances by Dayhoff was the creation of a publicly available database to store all known protein sequences.[16] This resource became the seed for today's massive databases of sequence information. 'I suspect that in years to come,' says Jones, 'her development of the first biological databases and some of the earliest tools for searching these databases will be seen as the biggest legacies.'[j,10]

By the 1990s, technology had advanced to the point where the entire DNA of organisms could be sequenced. 'Initially we were just sequencing the DNA of simple organisms such as bacteria,' says Jones 'but of course this eventually led to the publication of the complete human genome sequence in 2003. Today we have the complete genome sequences for over 1000 organisms, and within a few years we will have the complete genome sequences for thousands of individual humans. Not surprisingly, with this exponential growth in data, computing is more vital to modern biology than ever before.'[j,10]

Bioinformatics now comprises a wealth of computational tools that can identify the genes in a sequence of DNA, analyse gene and protein expression, regulation, and look at mutations in tumours. Bioinformatics researchers even analyse published scientific papers to derive summaries of the thousands of biological experiments published every year. The wealth of data produced by bioinformatics is essential for a growing list of applications, from drug development and insect resistance in crops to the forensic analysis of microbes and climate change studies.[k,11] Jones has direct experience of the impact of bioinformatics, for he is also a successful entrepreneur in the area. He was one of the founders of Inpharmatica, which specialized in computational tools and databases for the analysis of DNA, proteins, and drug discovery.[17] The highly successful company grew to over a hundred people and was sold in 2006 to drug discovery company Galapagos for 12.5 million euros.[18]

Bioinformatics continues to expand and provide vital data to related areas of research. 'The field is now moving well beyond just the sequence data,' says Jones. 'In systems biology, the ultimate goal is to build a mathematical model of a whole organism such as a single bacterial cell or ultimately the whole of a more complex organism. This involves many challenges—both in experimental biology and in computing.'[j,10]

Modelling biological systems is not a new idea. Perhaps surprisingly, the researcher who coined the term 'bioinformatics' has worked on this kind of modelling research from the beginning. 'In the beginning of the 1970s Ben Hesper and I defined bioinformatics as the study of informatic processes in biotic systems,'[19] says Paulien Hogeweg, Professor of Theoretical Biology and Bioinformatics at Utrecht University. 'It seemed to us that one of the defining properties of life was information processing. We therefore thought that in addition to biophysics and biochemistry, it was useful to distinguish bioinformatics as a research field. We recognized that in order to study informatic processes in biotic systems, computational methods were needed for both dynamical modelling and for pattern analysis.'[20]

From Hogeweg's perspective, the field narrowed as researchers concentrated on the vast amounts of genome data that was suddenly available. But with the data management, analysis, and prediction tools now maturing, it seems that more researchers are broadening their focus and exploiting all the information to understand living systems better. 'I am happy to see signs that our original meaning might be re-emerging,' says Hogeweg. 'We felt that the re-introduction of biologically inspired computational ideas back into biology was needed in order to begin to understand biological systems as information processing systems. In particular, a focus on local interaction leading to emergent phenomena at multiple scales seemed to be missing in most biological models.[21]

'Clearly there is an overlap between bioinformatics in our sense of the word and "artificial life,"' continues Hogeweg, 'which came into focus by the end of the eighties, and indeed I participated in the founding conferences. Profound differences are in purpose and constraints, where bioinformatics is much closer to biology in both respects.'[20]

Whether it is called bioinformatics, computational biology, systems biology, or even artificial life, this new form of interdisciplinary research is addressing some of the most fundamental questions in science. 'Who can not be interested in the question, "what is life?"' says Hogeweg. 'How did life originate from non-living matter? How did it evolve? How can simple interactions lead to such complex behaviour?'[20]

Hogeweg and researchers like her study many important problems that remain in biology. For example, they study evolution—how did complex genomes and complex organisms evolve? 'The primary process of evolution is known since Darwin: mutation and selection,' says Hogeweg. 'However the transformation from the level of mutations of DNA to the level of selection—the organism's shape, physiology and behavior—is a complex multilevel process. And this transformation itself evolved. To understand how evolution shaped this mapping, and how the mapping shapes evolution is a challenging project, on which major insights are being gained through computational methods.'[20]

The researchers also study how genes may regulate the expression of other genes in networks of interaction. 'In our work we have studied the evolution of gene regulatory networks in simulation models,' says Hogweg. 'These models show many unexpected results, for example that there may be large genomes early in evolution, and gene loss is an important process in adaptation.'[22] They even study morphogenesis— the generation of form as we develop from a single cell to our complex multicellular adult shape. 'Morphogenesis comes about by an intricate interplay between gene regulation and the physics of the cells/tissues,' says Hogeweg. 'By using a simple but fairly realistic representation of a biological cell, we have shown that intricate morphogenetic processes might in fact be the result of fairly simple regulation.'[20,23]

It's a difficult task, deriving the right data and learning how to use it to model a complex and ever-changing biological system. While we can model small fragments of living creatures, we are still unable to build accurate detailed models of an entire organism (even a single bacterium), but this may soon change.[24] 'The trick to doing this is to collect vast amounts of raw data on every aspect of the cells' behaviour under different conditions—levels of gene activation or amounts of protein produced for example—and then to integrate all these diverse sources data—everything from simple gene sequences to 3D image data—into a single computer model,' says Jones. 'Obviously if we are able to model all of the processes in a cell, or in a whole organism, the impact this would have not only in our understanding of life itself but also our ability to treat disease would be immense. Probably this will be a challenge finally met by the next generation of researchers, or possibly the generation after that, in computational biology, but we will see amazing developments even within the next ten years.'[10]

Computer medicine

The various flavours of bioinformatics impact biology and medicine in hugely important ways. But there is another kind of computer technology already used in just about every hospital you might visit, which helps save lives every day. It's the technology behind medical imaging.

The original medical imaging technology was X-ray, discovered by German physicist Wilhelm Conrad Röntgen in 1895 and used for surgery just a year later by British Major John Hall-Edwards. X-ray imaging continued to be the main way of looking inside the body until the late 1940s, when two new inventions emerged from the Second World War. The first was ultrasound, developed by English-American medical doctor John Wild after hearing about the use of high-frequency sounds for the detection of cracks in tank armour. He and an engineer named John Reid used fifteen Mhz sounds, allowing them to peer inside the bodies of patients and detect cancers. Like X-rays, ultrasound remains an important scanning technology used routinely to examine the developing foetus inside the mother. Around the same time, other scientists were developing the idea of injecting (or having patients swallow) small amounts of radioactive material and then using special gamma cameras to see where it went—a technique that become known as scintigraphy.[25]

Medical imaging continued using these methods until the late 1960s when British engineer Godfrey Hounsfield[x,26] (the designer of one of the first transistor-based computers) thought of an amazing idea. All the different imaging methods showed different features within the body, but they all suffered from the same limitation. They produced flat images. If the doctor needs to figure out where the problem lies in the body, taking a series of images from different angles might give them some idea. But wouldn't it be so much easier if you could see a three-dimensional image instead? 'People had been thinking for a long time about how to take X-ray images from lots of different of angles,' says David Hawkes, Professor of Medical Imaging Science at UCL. 'If you display those images as a movie you can see the three-dimensional structures of what's inside the body. Hounsfield came up with a method of doing this reconstruction with a computer.'[27] At around the same time, a South African researcher called Allan Cormack developed the theory behind the same concept.[y,25]

The result was the X-ray computed tomography (CT) scanner—an amazing computer-driven X-ray machine that produced full three-dimensional scans that could then be rotated and viewed at any angle. It was not the only advance. By now nuclear magnetic resonance had also been used to look within the human body. In this approach, massively powerful electromagnets are used to alter the very nuclei of the atoms in the body. These nuclei temporarily store and re-emit the electromagnetic energy at slightly different rates, which can then be detected, allowing an image of the soft tissues in our bodies to be imaged very accurately.[z] We thus had yet another kind of scanner—the magnetic resonance imaging (MRI) scanner. Even more advances followed. Computers were used to reconstruct many 2D images of special scintigraphy scanners into 3D, creating the positron emission tomography (PET) scanner and the single photon emission tomography (SPET) scanner.[y,25]

'That's when the revolution happened,' says Hawkes. 'Computers were linked in with the medical imaging technology and then things took off very rapidly.' In the subsequent decades, all the scanners were converted to digital, including ultrasound and X-ray. Accuracy was improved to the extent that some scanners can now detect individual cells, the speed of the scanners increased, and side effects to patients minimized. Today other forms of imaging provide yet more ways of seeing inside the body. Endoscopy allows us to use tiny optical cameras within us. 'The body is made up of many different types of tubes,' says Hawkes, 'and you can insert devices, often called an endoscope. With that endoscope we can observe what's happening in the lining of various structures. We can see through the mouth, down into the tubes that lead into the lung (bronchioles) and down into the tubes that leads into the stomach (oesophagus). Also going up the other end through the colon or through the urethra. So there are a number of ways of getting access into the internal structures. The linings are important because most cancers are what we call carcinomas. They are cancers that arise in the cells in the lining of tissue (epithelial tissue). And so we can interrogate them with optical techniques.'[aa,27] Today it's even possible to swallow a 'camera in a pill' (capsule endoscopy) and have it send photos wirelessly to a computer as it travels through the digestive system and out the other end of the patient.

None of these advances would be possible without the computer. We would not be able to generate the amazing quality medical scans without computers quietly performing trillions of calculations in the background. We would not have three-dimensional imaging at all without the computer performing reconstruction for us—not just gluing together a sequence of images to make a movie, but calculating the full three-dimensional structure from scans so we can view volumes of space, zooming in on organs of interest, and examining them from every angle. 'Computers were first used for image reconstruction,' says Hawkes. 'It's still an active area of research, taking the raw sensor information and trying to get something out of that in terms of an image.'[27]

But with the advances in scanning technology came a problem. There was just too much data. Too much to look at. If you are a doctor, having access to an amazing array of images and 3D reconstructions of your patient may be extremely useful, but if you have to watch the equivalent of several hours of movies for each patient, you may miss the crucial image that enables you to make the right diagnosis. 'Think of a movie camera that's producing an image fifty times a second,' says Hawkes. 'Each one is just a single two-dimensional image. Our MRI scanners are producing images but they're volume images at roughly the same rate. So in terms of the number of pixels, we might have 512 by 512 by 512, many times a second. There's a vast amount of data being produced. The radiologist who has been trained to look at one image at a time is now swamped with data.'[27]

To overcome this problem, the role of computers in medical imaging is now increasing further. Instead of simply producing the images, computers now are used to process the images, extracting information that the radiologist or doctor can use for diagnosis, condensing the bulk of information into a more digestible form. 'The classic tools that we develop are ways of segmenting,' says Hawkes, 'which means identifying a structure of interest. It literally means just cutting up the image—segmenting and labelling it into structures of interest. It might be the outline of the brain in an MRI scan. We want to label it, so we need to find its boundary. We want to identify the different parts of the brain so that we can perform some measurements. Is it getting smaller due to atrophy? Is there something like a tumour growing there? Segmentation is absolutely key to that.' Technologies developed in computer vision are borrowed and enhanced by the medical imaging researchers. But it remains an extremely difficult problem. 'It's hard to do as well as the trained observer,' says Hawkes. 'It's still an active research area and has been for the last twenty years. We are making some progress.'[27]

Computers are also used to match features between images using a technique known as image registration—an extremely useful tool for diagnostics. Given a feature such as a blood vessel or organ in one image, where is that in another image taken of the same patient? 'We want to do that because we want to measure the change in size of something,' says Hawkes. 'Is a tumour growing, is a blood vessel narrowing, is a bit of brain tissue shrinking? You need to establish that correspondence accurately and robustly and be able to follow changes over time. We've now got computers to do this much better than the human can.' Initial attempts at achieving this clever trick with computers involved identifying features, perhaps the tip of the nose or edges of the eyes, overlaying one image on top of the other, and lining up the features in both images. The problem was that the computer found it very hard to find the features in the first place. Today a better method is used. The information content of the two separate images is compared with that of the combined image. 'We found that the information content is similar for different modality images,' says Hawkes. 'If you have two images of a patient's head, somewhere in there are two eyes. The images may have difference contrasts, different characteristics, but both will have two eyes. When the images are misregistered, you end up with an image that has four eyes in the combined registered image. So by registering the image, what you're doing is simplifying it. You're minimising the information content. Minimising the joint entropy in relation to the sum of the combined two entropies.'[27, 28]

Registration is extremely useful for comparing two different images of a patient taken at different times. It can also help combine different types of scans together. 'If the patient has an MRI and a CT and an ultrasound, it can be quite difficult to relate the features with each other. You want to do that because those images give you complementary information in terms of structure,' says Hawkes.

Visualization is another area of computer science exploited in medical physics. Realistic renderings of internal organs derived from patient scans enable surgeons to understand what they may be about to see.[bb] Combine this with modelling of the behaviour of the organs, and surgeons may one day even be able to practise their more complex operations on a realistic virtual version of you before trying for real. It may also make less invasive forms of surgery using laparoscopes[cc] more viable for a larger range of surgeries. 'I would like to see a combination of medical imaging, acquired before the patient, processed so that you can build computational models of the anatomy. You can move them around, even make them function as they should—the heart has to beat, the lungs have to breathe,' says Hawkes. 'Combine the imaging technology with computational modelling technology with imaging techniques that you can use during the technique that are not invasive. Bring that all together.'[27,29]

There seems to be no limit to the number of techniques from computer science that can be applied to medical imaging. Perhaps one of the most exciting in the future may be machine learning methods for prediction. With routine scans being performed for women to screen for breast cancer, there are millions of images being produced. Only a tiny proportion, perhaps five in 1000 will have cancer. But with so much data, there is a real possibility that computers could be used to learn the difference between normal breasts, and those that appear abnormal. 'What we can get a computer to do is to look at the normal breasts, which have very different appearances depending on the size, shape and age of the person, and learn what the variation is in the normal patient,' says Hawkes. 'Perhaps—and this is a hypothesis that we haven't proven yet—we can detect if a lady's breast image is diverging from that norm. Perhaps that gives an indication of cancer. In patients with cancer we can actually see the calcification—spots in the image—and we see some distortion of the tissue associated with the growth of the cancer. That's only when it gets to be over 5 mm in size. Perhaps there's an earlier change we might find with machine learning.'[27]

Similar methods could be used for prostate cancer or even dementia. 'There are some extremely distressing forms of dementia, particularly Alzheimer's,' says Hawkes. 'MRI is certainly changing the way we're studying the disease. We know a lot now about how the structure changes in particular parts of the brain. For example, the hippocampus, a tiny structure within the brain associated with memory. That starts to shrink before other structures start to shrink. We can use image registration techniques to make accurate measurements. Then the machine learning techniques let us look at the trajectory of the change of all the different structures in the brain. Everyone's brains shrink beyond the age of twenty-two, but some people's brains shrink in a very different way. They're the ones to worry about because they're the ones that may lead to these dementias.'[27]

Machine learning methods are even used to help automatically find images of interest from the thousands produced with capsule endoscopy as it tumbles through the gut—removing all those hundreds of images where the camera was not pointing at anything very useful.[30]

The result of this exploitation of computer science in medicine is highly intelligent, accurate, and fast medical scanning techniques that are transforming medicine. We can now detect many forms of cancer earlier than ever before, allowing them to be treated more effectively. We can detect narrowing of the arteries better than ever before, enabling more effective management of cardiac disease. Treatment of all major internal diseases, disorders, and injuries has benefitted from this remarkable medical scanning technology.

It's still an exciting time of innovation. Because of mass production there are now highly sophisticated consumer electronic devices that are capable of supporting medicine. The latest generations of tablet computers and phones are powerful computers packed full of sensors. It seems likely that these could be used by nurses or even patients themselves to monitor important aspects of health. This long-term data would be much more useful for the doctors compared to a one-off measurement in a clinic. 'If you think of going in for a medical check-up,' says Hawkes. 'There they are, they take your blood pressure and write down two numbers at the state you happen to be in when you arrived at the doctor's surgery. You might be stressed, you might not be stressed. It may be the beginning of the day, you may have just had a large meal, whatever. And then they tell you if your blood pressure has gone up or down, That is so *not* the way to do it!'[dd]

There is also still much to do. 'We probably know more about what we don't know,' says Hawkes. 'There are still some big killers around where the imaging technology is not good enough.'[27]

Hawkes actively works to improve the technology. He is another example of scientist and entrepreneur, having co-founded the successful company IXICO[ee] with other key opinion leaders from different London institutes.[ff] The company specializes in technologies that support basic imaging research, clinical research studies, and imaging-based clinical trials. Thanks to researchers such as these and their remarkable exploitation of innovative new scanners, intelligent computing techniques, and mobile technologies, we are improving medicine and helping to save lives every day.

Computer detectives

Medical imaging is one of the real success stories of computer science. It provides a wonderful example of how computers impact our lives and help us when we are at our most vulnerable. But computers are more than medical marvels, enlighteners of natural sciences, or conveyors of culture. Computers are big business. In finance, the everyday miracles of technology that you take for granted may be worth staggering sums of money. If you are an entrepreneur, the trick is often to get there first.

'It was a very exciting time in Computer Science,' says self-made millionaire Jason Kingdon. 'That period at the end of the 1980s was the first time access to technology had been democratized. You could run your own experiment. You didn't need permission. You didn't need to queue up in a lab and have a hundred people vet what you were doing. You actually had access to the stuff, you could program it yourself, and get on and do things.'[31]

Kingdon was one of a new type of AI researcher working in the midst of the last AI winter. These computer scientists were not driven by a desire to understand intelligence. They wanted to solve hard problems using clever software. 'We wanted to see if there was a way to harness this new computing power, taking biologically inspired algorithms, and applying them in a way that delivered a different type of result.' At the end of the 1980s nonlinear, stochastic optimization and search algorithms were suddenly in vogue. Methods such as genetic algorithms and artificial neural networks were emerging as the new hot topics for research. 'The differences were that it was data-driven,' says Kingdon, 'it was based on an understanding of how an algorithm explored a space, and it was results-oriented. It was attempting to deliver something that otherwise you couldn't do.'[31]

Kingdon and his fellow PhD students were at the cutting edge of this new form of applied AI research. Professor Philip Treleaven, the head of the Intelligent Systems Group, UCL, helped drive their work towards industry. 'I'm a very applied researcher,' he says, 'Always have been. It's better to be application driven. When we started at UCL the financial industry was nearby so it was natural to work with them.'[31]

The group comprised several PhD students, including Ugur Bilge, Konrad Feldman, Suran Goonatilake, Sukhdev Khebbal, Jason Kingdon, and Anoop Mangat. It was just one of many such groups emerging in computer science departments around the world. But with funding difficult to obtain, and Treleaven's (and UCL's) policy of actively working with industry, this group of researchers was soon unique in its access to real-world financial data. By the early 1990s, the group was well established with collaborations between several banks, insurance companies, and other major companies. The researchers were using neural networks, genetic algorithms, and fuzzy logic to spot anomalous transactions and fraud. They were studying how combinations of the techniques could provide decision support tools for finance.

In 1993, an article about one of the projects was published in the British newspaper, *The Daily Telegraph*. It triggered massive interest. 'The phone rang off the hook that whole week,' says Kingdon. 'We had a lot of people approaching us, asking if there was research work we would undertake. A portion of those started saying, "We think this could be a major competitive advantage for us. We don't want you to publish the results, we want you do it as a piece of consultancy." [31] On that basis, several members of the group decided to start a company. They called it Searchspace Ltd.[gg]

For the first two years they worked from the university as consultants. Treleaven recalls the time. 'First they were working for me and I was paying them, then they were working for themselves and I was paying them! Then they were just working for themselves.' [32] They moved into their own London-based office in 1995.

The founders were inspired by the first wave of Silicon Valley entrepreneurs[hh] who seemed to have created amazing technologies and become extremely wealthy. 'That was very relevant to what you thought you could end up doing,' says Kingdon. The Searchspace team had big ambitions. 'For Searchspace, when we formed it, we thought there's got to be a Tyrell Corporation.[ii] It's not been made yet! Who's going to do it?' Kingdon's voice shows his excitement. 'Wow, what a fantastic job, if you can build something like that, you know? You're experimenting, with the resources to do it, the freedom to do it, and you're applying it in a way that engages and impacts the world.' But with such big ambitions, what was the right industry for their clever AI computer methods? The Searchspace team didn't know, but they were being approached by more and more different companies, so they developed clever software for each new customer. Soon the array of different applications was astonishing. They analysed the electricity market in the UK, created smart Web sites for a travel agent and a major brewery. They modelled flooding risk for an insurance company, and analysed ice-cream sales for a major supermarket.[31]

Searchspace had grown to be a highly successful company. But the range of applications was eclectic. One of the easiest ways they could move forward would be to produce a programming environment that could provide such analytic capabilities for many applications. It was a route that other companies were taking, but the Searchspace team had other ambitions. 'We wanted to do something a lot more immediate, for business use,' says Kingdon. 'And when the London Stock Exchange approached us and said, "'if you can use this stuff for financial analysis, can you use it for detecting insider dealing, market manipulation?" We said we'd give it a go.'[31]

They were given six months of financial data and asked to see what they could find hidden within it. Would those involved in illegal activity leave detectable 'digital fingerprints' behind? The results from this early trial were amazingly successful. 'We came back with nineteen investigations that we would have done over that six month period,' recalls Kingdon. 'Over the same period they investigated seventeen. The seventeen were included in the nineteen we found and the additional two they would have looked at, had they found them.

'It totally transformed their attitudes,' he continues. 'Historically, they approached the problem as an investigatory problem. They would employ people like ex-policemen that would be embedded in the community, ear to the ground, seeing what's going on. It was very people-centric. Suddenly they were saying, "Wow! It's actually in the data!"' Kingdon smiles. 'And this data is shouting at you.'[31]

From the work with the London Stock Exchange, the Searchspace team had the idea of a transaction monitoring framework which performed statistical profiling of the data. Into the framework they placed monitoring modules (quickly renamed to 'sentinels' for marketing purposes). Each sentinel looked for specific issues, like a reporting officer. Each would be built with some business function and domain-specific knowledge for that task. The technology was first used for the detection of money laundering and fraud in banks. Their software statistically models every activity through that bank, in the context of an individual.[33] 'So Peter Bentley's five HSBC accounts,' says Kingdon. 'Each of those has an individual profile. There is a statistical profile of the normal transaction amounts. What an outlier looks like, what an average amount looks like, what a payment frequency looks like, what trend lines look like, what individual transactions look like, and the type of those transactions. For each of those five different dimensions and from the way they are aggregated. So you can imagine you've got this huge statistical stew that's being constantly added to and built and maintained. The characterisation is constantly updating and adjusting in line with your activity.'[31]

It's a clever idea. If one of the sentinels detects any form of transaction that appears different from the norm, then it is flagged as anomalous. It might be that you have just gone on holiday somewhere new and are withdrawing money. But it might also mean that your account details or bankcard have been stolen and the transaction is fraudulent. 'It provides a very sensitive listening device for activity in your environment,' says Kingdon. 'It's self correcting and it can be tuned in a very fine way. You can have a sentinel for money laundering, another for credit card fraud, another for debit card fraud, another one for mortgage fraud, all the way through to marketing opportunities. The guy has just got married, had a baby, or lost his job. All of these events—fortunately or unfortunately—are available through this kind of analysis.'[31]

The success of their approach was partly because they were not afraid to use a mixture of different computational methods. 'When you start building AI systems for businesses, a generalist system has very little value to an organisation, unless it has the capacity to learn a specialism very quickly,' explains Kingdon. 'It's much more likely that you'll have to pack it with contextual deep knowledge of that particular area. Our anti-money laundering Sentinel knew a lot about money laundering.'[31]

Searchspace became the sole provider of transaction monitoring software for the London Stock Exchange, followed by the New York Stock Exchange. Suddenly they were the global leader in financial transaction monitoring for stock exchanges. The company began receiving media attention and before long they were introducing anti-money-laundering software to the Royal Bank of Scotland. Again their solution was market-leading and Searchspace became the world leader in anti-money-laundering detection. 'The company got there first, and I think helped to start a whole industry,' says Treleaven.[32] Around sixty per cent of all top tier banks became Searchspace clients. Their product was market leading in the USA, Europe, South Africa, and Japan.

Searchspace had grown from five people to 250 in just ten years. During that time they had been one of the top twenty European enterprise companies, and consistently one of the fastest growing companies in the UK and in Europe. 'It was a great ride,' says Kingdon. 'Things evolved very naturally and it just worked out. The core of it was that we had produced a brand new technology, which people could see made a lot of sense. If you've got this industrial statistical analysis going on, that's going to be a useful thing. It's going to find stuff that others can't. I think it's the only technology that has found terrorist financing.' Indeed Searchspace found a number of instances in the USA, leading to investigations by various agencies. They also assisted UK banks in the investigation of the terrorists involved in the 7/7 bombing of London. 'The people involved with that were absolute outliers,' says Kingdon. 'In fact they'd been detected by the system as credit card fraudsters. To this day I really don't understand why the idea of following the money hasn't been taken to a much greater degree than it appeared to us that it had been.'[31]

The transaction and fraud protection pioneered by Searchspace is a technology that benefits every country in the world, and directly protects us every day. 'I think there is something in that,' says Kingdon. 'In this interconnected, anonymized world, all this infrastructure has been put in place. You arrive in New York, you effortlessly take money from the ATM. Same thing in Hong Kong. It works because it's automated by computers. People are out of the way. Our argument is that something needs to step in—hang on a sec, should this guy be doing this? It's almost like a duty of care.'[31]

The spectacular success of the computer software company means that Searchspace is now used as a role model for other businesses. But after ten years, the founders decided the technology was mature enough for it to continue without them. 'We eventually sold the business in 2005 for 148 million dollars,' says Kingdon. 'From our perspective, we set up to make a general purpose technology company. We ended up being absolute kings in this domain of anti-money laundering and fraud detection. To an extent we felt that we had run our course. We could move on and let them get on with it.'[31] The technology remains the market leader in anti-money-laundering and anti-fraud software today.[jj]

The founders of Searchspace have gone their separate ways, but continue to be highly successful. Kingdon remains unequivocally enthusiastic about the potential for computers. 'The fact that you and I could have an idea this afternoon,' he says, 'We could have something that is available to a global market by tomorrow. We could be online, putting that out tomorrow. That's just phenomenal.'[31]

Treleaven agrees. 'The spread of technology and availability of information has helped democratize the world. Someone in a remote village in Africa can educate themselves using Wikipedia now. Our societies have been transformed by computers.'[32]

'There is no time like it in terms of technology,' says Kingdon. 'Anybody who is involved in this, you are in the white hot centre of *the* revolution that is taking place. Maybe this is something absolutely decisive in the history of mankind.'[31]

ENDNOTES

Chapter 000

a. Some computer scientists are actively working to give computers emotions, as we'll see in later chapters.

b. You can still see the very first—and rather basic—Web pages from 1992 archived online here: http://www.w3.org/History/19921103-hypertext/hypertext/WWW/TheProject.html

c. And the fastest growing advances in medicine are all enabled by computers.

d. Here are a few more responses:

Joel Jorden, a PhD student at UCL performing research into technology enabling touch to be transmitted over the Internet, responded with a succinct, 'Computer Science is Mathematical Engineering.'

Professor Katharina Morik, who works on machine learning and data mining at the Technische Universität Dortmund, stated, 'Computer science is the art of describing processes formally such that we can reason about them and their properties and the descriptions can be executed in the real world.'

Rob Pefferly, a mathematician at the Estonian Business School said, 'Computer Science is the technical art of data manipulation that empowers mankind's ability to process information and distill knowledge from chaos.'

Professor Robert van de Geijn at the University of Texas at Austin focuses on a branch of mathematics called linear algebra combined with parallel computers. He replied, 'A favorite definition of mine of Science is "Knowledge that has been made systematic." By that definition, computer science is a science: we take knowledge and try to make it systematic to the point where it can be made mechanical (automatic).'

Professor S. Sitharama Iyengar works in the area of sensor networks and robotics at Louisiana State University and gave a different answer: 'Computer Science is the science of logic that pervades every aspect of human life—it personifies the art of living.'

Professor M. Alojzy Kłopotek, who works on artificial intelligence and reasoning at the Polish Academy of Sciences replied (in several emails as he added to his answer): 'Computer science is a branch of science dealing with collecting, encoding and decoding, storing, processing, transmitting and visualizing information.'

e. I'm not saying we have no-one like this, however!

f. Likewise there's no way I can describe every computer scientist from the past or present—this does not mean their contributions are any less important! In this book, I've chosen to focus on a few familiar names and a few less familiar ones to help illustrate the diversity of the field.

Chapter 001

a. The direction of the lengthy pendulum's swing appears to change as the Earth turns.

b. Today the Turing Relay Race takes place along the riverside paths between Cambridge and Ely where he ran.

c. This theorem explains how the distribution of values may resemble a 'normal distribution'. For example, in a fair coin toss, the histogram of average proportion of heads over frequency will be normally distributed around 0.5. In other words, for most coin tosses, the coin will land heads-up fifty per cent of the time or close to fifty per cent of the time. Very infrequently will the coin appear to land heads-up less than or more than fifty per cent of the time.

d. Hilbert had actually set twenty-three major problems in 1900, but it was not until 1928 that he refined the *Entscheidungsproblem* sufficiently for mathematicians to tackle it.

e. It may seem strange to call a collection of physical objects a memory, but in reality that's what all memory is—physical things in one state or another, whether it's chemical concentrations and connections of your neurons or electrons in a memory chip. So you could regard the number of houses on the board or amount of money as akin to the concentration of chemicals in neurons or number of electrons in one part of a chip.

f. Today we would call this a finite state machine (FSM).

g. This clever type of Turing Machine is known as a Universal Turing Machine because it can simulate any other Turing Machine. It does this by reading a description of the machine and that machine's input. Today all computers have the ability to simulate any other computer—they are all Universal Turing Machines.

h. Researchers are still trying to think of exotic examples where this may not be true, perhaps sending spaceships into black holes with Turing Machines on them, which also likely to be impossible.

i. Lady Ada Lovelace worked with Charles Babbage on his mechanical computer and wrote the first algorithm intended to be processed by a machine in the 1840s.

j. The 'O' stands for 'order' so when we write $O(n)$ we are saying that the method has time complexity of order n.

k. and does not depend on the number multiplied by itself.

l. Assuming the age of the universe is 13.75 billion years.

m. For example instead of calculating the same thing many times you can just calculate it once, store the result and then retrieve it from memory when you need it again.

n. And the big-O notation, which allows us to figure out how fast the algorithm is likely to be before we even run it on a computer.

o. One is a problem first posed by Hilbert 100 years previously.

p. And the process of rewriting can be achieved in polynomial time.

q. http://www.satalia.com/

r. But not a random or probabilistic device.

s. Oracles may seem very informal and non-mathematical, but in fact the idea forms the basis of many important ideas in computability theory. Turing reduction is one example. A Turing reduction, from a problem A to a problem B, is a reduction which solves A, assuming B is already known. More formally, a Turing reduction is a function computable by an oracle machine with an oracle for B. If a Turing reduction of A to B exists then every algorithm for B can be used to produce an algorithm for A, by inserting the algorithm for B at each place where the oracle machine computing A queries the oracle for B. However, because the oracle machine may query the oracle a large number of times, the resulting algorithm may require more time and space.

t. Each process does not communicate with each other, except that if one of the processes finds a solution it sends a message to all of its brothers and sisters and says 'stop work'. It is possible for an ordinary Turing Machine to simulate this non-deterministic Turing Machine, but it will typically need exponential time to do it.

u. The Mandelbrot set was created because French-American mathematician Benoit Mandelbrot was interested in the oscillations of complex number series. In his simple equation, x and c were complex numbers and t was time. For any value of c, you could iteratively calculate the value of x_t, increasing t by 1 each time. Mandelbrot wanted to know which values of c would make the length of the imaginary number stored in x_t stop growing when the equation was applied for an infinite number of times. He discovered that if the length ever went above 2, then it was unbounded—it would grow forever. But for the right imaginary values of c, sometimes the result would simply oscillate between different lengths less than 2. Mandelbrot used his computer to apply the equation many times for different values of c. For each value of c, the computer would stop early if the length of the imaginary number in x_t was 2 or more. If the computer hadn't stopped early for that value of c, a black dot was drawn. The dot was placed at coordinate (m, n) using the numbers from the value of c: $(m + ni)$ where m was varied from -2.4 to 1.34 and n was varied from 1.4 to -1.4, to fill the computer screen. The result was the infinite complexity of the Mandelbrot set.

Chapter 010

a. In fact, Shannon was not the first to think of the idea—a Russian logician and electrical engineer called Victor Shestakov also made the same connection in 1935. However, he did not publish his work until 1941 (in Russian), three years after Shannon.

b. By Howard Gardner, Harvard Professor.

c. A relay works through magnetism. Pass an electric current through a relay and an internal electromagnet is powered, which operates its internal switch. (Your central heating controller may use a relay to switch the heating on and off—you will hear the little click when it switches.) Because they have moving mechanical parts, relays are slow and wear out quickly compared to other devices.

d. There were also many other relay-based computers, created by many pioneers before and during the war, including Howard Aiken at Harvard University, George Stibitz at Bell Telephone Laboratories, and Turing at Princeton University and Bletchley Park.

e. Thermionic valves (also known as vacuum tubes or electron tubes) look a little like light bulbs. They are made from a sealed glass envelope with no air inside, and internal electrodes. An electric current will heat one electrode (the cathode) resulting in a cloud of electrons in the vacuum, which are attracted to another electrode (the anode). The flow of electrons can be controlled by other electrodes (grids located between the cathode and anode). In this way electricity can be amplified, directed, or switched without needing mechanically moving parts. However, valves become very hot, consume a lot of electricity, and are prone to failure.

f. Together known as the *datapath*.

g. In 1945, Turing wrote a report describing his own design of a stored-program electronic computer, which even contained details such as logic circuit diagrams and an early form of programming language. His report referenced von Neumann's draft report. He presented the work to the National Physical Laboratory (NPL) Executive Committee in 1946, but was prohibited from making the ideas public because of the Official Secrets Act. Nevertheless his design was built, first as the Pilot Model ACE in 1950, leading to the MOSAIC, the Bendix Corporation's G-15 computer (1954) and the English Electric DEUCE (1955).

h. In the USA, these included the ORDVAC for the Army (1951), MANIAC for Government research (1952), ILLIAC at the University of Illinois (1952), AVIDAC for Government research (1953), IBM's 19 IBM 701 systems (from 1953 onwards), ORACLE for Government research (1953), JOHNNIAC at the Rand Corp (1954), MISTIC at Michigan State University (1957), and CYCLONE at Iowa State University (1959). In the meantime, other computers were being built elsewhere, including: Manchester University's SSEM (1948), Cambridge University's EDSAC (1949), Electronic Control's BINAC (1949), Turing's ACE for the UK National Physical Laboratory (1950), the National Bureau of Standards' SEAC (1950), MIT's WHIRL-WIND (1950), the University of Pennsylvania's EDVAC (1951), Ferranti's MARK 1 (1951), the UNIVAC 1 (1951), the CSIRO MARK 1, later CSIRAC (1951). As time progressed, other countries also built their own computers, such as BESK in Sweden (1953), WEIZAC in Israel (1955), SILLIAC in Australia (1956), EDB built nine systems in Sweden (from 1957), DASK in Denmark (1957), MUSASINO-1 in Japan (1957), FACOM built two FACOM 201 systems in Japan (1960), TRASK in Sweden (1965). All the designs were remarkably similar to the design described by von Neumann in his draft report, and most of the designers explicitly referenced von Neumann.

i. We'll return to this story in the next chapter.

j. A transistor is a device made from a 'semiconducting' material such as silicon. It has three terminals or electrical connections: the collector, emitter, and base. The power flows from collector to emitter, depending on how much electrical current is applied to the base. This means the transistor can act as a switch in digital electronics (or as an amplifier in analogue electronics).

k. Silicon chips are made by first growing special cylindrical rods (ingots) of silicon crystal, then slicing them into wafers about 0.75 mm thick, and polishing, to make them perfectly smooth. A layer of special chemical called photoresist is added and *photolithography* is used to project a pattern onto the wafer, with chemical processes used to etch away unexposed regions. This process is then repeated as many as fifty times to build the circuit and its components layer by layer. Because the whole circuit is made at once, there is no longer a problem of 'tyranny of numbers'. Integrated circuits are cheap to make, more reliable, use little material, and need far less power compared to circuits with discrete components.

l. Initally they wanted to call the company MooreNoyce, but this sounded too much like 'more noise' (and it's not good to have circuits that are electrically noisy—it means they interfere with other). Instead they settled on Intel, short for Integrated Electronics.

m. And it may be a self-fulfilling prophecy as chip manufacturers compete to improve their products.

n. RAID stands for Redundant Array of Inexpensive (or Independent) Disks. Instead of writing to a single hard disk, data is written to and often duplicated on several disks. It's a very common method used by businesses to protect their data—if one hard disk fails, another still has a copy of the data.

o. If you look in the settings of your computer you may see that part of your hard disk is used as a 'virtual memory'—this is used when the normal memory is a bit too full, so data and instructions overflow onto the hard disk rather than give you a nasty 'out of memory' error. You can often tell when memory is being swapped in and out of the hard disk—often using a method called *paging*—because everything slows down and you hear the disk chittering away non-stop.

p. Pipelining is actually a tricky thing to get right, because you don't always know which instructions the computer will follow next—especially if conditional statements are involved. If the hardware incorrectly predicts the next instruction then the pipeline may become invalid and need to be refilled—a lengthy process for many-stage pipelines.

q. http://nscc-tj.gov.cn/en/

r. To be more specific: 14,336 Xeon X5670 processors and 7168 Nvidia Tesla M2050 general-purpose graphics processing units (GPUs).

s. The generation after petascale computing is known as exascale—a thousand times faster than petascale. Research project are already underway to construct them.

t. The computer can also calculate how virtual lighting will affect the appearance of the objects and even add special effects—like making them look like paintings or cartoons. We'll return to graphics in a later chapter.

u. Easy because each task in a car can have a dedicated microprocessor and the job for that processor will never change.

v. Originally developed for Acorn desktop computers, the ARM processor is a reduced instruction set computer (RISC), which means its hardware only performs simpler instructions compared to other processors used in desktop computers. Because of this, the processor runs faster and needs less power, making it ideal for portable devices such as mobile phones.

w. We'll return to ideas of bio-inspired computing later in the book.

Chapter 011

a. We'll return to Shannon and many of these important ideas in the next chapter.

b. Erector sets with metal parts for model-making, still sold today. http://www.meccano.com/

c. He wasn't the only one working on these ideas. Williams and Kilburn in Manchester had built their own memory system which used a cathode-ray tube. Indeed, by 1948, in order to test their memory, they had built the world's first stored program computer, the Manchester Small-Scale Experimental Machine, or 'Baby'. But this was not a useable computer, as Wilkes was building.

d. Max Newman, Williams, and Kilburn came from Manchester to attend a conference on automatic computing machines the following month in Cambridge, during which the EDSAC was demonstrated.

e. Practical because it was used to solve real problems. An example of this was recalled by research student Shinn: 'Also working on the EDSAC in 1950 were Francis Crick and John Kendrew from the crystallographic department of the Cavendish Laboratory. I had no idea then that their work would become so important for absolutely everybody.'

f. Implemented using thirty-two mercury tanks, each containing sixteen thirty-five-bit words, although the amount actually available each day would vary because the memory was unreliable.

g. Mauchly and Eckert did implement subroutines on the ENIAC, but since this was not a stored-program machine, it was not quite the same concept.

h. We still use flow diagrams today to provide an overview of the functioning of a program.

i. In computer science a *variable* is like a numerical symbol in algebra—it's a parameter that represents a value, and that value may change, hence the name 'variable'. In hardware, a variable is just a specific location in memory.

j. This is modern-day assembly language for the x86 processor family.

k. Wilkes's team also pioneered the operating system on their computer. On the EDSAC this was a very simple program that was held in read-only memory and initiated reading of the program tape, and also looked after memory and control for subroutines. It was a program that looked after other programs, and made sure they loaded and ran correctly. All modern computers use operating systems—you may have heard of their names, which include: UNIX, MS DOS, Linux, Microsoft Windows, Mac OS X, Symbian OS, and iOS. Modern operating systems also include many other fancy features such as pretty windows-based environments, multi-tasking (providing the illusion of several programs running simultaneously by switching the attention of the processor between each program very quickly), and providing support for many different input and output peripherals (mice, keyboards, monitors, printers, modems). But underneath they all do the same job: they are programs which look after other programs on your computer, making sure they are loaded properly and have the memory and other resources that they require.

l. Interpreted programming languages did not die, however. Most varieties of BASIC are interpreted, as are languages such as Javascript, LISP, Matlab, and Mathematica. Some, like Java or Python, are first compiled into a new 'byte code' which is then interpreted.

m. Another example was the compiler A-0, designed by Grace Hopper for Eckert and Mauchly in 1951. Hopper's work helped lead to the first machine-independent programming languages. She is also known for her discovery of a moth in a relay of a Mark I computer in 1945, which is why we still refer to errors in computer programs as 'bugs' to this day.

n. Modern examples include: C++, Eiffel, and Java. Barbara Liskov was responsible for much of the early work that led to the design of object-oriented languages.

o. Examples include: Lisp, Haskell, and F#.

p. From http://www.c.happycodings.com/Sorting_Searching/code13.html

q. Magnetic tape and hard-disk systems were used from the 1950s to the present day (although storage capacities increased hugely and their physical sizes decreased).

r. Examples include the Codasyl Data Model or IBM's Information Management System (IMS).

s. Because SEQEL was a trademark of Hawker Siddeley, an aircraft company in the UK.

t. Some were indeed taken from architecture as Naur suggested, such as the notion of design patterns—templates of how to solve commonly occurring problems.

u. This model has lost support in recent years.

v. Including Euler, Algol W, Pascal, Modula, Modula-2, Oberon, Oberon-2, and Oberon-07.

w. We'll return to these exotic search methods in a later chapter.

x. Including the scrapping of a £300 million supply-chain management system for J. Sainsbury PLC, the cancellation of a $4 billion tax modernization effort for the US Internal Revenue Service, and the abandonment of Ford Motor Company's $400 million purchasing system after deployment.

y. The next chapter explores these issues.

Chapter 100

a. We'll return to Shannon's interests in artificial intelligence in the penultimate chapter of this book.

b. Shannon was the first to introduce the term in a published document, but he attributed its origin to John W. Tukey, in a Bell Labs memo written in 1947.

c. At the time, Shannon was also sharing an office with another pioneer Richard Hamming, who developed coding theory to detect and correct errors.

d. Conseil Europeen pour la Recherche Nucleaire, or in English: European Council for Nuclear Research.

e. Gerry Estrin.

f. He'd also met a bright research student at MIT called Larry Roberts.

g. Some twenty-five years later, Maurice Wilkes personally apologised to Kirstein for saying no. Kirstein describes this as 'incredibly generous and completely unnecessary'.

h. Such as NCP in the ARPANET, X.25, UUCP and later, DECnet and FidoNet.

i. Used on SERCnet and JANET X.25 academic networks from 1980 to 1992.

j. He is also winner of the 2012 IEEE Internet Award, for his contributions to Internet multicast, telephony, congestion control, and the shaping of open Internet standards and open-source systems in all these areas.

k. Such as the work by Douglas Engelbart at the Stanford Research Institute (SRI) during the 1960s who invented the computer mouse and software called the oNLine System, which enabled users to view information by clicking on hyperlinks. It also used screen windowing and presentation programs not unlike Powerpoint or Keynote software today.

l. That means it ran on several different operating systems, on different kinds of computers, including UNIX, Windows, PCs, and Macs.

m. Caching Web resources is rather like cache memory of a processor. It's a way of storing frequently read information locally to speed up access.

n. Wiki is Hawaiian for fast. Ward Cunningham created the first wiki in 1994, which he named WikiWikiWeb, inspired by the Wiki Wiki Shuttle bus in Honolulu, Hawaii.

o. The idea of online diaries dates back to the beginnings of the Internet, but the term 'blog' (short for weblog) was only coined in the late 1990s.

p. Sue Black is a strong proponent of this new form of social media. 'To me social media is currently the most important thing in computer science,' she says. 'It is changing power structures, invalidating laws, contributing to the overthrowing of governments and changing society. It will have an increased effect as we go into the future.'

q. The Semantic Web aims to add new tags to HTML that allow meanings to be linked to resources. Instead of just having a hyperlink to a new page, a word may be linked to information about the meaning of that word. This could then permit computers to search ideas and deduce concepts, rather than just present raw data.

r. The practice of sending emails that pretend to be from trustworthy sources in order to scam you into giving passwords or bank details is known as 'phishing'.

s. Information on market capital accessed April 2011 from: http://uk.finance.yahoo.com/

t. Perhaps bizarrely, in addition to starring in eighteen movies and marrying six different men, the Austrian-American actress Hedy Lamarr renowned for her on-screen beauty invented and patented frequency hopping. It's a method of enabling wireless communication to work effectively while being difficult to discover or decipher, widely used today in WiFi and some cordless phones.

Chapter 101

a. Bob soon joined ARPA and led the ARPNET project as we saw in the previous chapter.

b. The same Licklider who had dreamed of linking computers into a global network.

c. Engelbart's mouse was made of wood, and had two wheels underneath mounted at a right angle to each other. As the mouse was moved, the wheels turned or dragged over the surface, allowing the computer to figure out how far the mouse was travelling, and move the on-screen pointer by the same amount. Later versions shrunk the two wheels inside the device and used a ball to roll over the surface. Modern computer mice are normally optical—they have a simple camera underneath that looks at the table surface and they use the changing image to figure out where they are moving.

d. However, Engelbart was so ahead of his time that many people in the audience didn't understand what they were seeing. 'It's hard to believe now,' says Bill Paxton, a fellow researcher who assisted in the demo, 'but at the time, even we had trouble understanding what he was doing. Think of everyone else out there.'

e. Who had moved from ARPA to Xerox Parc in 1970 and took over as manager of the computer science lab in 1977.

f. Microsoft Disk Operating System.

g. And the associated improvements in touch-sensitive displays, batteries, memory, and processors.

h. The next chapter will explore artificial intelligence.

i. Often referred to as vertices and edges, respectively.

j. Invented by Sutherland's PhD student, and co-founder of Pixar, Edwin Catmull.

k. There is an increasing number of these, often known as pixel shaders, which can calculate effects such as reflections, fog, smoke, or changing textures.

l. A free online virtual world, where anyone can create their own characters and environment, and interact with those created by everyone else. http://secondlife.com/

m. http://www.xbox.com/en-US/kinect

n. The condition was greatly over-hyped in the British tabloid press in 2008. The true seriousness of the condition is not known.

o. Which we'll return to in the next chapter.

p. Also described in the next chapter.

Chapter 110

a. His appearance in this newsreel film was just another example of the interest in his most recent work on intelligent machines. *Life* and *Popular Science* magazines ran feature stories on Shannon's amazing learning mouse in 1952.

b. The work was also inspiring enough for the two Sutherland brothers to help build a similar device a few years later for Edmund Berkeley, as we saw in the previous chapter.

c. The work was spread around the world in an article in the popular magazine *Scientific American*.

d. Which was itself based on work by von Neumann back in 1928.

e. More specifically: a game with two players, with a limited number of possible moves, where the game is 'zero sum' (when one player gains, the other loses by exactly the same amount).

f. Shannon's heuristics were based on an understanding (and some assumptions) of chess. For example, he thought that in the first ten moves it is important to develop pieces to good positions, in the 'middle game' it is good to take as many of your opponent's pieces as possible, and when there are few pieces left, it is important to promote pawns and consider the king. Shannon's machine only focused on the middle game.

g. From the early 1950s, Arthur Samuel pioneered computer checkers, on IBM's first commercial computer, the 701. His program used Shannon's minimax algorithm, but also included the ability to learn which moves were more successful than others.

h. Turing would perhaps have been disappointed that a decade beyond the end of the century, general educated opinion would still find it difficult to accept that machines could think, let alone be intelligent enough to converse with us.

i. In addition to Turing, its members included the likes of Grey Walter and Harold Shipton, pioneers in electroencephalography (EEG) and robotics, Eliot Slater (an eminent psychiatrist), Ross Ashby (a pioneer of cybernetics), Jack Good (a pioneer in artificial intelligence), and many others.

j. The new area of research called *cybernetics*, explored by Wiener in his book published in 1948.

k. One important example was the Logic Theorist created by Newell, Simon, and Shaw in 1955. They created a special language IPL (Information Processing Language) to process lists of symbols, allowing their program to prove theorems by search and the application of rules.

l. Minsky also worked for Shannon in the summer of 1952.

m. These more complex types of neural network were later to become known as self-organizing random networks.

n. Time-sharing is the idea of dividing the time of computers into small slices in order to enable many programs to be run on a single computer simultaneously. It is used universally in almost every computer system today—it's how you can run many programs at the same time with just a single computer processor.

o. Which was created in 1972 by Alan Colmeraurer.

p. The semantic network was invented by Richard Richens. In its most basic form it is simply a list of associations between items, which form a network of meaning between those items. For example: ((seal (is_a mammal) (eats fish)) (mammal (is_a vertebrate) (feeds_children milk))

q. http://www.cyc.com/

r. Such as Japan's Fifth Generation Computer Systems Project which built several parallel processing, logic-programming-based 'inference machines'. Other examples include the dedicated LISP machines (specialized computers for running LISP) or the Connection Machines made by companies such as Thinking Machines Corporation, which were quickly surpassed by ordinary computers.

s. The Neats used logic to reason about information, for example, in expert systems or chatterbots. The Scruffies used heuristic rules to plan, process, or derive knowledge in frames. But all such information was stored as labels with no link to the real world. A 'chair' may have symbolic links to a 'person' or a 'table' but the computer has no idea how a real chair looks and feels, and that it might be substantially different from a spoon, for example.

t. Even today, chatterbots based on symbolic processing illustrate Searle's point very well. They simply cannot produce the right responses by clever symbol manipulations alone; they need to know what the words mean. As an example, here's a conversation I had with iGod in 2011, a chatterbot available at http://www.titane.ca/ The bot makes a great start, but it is not long before it reveals itself to be nonsense. *Me: I am writing about Artificial Intelligence. God: Will you include me in your essay? Me: I was thinking that I might. God: How do I know that you were really 'thinking'? Me: That is for you to decide. God: Does it have any other purpose? Me: Who is right, Minsky or McCarthy? God: Not a robot. Probably a human. Maybe a celebrity? Have you tried a web search?*

u. Indeed Turing wrote a remarkable letter to Ashby, beginning with the words, 'Sir Charles Darwin has shown me your letter, and I am most interested to find that there is somebody working along these lines. In working on the ACE I am more interested in the possibility of producing models of the action of the brain than in the practical applications to computing. I am most anxious to read your paper.' (This Darwin was a mathematician and the grandson of *the* Charles Darwin.)

v. Fascinatingly, even the very first computers were used for Alife studies. One such example is Nils Als Barricelli's Numerical Symboorganisms program, produced in 1953 on von Neumann's IAS machine.

w. I was in the audience of the 1994 conference on Simulation of Adaptive Behaviour in Brighton, UK, when Karl Sims first spoke about his work (he had been 'poached' from the conference at which he was presenting the work). It was the first and last time I've ever witnessed a large hall of normally staid academics give a speaker a standing ovation for a piece of work.

x. 'It is easy to understand why everybody called him Johnny,' says Holland. 'He was a very friendly, nice person.'

y. An allele is a specific form of a gene. You can think of the gene for eye colour having an allele for blue and another for brown.

z. In a process called crossover, which is the basis for crossbreeding. This was the major new feature of genetic algorithms. Previous evolutionary algorithms relied solely on mutation without any crossover between parents.

aa. He was inspired in part by the final unfinished works of von Neumann that were edited by his mentor Art Burks. These papers and eventually a book described von Neumann's self-reproducing automata—a remarkable idea that described cellular automata (CA) (grids of cells whose contents were controlled by local neighbourhood rules), and self-reproducing machines called universal constructors that lived within these strange worlds. The ideas were later taken up and studied in depth by mathematicians such as John Conway and by computer scientists such as Chris Langton and Stephen Wolfram. Today CAs are used extensively for modelling many natural phenomena, including fluid dynamics, the spread of fire, or the growth of tumours. Some computer science researchers believe that computers with architectures similar to cellular automata may enable fault-tolerant or self-repairing processors.

bb. Holland's genetic algorithms were not the only evolutionary algorithms invented in the 1960s and early 1970s. Also in the USA, Lawrence Fogel studied the use of artificial evolution to modify finite state machines and enable them to make predictions, with the intention that this would lead to artificial intelligence. In Germany, Ingo Rechenberg created the *evolutionsstrategie* and used it for optimization, such as aerodynamic wing designs. Today all three approaches are merged into the single field of evolutionary computation.

cc. This is another area which Turing investigated in one of his final works: 'The Chemical Basis for Morphogenesis'.

dd. At least not without cheating. Humphrys claims to have created a program that did successfully fool a human, but that seems to have been mainly achieved through the program repeatedly using an impressive array of filthy language and provoking an argument.

ee. For example, radial basis function networks, Kohonen self-organizing networks, the Boltzmann Machine, deep learning, spiking neural networks, cascading neural networks, the reservoir model, and many other variations and combinations.

Chapter 111

a. Influenced by Cezanne and Dutch Still Life Painting.

b. Such as Kenneth Martin who used randomness (dice or numbers drawn from a hat) to generate art.

c. IBM UK Ltd's Scientific Research Centre.

d. Jon uses generative processes extensively in his own work. 'I read Dawkins' *Blind Watchmaker* book and was immediately inspired to use evolutionary and generative processes in my work.'

e. An evolutionary or generative art system has a cousin, known as interactive art, for which computers are also commonly used. Instead of the artist using their system to generate the art and then exhibiting a finished product, interactive art enables the artist to create a process and then participants may interact with and change the artwork in the exhibition. It's an exciting idea for many artists. 'Interactivity brought the biggest change in thousands of years of art history by replacing objects with real-time generated processes that depend on and react to the participants' behaviour,' says Novakovic. 'Such things never existed before. This challenges our understanding of what art is, and of the roles of the artist and the audience (who is actually responsible for the act of creation—the artist, the audience, or both?), and even the place of art in society.'

f. A laborious process where each frame had to be rendered one by one onto film.

g. A psychedelic-influenced electronic rock-dance band, known for having a pro-Ecstasy stance.

h. Latham didn't use IBM computers again for the band, but he did direct several more Shamen videos and provided album cover artwork; he also worked on the movie *Hackers*.

i. Albeit in the style of William Latham.

j. Including myself, with an interactive virtual reality artwork based on a model of the immune system, called Fugue.

k. The use of computers for art dates back to the early days of computer science. Pioneering artists include: Michael Noll, Georg Nees, Frieder Nake,

Vera Molnar, Manfred Mohr, John Whitney, and Charles Csuri. Some of the seminal exhibitions include Generative Computergrafik (1965) and Cybernetic Serendipity (1968). Indeed, cybernetics formed an early influence for many, such as the cybernetic sculptor Edward Ihnatowicz and the telematic pioneer Roy Ascott. Later, the use of PCs and the Internet brought New Media in the late 1980s and 1990s with the work of Paul Brown, Paul Sermon's tele-presence, Stelarc's robotic art, and Jeffrey Shaw's interactive art.

l. 'There is a subtle distinction between "automated aesthetic judgment" and "creativity",' says McCormack, to clarify his comments. 'Being able to make aesthetic judgments is not the same as being creative (although there may be a relation between the two concepts). It's the old 'I don't know much about art, but I know what I like' argument. The examples I have given are more about automated aesthetic judgement, not real creativity. However, I'd argue that through evolutionary methods a machine can effectively modify itself so the judgements no longer necessarily represent those of the original programmer, hence opening the possibility for the machine to make new creative decisions.'

m. Computer Artworks first released an interactive screensaver version of the IBM software called Organic Art (published by Warner Interactive), which allowed PC users to evolve their own art. It was massively successful and before long Latham was famous again. 'I remember being on holiday in Greece, and a guy came up to me. "I run a garage. I've got your screensaver running day and night. It's fantastic!" I'd have chance meetings with people from all walks of life who would say that.' They followed with a computer game called Evolva in which players could mutate their own creatures. This was followed by a game commissioned by Universal, based on the horror movie The Thing. But in December of 2000, Vivendi, a major French media conglomerate, bought Universal Studios and formed Vivendi Universal Entertainment. Latham's company was offered a deal to develop a sequel to their last game, but it fell through as Universal cleared their catalogue. Computer Artworks couldn't survive the loss of such a massive contract, and the company was forced to close in 2003.

n. Kelley and Jefferys had William's Mutator Artworks on their walls as BSc students and had always thought the rule-based 'spiralling' approach used in Form Grow could be applied in the rule-based world of Proteomics.

o. http://www.foldsynth.com/

p. http://www.wwpdb.org/

q. A 3D game development tool. http://unity3d.com/

r. Some aspects of the problem are NP-complete.

s. The Simple Electronic Computer (SEC).

t. After graduating, Norman Kitz moved to English Electric and worked at NPL on the DEUCE computer. Later he worked at Bell Punch and designed the world's first electronic desktop calculator, called ANITA. Meanwhile Andrew Booth created the All-Purpose Electronic Computers (APEC).

u. By Frederic Sanger in 1955.

v. More specifically, the differences between those protein sequences with a high likelihood of common ancestry (homologous proteins) could imply the rate of evolutionary change at the molecular level.

w. PAM (point accepted mutation) uses matrices of probabilities that say how likely it is for one sequence to mutate into another based on observations. From these the likelihood of similarity of different sequences can be calculated.

x. Perhaps surprisingly, Hounsfield was working for EMI at the time. Some claim that it was because of the success of the Beatles pop group that EMI was able to fund research such as this.

y. Both Hounsfield and Cormack were awarded the Nobel Prize in Physiology or Medicine in 1979 for their work.

z. Peter Mansfield, the British physicist and inventor of the approach, was also awarded the Nobel Prize for his work.

aa. Where the problems include recognizing car number plates or finding faces in images.

bb. Graphics processors are also used to help speed up many of the complex calculations needed throughout the reconstruction, segmentation, and registration processes.

cc. Or even remote surgeries where the doctors are elsewhere and operate through robots—a technology now being used for some operations.

dd. I have personal experience of using mobile devices for medical purposes. In one of my research projects I have been working with cardiologists and machine learning experts to produce a technology that allows everyone to sample their own heart sounds and provide this data to their doctors. I created an iPhone app called *iStethoscope Pro* to achieve this. The app received a massive amount of publicity on radio and television and briefly became the number one bestselling program out of several hundred thousand others—showing the level of interest from people around the world in this form of technology.

ee. http://www.ixico.com/

ff. Including Professor Derek Hill, who we met in the first chapter.

gg. 'The name was a geeky reference to the mathematical concept of a search algorithm's set of candidate solutions,' says Kingdon.

hh. Such as the creators of Apple, Adobe, Cisco, Intel, Sandisk, Symantec, and many others.

ii. The fictional technology corporation in Philip K. Dick's *BladeRunner*, which created amazing technologies such as humanoid robots.

jj. http://www.actimize.com/

BIBLIOGRAPHIC NOTES

Chapter 000

1. McDonalds Corporation. (2008) Stock Control at McDonald's. Published online at: http://www.mcdonalds.co.uk/static/pdf/aboutus/education/mcd_stock_control.pdf
2. Micros Case Study. (2006) System Makeover Re-Energizes Pizza Giant's Sales and Productivity. Published online at: http://www.micros.com/nr/rdonlyres/49a20e3e-02ec-4e0e-9986-72b0511b0df5/0/pizza-hutuk.pdf
3. Michel, J-B., Shen, Y. K., Aiden, A. P., Veres, A., Gray, M. K., The Google Books Team, Pickett, J. P., Hoiberg, D., Clancy, D., Norvig, P., Orwant, J., Pinker, S., Nowak, M. A., and Aiden, E. L. (2010) Quantitative Analysis of Culture Using Millions of Digitized Books, *Science*, 1199644. Published online 16 December. DOI: 10.1126/science.1199644.
4. Chao, E. L. and Hall, K. (2008) Occupational Projections and Training Data 2008–09 Edition. US Department of Labor and Bureau of Labor Statistics. February, Bulletin 2702.
5. Forbes Rich List 2010: World's 100 Wealthiest, *This is Money*. Published online 11 March 2010. http://www.thisismoney.co.uk/news/article.html?in_article_id=500941

Chapter 001

1. Hodges, A. (1992) *Alan Turing: The Enigma*. UK paperback: Vintage, Random House, London.

2. Hodges, A. (1997) *Alan Turing: A Natural Philosopher*. Weidenfeld & Nicolson, London.

3. O'Connor, J. M. (2000) Alan Turing—Enigma, *British Heritage Magazine*.

4. Wilkinson, J. H. (1971) Some Comments from a Numerical Analyst, 1970 Turing Award lecture, *Journal of the ACM*, 18:2, February, pp. 137–47.

5. Russell, B. (1903) *The Principles of Mathematics*. W. W. Norton, New York (1996 edition).

6. Bentley, P. J. (2008) *The Book of Numbers: The Secrets of Numbers and How They Created Our World*. Cassell Illustrated, London.

7. Gödel (1931) Über formal unentscheidbare Sätze der Principia Mathematica und verwandter Systeme, I. Monatshefte für Mathematik und Physik 38: 173–98. Also available in English as: Gödel (2000) On Formally Undecidable Propositions of Principia Mathematica and Related Systems I. A modern translation by Martin Hirzel. http://www.research.ibm.com/people/h/hirzel/papers/canon00-goedel.pdf

8. Turing, A. M. (1936) On Computable Numbers, With an Application to the Entscheidungsproblem, Proceedings of the London Mathematical Society 42. Reprinted in Martin Davis ed. (1965) *The Undecidable*. Raven Press, Hewlett, NY, pp. 115–54.

9. Turing, A. M. (1938) On Computable Numbers, with an Application to the Entscheidungsproblem: A Correction, Proceedings of the London Mathematical Society 43:2, pp. 544–6, 1937; doi:10.1112/plms/s2-43.6.544). Reprinted in Martin Davis (ed.) (1965) *The Undecidable*. Raven Press. Hewlett, NY, pp. 115–54.

10. Church, A. (1937) Reviewed Work: On Computable Numbers, with an Application to the Entscheidungsproblem by A. M. Turing, *The Journal of Symbolic Logic*, March, 2:1, pp. 42–3.

11. Rota, G-C. and Palombi, F. (1997) *Indiscrete Thoughts*. Modern Birkhäuser Classics, Boston, MA.

12. Marans, D. (2010) Logic Matters 2.5. Notable Thinkers, Images and Quotations. Lecture Notes. St. Thomas University, Miami, FL. Available at: http://www.slideshare.net/guest02c582a/logic-matters-25

13. Spencer, C. (2009) Profile: Alan Turing. BBC News Friday, 11 September. Available online at: http://news.bbc.co.uk/1/hi/uk/8250592.stm

14. Hodges, A. (1998) Unveiling the Official Blue Plaque on Alan Turing's Birthplace. Transcript of oration, available on: http://www.turing.org.uk/bio/oration.html

15. http://www.bletchleypark.org.uk/

16. Author interview with Sue Black, January 2011.

17. Brown, G. (2009) Apology to Alan Turing, *The Daily Telegraph*, 10 September.

18. Author interview with Mark Herbster, January 2011.

19. Author interview with Robin Hirsch, January 2011.

20. Jaffe, A. M. (2006) The Millennium Grand Challenge in Mathematics, *Notices of the AMS*, 53:6, pp. 652–60.

21. (2000) P = NP Challenge Description. Clay Mathematics institute. http://www.claymath.org/millennium/P_vs_NP/

22. Kaye, R. (2000) Minesweeper is NP-complete, *Mathematical Intelligencer*, 22:2, pp. 9–15.

23. Garey, M. R. and Johnson, D. S. (1990) *Computers and Intractability: A Guide to the Theory of NP-Completeness*. W. H. Freeman, New York.

24. Sipser, M. (2005) *Introduction to the Theory of Computation*. Course Technology Inc., Boston, MA.

25. Author interview with Daniel Hulme, January 2011.

26. Rogers, H. (1987) *Theory of Recursive Functions and Effective Computability*. MIT Press, Cambridge, MA.

27. Rice, H. G. (1953) Classes of Recursively Enumerable Sets and Their Decision Problems, *Transactions of the American Mathematical Society*, 74, pp. 358–66.

28. Kolmogorov, A. N. (1963) On Tables of Random Numbers, *Theoretical Computer Science*, 207:2, pp. 387–95. doi:10.1016/S0304-3975(98)00075-9.

29. Mandelbrot, B. (1982) *The Fractal Geometry of Nature*. W. H. Freeman, San Francisco.

30. Pearlman, W. A. and Said, A. (2011) *Digital Signal Compression: Principles and Practice*. Cambridge University Press, Cambridge.

Chapter 010

1. Hodges, A. (1992) *Alan Turing: The Enigma*. UK paperback: Vintage, Random House, London.

2. Sloane, N. J. A. and Wyner, A. D. (Eds) (1993) *Claude E. Shannon: Collected Papers*. Wiley-IEEE Press, Hoboken, NJ.

3. Shannon, C. E. (1940) A Symbolic Analysis of Relay and Switching Circuits. M.Sc. Thesis. Advisor: Frank L. Hitchcock. MIT. Dept. of Electrical Engineering. Publisher: MIT.

4. Bazhanov, V. and Volgin, L. (2001) I. Shestakov and C. Shannon: The Fate of One Brilliant Idea, *Scientific and Technical Kaleidoscope*, N2, pp. 43–8 (Russian).

5. MIT Professor Claude Shannon Dies; Was Founder of Digital Communications. *MIT News*. 27 February 2001. Available online at: http://web.mit. edu/newsoffice/2001/shannon.html

6. Claude Shannon, Father of Information Theory, Dies at 84. Obituary published in *Bell Labs* news, 26 February 2001. Available online: http://www. bell-labs.com/news/2001/february/26/1.html

7. Macrae, N. (2000) *John von Neumann: The Scientific Genius who Pioneered the Modern Computer*. American Mathematical Society, Providence, RI.

8. Deane, J. (2006) SILLIAC—Vacuum Tube Supercomputer. A History of SILLIAC. Published by the Science Foundation for Physics and the Australian Computer Museum Society. Content available online: http://www. physics.usyd.edu.au/foundation.old/silliac/book.html

9. Halmos, P. R. (1973) The Legend of John von Neumann, *American Mathematical Monthly*, 80: 382–94.

10. O'Connor, J. and Robertson, E. (2003) *John von Neumann Biography*. MacTutor Biographies. School of Mathematics and Statistics, University of St. Andrews, St. Andrews. http://www-history.mcs.st-and.ac.uk/Biographies/Von_Neumann.html

11. Copeland, J. (2000) A Brief History of Computing. AlanTuring.net Reference Article. Available at: http://www.alanturing.net/turing_archive/pages/Reference%20Articles/BriefHistofComp.html

12. Rheingold, H. (1985) *Tools For Thought: The People and Ideas of the Next Computer Revolution*. Simon & Schuster, New York.

13. von Neumann, J. (1945) First Draft of a Report on the EDVAC. Moore School of Electrical Engineering, University of Pennsylvania. Developed under contract W-670-ORD-4926 between the United States Army Ordenance Department and the University of Pennsylvania.

14. Randell (1972) On Alan Turing and the Origins of Digital Computers, in Meltzer, B., Michie, D. (eds) *Machine Intelligence 7*. Edinburgh University Press, Edinburgh, p. 10.

15. Carpenter, B. E. and Doran, R. W. (1986) *A. M. Turing's ACE Report of 1946 and Other Papers*. MIT Press, Cambridge, MA.

16. Copeland, J. (2006) *Colossus: The Secrets of Bletchley Park's Codebreaking Computers*. Oxford University Press, Oxford.

17. Author interview with Bruce Damer, December 2010.

18. Wilkes, M. (1986) The Genesis of Microprogramming, *Annals of the History of Computing*, 8:2, pp. 115–26.

19. Bell Labs. History of The Transistor (the 'Crystal Triode') Bell Systems Memorial pages. Available at: http://www.porticus.org/bell/belllabs_transistor.html

20. Lavington, S. (1998) *A History of Manchester Computers* (2nd edition). The British Computer Society, London.

21. Texas Instruments. The Chip that Jack Built. Web page: TI People, Jack Kilby. http://www.ti.com/corp/docs/kilbyctr/jackbuilt.shtml

22. Halmos P. R., (1973) The Legend of John von Neumann, *American Mathematical Monthly*, 80, pp. 382–94.

23. Heppenheimer, T. A. (1990) How von Neumann Showed the Way, *American Heritage* 6:2.

24. Transcript of Intel Developers' Forum, 8.18.07, Afternoon Session. Available online at: http://download.intel.com/pressroom/kits/events/idffall_2007/TranscriptMoore-Gelsinger.pdf

25. Moore, G. E. (1965) Cramming More Components onto Integrated Circuits, *Electronics*, 38:8, 19 April.

26. Intel (2005) Excerpts from A Conversation with Gordon Moore: Moore's Law. Available online: ftp://download.intel.com/museum/Moores_Law/Video-Transcripts/Excepts_A_Conversation_with_Gordon_Moore.pdf

27. Kanellos, M. (2003) Moore's Law to Roll on for Another Decade. *CNET News*, 10 February.

28. Author interview with David Patterson, February 2011.

29. Ostrander, F. (2000) The Serious Business of Sound for Toys (or How I Went from HLA to Amazing Amy) by Presented at the Los Angeles AES Chapter Meeting, 25 April.

30. Hennessy, J. L. and Patterson, D. A. (2007) *Computer Architecture: A Quantitative Approach* (4th edition) Morgan Kaufmann, New York.

31. Asanovic, K., Bodik, R., Catanzaro, B. C., Gebis, J. J., Husbands, P., Keutzer, K., Patterson, D. A., Plishker, W. L., Shalf, J., Williams, S. W., and Yelick, K. A. (2006) The Landscape of Parallel Computing Research: A View from Berkeley. Electrical Engineering and Computer Sciences, University of California at Berkeley, Technical Report No. UCB/EECS-2006-183. http://www.eecs.berkeley.edu/Pubs/TechRpts/2006/EECS-2006-183.html

32. Patterson, D. (2010) The Trouble With Multicore: Chipmakers are Busy Designing Microprocessors that most Programmers can't Handle, *IEEE Spectrum*, July.

33. What is AWS? Amazon Web Services webpage: http://aws.amazon.com/what-is-aws/

34. Barnatt, C. (2010) *A Brief Guide to Cloud Computing: An Essential Introduction to the Next Revolution in Computing*. Robinson Publishing, London.

35. Turley, J. (2003) Motoring with Microprocessors. EE Times: Significant Bits. Available online: http://www.eetimes.com/discussion/other/4024611/Motoring-with-microprocessors

36. Rubenstein, R. (2010) How ARM Processors are Enabling a Massively Parallel Neural Network, *New Electronics Magazine*. Available online at: http://www.newelectronics.co.uk/article/26279/Modelling-the-brain.aspx

37. Teuscher, C. and Adamatzky, A. (eds) (2005) *Unconventional Computing 2005: From Cellular Automata to Wetware*. Luniver Press, Beckington.
38. Author interview with Andy Tyrrell, February 2011.

Chapter 011

1. Davis, D. (2008) Of Note: The Moore School Lectures 1946, *Penn Engineering News*, pp.6–8.
2. Mauchley, J. (1942) The Use of High Speed Vacuum Tube Devices for Calculating. Internal memo, reproduced in Randell, B. (1982) *The Origins of Digital Computers: Selected Papers*. Birkhäuser, Basel.
3. Frank M. Verzuh: Moore School of Electrical Engineering lecture notes (CBI 51), Charles Babbage Institute, University of Minnesota, Minneapolis, MN.
4. Gallager, R. G. (2001) Claude E. Shannon: A Retrospective on His Life, Work, and Impact, *IEEE Transactions on Information Theory*, 47:7, pp. 2681–95.
5. Wilkes, M. V. (1985) *Memoirs of a Computer Pioneer*. The MIT Press, Cambridge, MA.
6. Hartley, D. (Ed) (1999) EDSAC 1 and After—A Compilation of Personal Reminiscences. Compiled for the EDSAC 99 Meeting (50th anniversary of the EDSAC). Available online at: http://www.cl.cam.ac.uk/conference/EDSAC99/reminiscences/
7. David J. Wheeler, OH 132. Oral History Interview by William Aspray, 14 May 1987, Princeton, NJ. Charles Babbage Institute, University of Minnesota, Minneapolis, MN.
8. Malik, M. A. (1998) Evolution of the High Level Programming Languages: A Critical Perspective, *ACM SIGPLAN Notices*. V, 33:12, pp. 72–80.
9. Ponton, J. The Autocodes: Sirius to IMP, a User's Perspective. Available online: http://www.chemeng.ed.ac.uk/people/jack/history/autocodes/
10. Knuth, D. E. and Pardo, L. T. (1977) Early Development of Programming Languages, in Belzer, J., Holzman, A. G., and Kent, A. (eds) *Encyclopedia of Computer Science and Technology*, 7. Marcel Dekker, New York, pp. 419–93.

11. McJones, P. (ed.) (2010) History of FORTRAN and FORTRAN II. Software Preservation Group, Computer History Museum. Available at: http://www.softwarepreservation.org/projects/FORTRAN/

12. Author interview with David Patterson, February 2011.

13. Father of British Computing Sir Maurice Wilkes Dies, *BBC News*, 30 November 2010.

14. Codd, E.F. (1970) A Relational Model of Data for Large Shared Data Banks, *Communications of the ACM*, 13:6, 377–87. doi:10.1145/362384.362685

15. Date, C. J. (2004) *An Introduction to Database Systems*. Addison Wesley.

16. Oppel, A. (2004) *Databases Demystified*. McGraw-Hill Osborne Media, New York.

17. Paragon Corporation (2005) SQL Cheat Sheet: Query By Example, 2 July 2005. Available online at: http://www.paragoncorporation.com/ArticleDetail.aspx?ArticleID = 27

18. P. Naur and B. Randell (eds.) (1969). Software Engineering: Report of a Conference Sponsored by the NATO Science Committee, Garmisch, Germany, 7–11 October 1968, Brussels, Scientific Affairs Division, NATO, 231 pp.

19. B. Randell and J. N. Buxton (eds.) (1970) Software Engineering Techniques: Report of a Conference Sponsored by the NATO Science Committee, Rome, Italy, 27–31 October 1969, Brussels, Scientific Affairs Division, NATO, 164 pp.

20. Sommerville, I. (2010) *Software Engineering* (9th edition). Addison Wesley, Boston, MA.

21. Author interview with Ian Sommerville, March 2011.

22. Randell, B. (1996) The 1968/69 NATO Software Engineering Reports. Dagstuhl-Seminar 9635: 'History of Software Engineering' Schloss Dagstuhl, 26–30 August.

23. Author interview with Anthony Finkelstein, March 2011.

24. Wirth, N. (1995) A Plea for Lean Software, *Computer* 28:2, pp. 64–8. doi:10.1109/2.348001

25. Kennedy, R. C. (2008) Fat, Fatter, Fattest: Microsoft's Kings of Bloat. *InfoWorld Applications*, 14 April.

26. Author interview with Mark Harman, March 2011.

27. Charette, R. (2005) Why Software Fails. We Waste Billions of Dollars Each Year on Entirely Preventable Mistakes, *IEEE Spectrum*, September.

Available online: http://spectrum.ieee.org/computing/software/why-software-fails

Chapter 100

1. Macquarrie, K. (1998) *Peru's Amazonian Eden: Manu National Park and Biosphere Reserve* (2nd edition). Francis O. Patthey & Sons, Barcelona.

2. Author interview with Peter Kirstein, March 2011.

3. Hamming, R. (1986) You and Your Research. Transcript of seminar in the Bell Communications Research Colloquia Series given on 7 March. (Transcripted by J. F. Kaiser).

4. Shannon, C. E. (1948) A Mathematical Theory of Communication, *Bell System Technical Journal*, 27, pp. 379–423, 623–56.

5. Author interview with Jon Crowcroft, April 2011.

6. Price, R. (1985) A Conversation with Claude Shannon: One Man's Approach to Problem Solving, *Cryptologia*, 9:2, pp. 167–75. R Price (1984) A Conversation with Claude Shannon: One Man's Approach to Problem Solving, *IEEE Communications Magazine*, 23:5, pp. 123–6.

7. Licklider, J. C. R. (1960) Man–Computer Symbiosis, *IRE Transactions on Human Factors in Electronics*, HFE-1, pp. 4–11, March.

8. Davies, D. W., Bartlett, K. A., Scantlebury, R. A., and Wilkinson, P. T. (1967) A Digital Communications Network for Computers Giving Rapid Response at Remote Terminals, ACM Symposium on Operating Systems Problems, October.

9. Kirstein, P. T. Early Experiences With the ARPANET and Internet in the UK. Available online: http://nrg.cs.ucl.ac.uk/internet-history.html

10. Cerf, V. G. and Kahn, R. E. (1974) A Protocol for Packet Network Intercommunication, *IEEE Transactions on Communications*, 22:5, May, 1974 pp. 637–48.

11. Cooper, C. S. (2010) *JANET: The First 25 Years*. The JNT Association, Didcott.

12. Cerf, V. and Kirstein, P. (1978) Issues in Packet to Packet Interconnection. Proceedings of the *IEEE*, 66:11, pp. 1386–408.

13. Zhou, S. and Mondragon, R. J. (2004) The Rich-Club Phenomenon in the Internet Topology, *IEEE Communications Letters*, 8:3, pp. 180–2.

14. Zhou, S. (2009) Why the Internet is so 'Small'? in Rashid, M., Eduardo, C., and Radoslaw, P., and Imrich, C. (eds) *Communications Infrastructure, Systems and Applications in Europe* (4–12). Springer, Berlin/Heidelberg.

15. Author interview with Shi Zhou, April 2011.

16. Crowcroft, J. (2010) Peter Kirstein and the role of the UK in the History of the Internet. From 1973 Until the Present Day, and On into the Future.

17. *UCL News* (2003) UCL celebrates Internet pioneers. Available online at: http://www.cs.ucl.ac.uk/csnews/internet_pioneers.html

18. Hoffman, P. and Harris, S. The Tao of IETF: A Novice's Guide to the Internet Engineering Task Force. Request for Comments: 4677. Network Working Group. Available online at: http://www.rfc-editor.org/rfc/rfc4677.txt

19. Author interview with Mark Handley, April 2011.

20. Vint Cerf on the Future of the Internet. July 2009 lecture at Singularity University. Available online at: http://www.datacenterknowledge.com/archives/2009/10/12/vint-cerf-on-the-future-of-the-internet/

21. Greenemeier, L. (2009) The Origin of the Computer Mouse, *Scientific American*. Available online at: http://www.scientificamerican.com/article.cfm?id = origins-computer-mouse

22. Berners-Lee (1994) A Brief History of the Web (Written for a possible book in around 1993/4. Written in Microsoft word, copied to HTML and salvaged by hand.) Available online at: http://www.w3.org/DesignIssues/TimBook-old/History.html

23. Schonfeld, E. (2010) Web Video Hogs Up 37 Per cent of Internet Traffic During Peak TV Hours, *TechCrunch*. Available online: http://techcrunch.com/2010/11/19/web-video-37-percent-internet-traffic/

24. Fielding, R. T., Gettys, J., Mogul, J. C., Frystyk, H., Masinter, L., Leach, P. J., Berners-Lee, T. (1999) Hypertext Transfer Protocol—HTTP/1.1. Network Working Group. Request For Comments: 2616. Standards Track, June.

25. Berners-Lee, T., Hendler, J., and Lassila, O. (2001). The Semantic Web, *Scientific American*, 17 May.

26. Except from Tim Berners Lee FAQ, reproduced with permission. http://www.w3.org/People/Berners-Lee/FAQ.html

27. Naone, E. (2009) First Test for Election Cryptography, *Technology Review*. MIT. Available online at: http://www.technologyreview.com/web/23836/?a = f

28. Shannon, C. (1949) Communication Theory of Secrecy Systems, *Bell System Technical Journal*, 28:4, pp. 656–715.

29. Author interview with Nicolas Courtois, March 2011.

30. Courtois, N. (2002) Comment tout dire sans rien révéler, *Dossiers De pour la science, pour la science* (French Edition of *Scientific American*), 36.

31. Courtois, N. and Meier, W. (2003) Algebraic Attacks on Stream Ciphers with Linear Feedback, *Advances in Cryptology—EuroCrypt 2003*, Lecture Notes in Computer Science, 2656, Springer-Verlag, Berlin, pp. 345–59. doi: 10.1007/3-540-39200-9_21.

32. Cocks, C. (2001) An Identity Based Encryption Scheme Based on Quadratic Residues, Cryptography and Coding, 8th IMA International Conference, pp. 360–3.

33. Diffie, W. and Hellman, M. (1976) New Directions in Cryptography. *IEEE Transactions on Information Theor*, 22:6, pp. 644–54.

34. Rivest, R., Shamir, A., Adleman, L. (1978) A Method for Obtaining Digital Signatures and Public-Key Cryptosystems, *Communications of the ACM*, 21:2, 120–6. doi:10.1145/359340.359342

35. McQuade, S. C. (2008) *Encyclopedia of Cybercrime*. Greenwood Press.

36. Danchev, D. (2008) Coordinated Russia vs Georgia Cyber Attack in Progress, *ZNet.com*, 11 August, 4:23p.m PDT. Available online at: http://www.zdnet.com/blog/security/coordinated-russia-vs-georgia-cyber-attack-in-progress/1670

37. Halliday, J. and Julian Borger, J. (2010) Iranian Nuclear Plants Likely Target of Foiled Cyber Sabotage. *The Guardian*, Saturday 25 September. Available online at: http://www.guardian.co.uk/world/2010/sep/25/iran-cyber-hacking-nuclear-plants

38. Office of Audits (2011) Inadequate Security Practices Expose Key NASA Network to Cyber Attack. Report No. IG-11-017 (Assignment No. A-10-011-00). Available online at: http://www.scribd.com/doc/51838938/NASA-Cybersecurity-Report

39. Lowenstein, R. (2004) *Origins of the Crash: The Great Bubble and Its Undoing*. Penguin Press, Harmondsworth.

40. BT 21CN—Network Topology & Technology. An Overview of BT's 21st Century Network Technology and Topology. Available online at: http://www.kitz.co.uk/adsl/21cn_network.htm

41. Boone, L. E. and Kurtz, D. L. (2007) *Contemporary Marketing* (13th edition). South-Western College Publications, Cincinnati, OH.

Chapter 101

1. MouseSite at Stanford. The Demo—Streaming Clips of Engelbart's 1968 Demonstration. Available online at: http://sloan.stanford.edu/MouseSite /1968Demo.html

2. Stanford and the Silicon Valley Oral History Interviews. Douglas Engelbart Interview 1, 19 December 1986. Conducted by H. Lowood and T. Adams, Stanford. Available online at: http://www-sul.stanford.edu/depts/hasrg/histsci/ssvoral/engelbart/main1-ntb.html

3. Bush, V. (1945) As We May Think, *The Atlantic Monthly*, July. Reprinted in *Life* magazine, 10 September 1945.

4. Engelbart, D. C. (1962) Augmenting Human Intellect: A Conceptual Framework. Stanford Research Institute, Menlo Park, CA 94,025. USA. AFOSR-3233 Summary Report. Prepared for: Director of Information Sciences, Air Force Office of Scientific Research, Washington, DC, 25, D.C. Contract AF49(638)-1024. SRI Project No. 3578. Available online at: http://www.1962paper.org/web.html

5. Metz, C. (2008) The Mother of All Demos—150 Years Ahead of Its Time. The Register. Posted in Software, 11th December. Availableonline at: http://www.theregister.co.uk/2008/12/11/engelbart_celebration/

6. Hiltzik, M. A. (1999) *Dealers of Lightning: Xerox PARC and the Dawn of the Computer Age*. HarperCollins, New York.

7. Linzmayer, O. (2004) *Apple Confidential 2.0: The Definitive History of the World's Most Colorful Company: The Real Story of Apple Computer, Inc.* No Starch Press, San Francisco, CA.

8. Brad A. Myers. (1998) A Brief History of Human Computer Interaction Technology, *ACM Interactions*, 5:2, pp. 44–54.

9. Doug Engelbart Institute: Doug's Vision Highlights. Adapted from Doug Engelbart's Augmenting Society's Collective IQ, the abstract for his Keynote Speech at Hypertext 2004 (AUGMENT,133,319,). Available online at: http://www.dougengelbart.org/about/vision-highlights.html

10. New Media Consortium (2009) *Doug Engelbart Tribute Video*. (Interview clips from 2002.) http://www.youtube.com/watch?v = lAv-5Z7TPHE

11. Licklider, J. C. R. (1960) Man–Computer Symbiosis. *IRE Transactions on Human Factors in Electronics HFE-1*, pp. 4–11.

12. Oral history interview of R. W. Taylor, OH 154, by William Aspray, 28 February 1989, San Francisco, CA. Charles Babbage Institute, University of Minnesota, Minneapolis, MN.

13. Berkeley, E. C. (1949) *Giant Brains Or Machines That Think*. John Wiley & Sons, New York.

14. Frenkel, K. A. (1989) An Interview with Ivan Sutherland, *Communications of the ACM*, 32:6, June.

15. Aspray, W. (1989) An Interview with Ivan Sutherland OH 171. Charles Babbage Institute Center for the History of Information Processing University of Minnesota, Minneapolis, MN. Copyright, Charles Babbage Institute.

16. Hoggett, R. (2010) 1953—'Franken' Maze-Solving Machine—Ivan and Bert Sutherland. Article with scans of original notes and reports, posted on cyberneticzoo.com, Monday, 3 May. Available online at: http://cyberneticzoo.com/?tag = robert-bert-sutherland

17. Sutherland, I. E. (1963) Sketchpad: A Man-Machine Graphical Communication System. Technical Report No. 296, Lincoln Laboratory, MIT, Cambridge, MA.

18. Sutherland, I. E. (1968) A head-mounted three dimensional display. In Proceedings of the 9–11 December, Fall Joint Computer Conference, part I (AFIPS '68 (Fall, part I)). ACM, New York, 757–64. doi = 10.1145/1476589.1476686 http://doi.acm.org/10.1145/1476589.1476686

19. Masson, T. (2007) *CG101: A Computer Graphics Industry Reference* (2nd edition). Published by Digital Fauxtography Inc, San Rafael, CA.

20. ABOWD team Shopper's Assistant. Class Assignment. Biography of a Luminary: Dr Ivan E. Sutherland. Available online at: http://www.cc.gatech.edu/classes/cs6751_97_fall/projects/abowd_team/ivan/ivan.html

21. Asynchronous Research Center. Roncken and Sutherland to Join PSU's Dynamic Intellectual Community. Available online at: http://arc.cecs.pdx.edu/about

22. Slater, M., Chrysanthou, Y., and Steed, A. (2001) *Computer Graphics and Virtual Environments: From Realism to Real-time*. Addison Wesley, Boston, MA.

23. Möller, T., Haines, E., and Hoffman, N. (2008) *Real-Time Rendering*. A. K. Peters/CRC Press, Boca Raton, FL.

24. Deering, M. F. (1993) Making Virtual Reality more Real, Experience with the Virtual Portal, in Proc. Graphics Interface '93.

25. Burkeman, O. (2001) The Guardian Profile: Jaron Lanier, The Virtual Visionary. *The Guardian*, Saturday 29 December. Available online at: http://www.guardian.co.uk/technology/2001/dec/29/games.academicexperts

26. Author interview with Mel Slater, April 2011.

27. Wellcome Trust (2008) Paranoid Thoughts. Video starring Daniel Freeman, Institute of Psychiatry. Available online at: http://www.iop.kcl.ac.uk/apps/paranoidthoughts/research/default.aspx

28. Author interview with Angela Sasse, April 2011.

29. Author interview with Nadia Berthouze, April 2011.

30. Norman, D. (2002) *The Design of Everyday Things*. Basic Books, New York.

31. Author interview with Ann Blandford, April 2011.

32. Damasio, H., Grabowski, T. Frank, R., Galaburda, A. M., and Damasio, A. R. (1994) The Return of Phineas Gage: Clues About the Brain from the Skull of a Famous Patient, *Science*, 20 May, 264:5162, pp. 1102–5, doi: 10.1126/science.8178168

33. Picard, R. (2000) *Affective Computing*. MIT Press, Cambridge, MA.

Chapter 110

1. Claude Shanon—Father of the Information Age. UC Television documentary, available online at: http://www.youtube.com/watch?v=z2Whj_nL-x8&NR=1

2. *Life Magazine*, 28 July 1952. Described online at: http://cyberneticzoo.com/?p=2552

3. Shannon, C. (1951) Presentation of a Maze-Solving Machine. Group Interchange. In Transactions of the Eighth Conference on Cybernetics, 15–16 March 1951, Josiah Macy, Jr Foundation, New York, pp. 173–80.

4. Shannon, C. (1950) Programming a Computer for Playing Chess 1, *Philosophical Magazine*, Series 7, March, 41: 314.

5. von Neumann, J. and Morgenstern, O. (1944) *Theory of Games and Economic Behavior*. Princeton University Press, Princeton, NJ.

6. von Neumann, J. (1928) 'Zur Theorie der Gesellschaftsspiele', *Mathematische Annalen*, 100, pp. 295–300.

7. Hodges, A. (1992) *Alan Turing: The Enigma*. Vintage, Random House, London.

8. Newborn, M. (1997) *Kasparov versus Deep Blue: Computer Chess Comes of Age*. Springer, New York.

9. Turing, A. (1950) Computing Machinery and Intelligence, *Mind*, 59:236, pp. 433–60.

10. Weiner, N. (1948) *Cybernetics, or Control and Communication in the Animal and the Machine*. MIT Press, Cambridge, MA.

11. Husbands, P., Holland, O., and Wheeler, M. (eds) (2008) *The Mechanical Mind in History*. MIT Press, Cambridge, MA.

12. Newell, A. and Simon, A. H. (1956) The Logic Theory Machine: A Complex Information Processing System, *IRE Transactions on Information Theory IT-2*, pp. 61–79.

13. McCarthy, J., Minsky, M., Rochester, N., Shannon, C. (1955), A Proposal for the Dartmouth Summer Research Project on Artificial Intelligence. Available online at: http://www-formal.stanford.edu/jmc/history/dartmouth/dartmouth.html

14. Aspray, W. (1989) An Interview with Ivan Sutherland OH 171. Charles Babbage Institute Center for the History of Information Processing University of Minnesota, MN. Copyright, Charles Babbage Institute.

15. Bernstein, J. (1981) Profiles: AI. An Interview with Marvin Minsky, *The New Yorker Magazine*, 14 December.

16. McCulloch, W. and Pitts, W. (1943) A Logical Calculus of the Ideas Immanent in Nervous Activity, *Bulletin of Mathematical Biophysics*, 7, pp. 115–33.

17. Hebb, D.O. (1949) *The Organization of Behavior*. John Wiley & Sons, New York.

18. Author interview with Robin Hirsch, January 2011.

19. Minsky, M. (1974) A Framework for Representing Knowledge. MIT-AI Laboratory Memo 306, June Reprinted in P. Winston (ed.), *The Psychology of Computer Vision*. McGraw-Hill, New York, 1975.

20. Winograd, T. (1972) *Understanding Natural Language*. Academic Press, New York.

21. Simon, H. A. (1965) *The Shape of Automation for Men and Management*. Harper & Row, New York.

22. Minsky, M. (1967) *Computation: Finite and Infinite Machines*. Prentice-Hall, Englewood Cliffs, NJ.

23. Rosenblatt, F. (1957) The Perceptron—A Perceiving and Recognizing Automaton. Report 85-460-1, Cornell Aeronautical Laboratory, Buffalo, NY.

24. Minksy, M. and Papert, S. (1969) *Perceptrons: An Introduction to Computational Geometry*. MIT Press, Cambridge, MA.

25. Author interview with John Shawe-Taylor, May 2011.

26. Lighthill, J. (1973) Artificial Intelligence: A General Survey, *Artificial Intelligence: A Paper Symposium*, Science Research Council, Swindon.

27. Nilsson, N. J. (2009) *The Quest for Artificial Intelligence: A History of Ideas and Achievements*. Cambridge University Press, Cambridge.

28. Searle, John. R. (1980) Minds, Brains, and Programs, *Behavioral and Brain Sciences*, 3:3, pp. 417–57.

29. Brooks, R. A. (1990). Elephants Don't Play Chess, in P. Maes (ed.) *Designing Autonomous Agents: Theory and Practice from Biology to Engineering and Back*. MIT Press, Cambridge, MA, pp. 3–16.

30. Brockman, J. (1997) 'The Deep Question': A Talk With Rodney Brooks. Interview by John Brockman, 19 November. Available online at: http://www.edge.org/3rd_culture/brooks/brooks_p1.html

31. R. A. Brooks (1991) Intelligence Without Representation, *Artificial Intelligence*, 47, pp. 139–59.

32. Brooks, R. A. (1986) A Robust Layered Control System for a Mobile Robot, *IEEE Journal of Robotics and Automation*, 2:1, pp. 14–23; also MIT AI Memo 864, September 1985.

33. Letter from Alan Turing to Ross Ashby, 1946. Available online at: http://www.rossashby.info/letters/turing.html

34. Science: The Thinking Machine, *Time*, 24 January 1949. Available online at: http://www.time.com/time/magazine/article/ 0,9171,799721,00.html

35. Holland, O. (2003) Exploration and High Adventure: The Legacy of Grey Walter, *Philosophical Transactions of the Royal Society, London*, A 361, pp. 2085–121.

36. Wilson, S. (1991) The Animat Path to AI, in J. A. Meyer and S. W. Wilson (eds), *From Animals to Animats: Proceedings of the First International Conference on the Simulation of Adaptive Behavior*, MIT Press/Bradford Books, Cambridge, MA.

37. Barricelli, N. A. (1953) Experiments in Bionumeric Evolution Executed by the Electronic Computer at Princeton, N.J. Archives of the Institute for Advanced Study, Princeton, NJ.

38. Karl Sims (1994) Evolving Virtual Creatures, *SIGGRAPH '94 Proceedings*, pp. 15–22.

39. Karl Sims (1994) Evolving 3D Morphology and Behavior by Competition, in R. Brooks and P. Maes (eds) *Artificial Life IV Proceedings*. MIT Press, Cambridge, MA, pp. 28–39.

40. Author interview with John Holland, May 2011.

41. Rochester, N., Holland, J. H., Habit, L. H. and Duda, W. L. (1956) Tests on a Cell Assembly Theory of the Action of the Brain, Using a Large Digital Computer, *IRE Transactions on Information Theory*, 2, pp. 80–93.

42. Arthur W. Burks and Alice R. Burks, OH 75. Oral history interview by Nancy B. Stern, 20 June 1980, Ann Arbor, MI. Charles Babbage Institute, University of Minnesota, MN.

43. Fisher, R. A. (1930) *The Genetical Theory of Natural Selection*. Clarendon Press, Oxford.

44. von Neumann, J. and A. W. Burks (1966) *Theory of Self-Reproducing Automata*. University of Illinois Press, URB.

45. Holland, J. H. (1975) *Adaptation in Natural and Artificial Systems*. University of Michigan Press, Englewood Cliffs, NJ.

46. Goldberg, D. E. (1989) *Genetic Algorithms in Search, Optimization, and Machine Learning*. Addison Wesley.

47. Fogel, L.J., Owens, A.J., Walsh, M.J. (1966) *Artificial Intelligence through Simulated Evolution*. John Wiley & Sons, New York.

48. Rechenberg, I. (1971) Evolutionsstrategie—Optimierung technischer Systeme nach Prinzipien der biologischen Evolution (PhD thesis). Reprinted by Fromman-Holzboog (1973).

49. Bonabeau, E., Dorigo, M., and Theraulaz, G. (1999) *Swarm Intelligence: From Natural to Artificial Systems* (Santa Fe Institute Studies on the Sciences of Complexity). Oxford University Press, New York.

50. D'haeseleer, P., Forrest, S., and Helman, P. (1996) An Immunological Approach to Change Detection: Algorithms, Analysis, and Implications. In Proceedings of the 1996 IEEE Symposium on Computer Security and Privacy.

51. Langton, C. G. (1998) *Artificial Life: An Overview*. MIT Press, Cambridge, MA.

52. Turing, A. (1952) The Chemical Basis of Morphogenesis, *Philosphical Transactions of the Royal Society London*, B, 14 August 237:641, pp. 37–72.

53. Humphrys, M. (2008) How My Program Passed the Turing Test, in R. Epstein, G. Roberts, and G. Beber (eds), *Parsing the turing Test: Philosophical and Methodological Issues in the Quest for the Thinking Computer*, Springer, New York.

54. Koza, J. (1992) *Genetic Programming: On the Programming of Computers by Means of Natural Selection*. MIT Press, Cambridge, MA.

55. Author interview with Bill Langdon, May 2011.

56. Bishop, C. (1996) *Neural Networks for Pattern Recognition*. Oxford University Press, New York.

57. Hinton, G. E., Osindero, S., and Teh, Y. (2006) A Fast Learning Algorithm for Deep Belief Nets, *Neural Computation* 18:7, pp. 1527–54. doi:10.1162/neco.2006.18.7.1527

58. Author interview with Geoff Hinton (originally conducted for *Digital Biology*), 1999.

59. Cristianini, N. and Shawe-Taylor, J. (2000) *An Introduction to Support Vector Machines and Other Kernel-Based Learning Methods.* Cambridge University Press, Cambridge.

60. Shoham, Y. and Leyton-Brown, K. (2009) *Multiagent Systems: Algorithmic, Game-Theoretic, and Logical Foundations.* Cambridge University Press, Cambridge.

61. Author interview with Owen Holland, May 2011.

Chapter 111

1. Author interview with William Latham, June 2011.

2. Todd, S. and Latham, W. (1992) *Evolutionary Art and Computers.* Academic Press/Harcourt Brace Jovanovich, New York.

3. Latham, W. (1988) *The Conquest of Form: Computer Art by William Latham.* Arnolfini Gallery, Bristol.

4. Author interview with Jon McCormack, June 2011.

5. Author interview with Gordana Novakovic, June 2011.

6. Jon McCormack (2004) *Impossible Nature: The Art of Jon McCormack.* Australian Centre for the Moving Image, Melbourne.

7. Latham, W., Shaw, M., Todd, S., Leymarie, F., Kelly, L., and Jefferys, B. (2007) From DNA to 3D Organic Art Forms, SIGGRAPH 2007 Sketch in *The Viz Bus.* doi: 10.1145/1278780.1278786.

8. Lesk, A. (2005) *Introduction to Bioinformatics.* Oxford University Press, Oxford.

9. Johnson, R. (2008) Computer Science at Birkbeck College: A Short History. Presented at 50th anniversary celebration, Birkbeck College, London, May. Available online at: http://www.dcs.bbk.ac.uk/~rgj/Computer%20 Science%20at%20Birkbeck%20College%20comp

10. Author interview with David Jones, June 2011.

11. Mount, D. W. (2004) *Bioinformatics: Sequence and Genome Analysis* (2nd revised edition). Cold Spring Harbor Laboratory Press, Cold Spring Harbor, NY.

12. Needleman, S. B. and Wunsch, C. D. (1970) A General Method Applicable to Search for Similarities in the Amino Acid Sequence of Two Proteins, *Journal of Molecular Biology,* 48:3, pp. 443–53. doi:10.1016/0022-2836(70) 90057-4. PMID 5420325.

13. Dayhoff, M. O. and Ledley, R. S. (1963) Comprotein: A Computer Program to Aid Primary Protein Structure Determination, *Proceedings of the Fall Joint Computer Conference, 1962*, American Federation of Information Processing Societies, Santa Monica, CA, 262–74.

14. Eck, R. V. and Dayhoff, M. O. (1966) Evolution of the Structure of Ferredoxin Based on Living Relics of Primitive Amino Acid Sequences, *Science*, 152, pp. 363–6.

15. Schwartz, R. M. and Dayhoff, M. O. (1978) Detection of Distant Relationships Based on Point Mutation Data, in H. Matsubara and T. Yamanaka, eds., *Evolution of Protein Molecules*. Center for Academic Publications Japan/ Japan Scientific Societies Press, Tokyo, pp. 1–16.

16. Dayhoff, M. O., Eck, R. V., Chang, M. A., and Sochard, M. R. (1965) *Atlas of Protein Sequence and Structure*. National Biomedical Research Foundation, Silver Spring, MD. (Black Cover), 93 printed one-sided pages.

17. Kenward, M. (2001) Inpharmatica: Number Crunching on a Massive Scale, *FTIT*, 21 February, Health & Medicine case studies. Available online at: http://specials.ft.com/february2001/ftit/FT3CRO7YCJC.html

18. Martino, M. (2006) Press Release: Galapagos to acquire Inpharmatica, *FierceBiotech*. Available online at: http://www.fiercebiotech.com/node/ 4829#ixzz1Q6GX1B3r

19. Hesper, B., Hogeweg, P. (1970) Bioinformatica: een werkconcept. *Kameleon*, 1:6, pp. 28–9. (In Dutch.) Leidse Biologen Club: Leiden.

20. Author interview with Paulien Hogeweg, June 2011.

21. Hogeweg P. (2011) The Roots of Bioinformatics in Theoretical Biology, *PLoS Comput. Biol*, 7:3, e1002021. doi:10.1371/journal.pcbi.1002021

22. Crombach, A. and Hogeweg, P. (2008) Evolution of Evolvability in gene Regulatory Networks. *PLoS Comput. Biol*, 4:7, e1000112. Available online as: http://www.ncbi.nlm.nih.gov/pubmed/18617989

23. Marée, A. F. and Hogeweg, P. (2001) How Amoeboids Self-Organize into a Fruiting Body: Multicellular Coordination, *Dictyostelium Discoideum*. Proceedings of the National Academy of Sciences, 27 March, 98:7, pp. 3879–83. Available online at: http://www.ncbi.nlm.nih.gov/pubmed/11274408

24. Segel, L. A. (2001) Computing an Organism, *Proceedings of the National Academy of Sciences*, 27 March, 98:7, pp. 3639–40. Available online at: http://www.ncbi.nlm.nih.gov/pubmed/11274380

25. Kevles, B. H. (1998) *Naked to the Bone: Medical Imaging in the Twentieth Century*. Basic Books, New York.

26. Timmis, B. (2005) The Beatles Greatest Gift...Is to Science. Summary of talk to Whittington Hospital NHS Trust. Available online at: http://www.whittington.nhs.uk/default.asp?c = 2804&t = 1

27. Author interview with David Hawkes, June 2011.

28. Studholme, C., Hill, D. L. G., and Hawkes, D. J. (1999) An Overlap Invariant Entropy Measure of 3D Medical Image Alignment, *Pattern Recognition*, 32, pp. 71–86.

29. Hawkes D. J., Barratt, D., Blackall, J. M., Chan, C., Edwards P. J., Rhode, K., Penney, G. P., and Hill, D. L. G. (2005) 'Tissue Deformation and Shape Models in Image-guided Interventions: A Discussion Paper *Medical Image Analysis*, 8:2, pp. 163–75.

30. Bashar, M. K., Kitasaka, T., Suenaga, Y., Mekada, Y., and Mori, K. (2010) Automatic Detection of Informative Frames From Wireless Capsule Endoscopy Images, *Medical Image Analysis*, 14:3, pp. 449–70. Epub 4 January 2010. PMID: 20137998

31. Author interview with Jason Kingdon, June 2011.

32. Author interview with Philip Treleaven, June 2011.

33. Kingdon, J. (2004) AI Fights Money Laundering, *IEEE Intelligent Systems*, 19:3, pp. 87–9, May/June. doi:10.1109/MIS.2004.1

INDEX

Adobe 152, 216, 261
Advanced Research Projects Agency
    (ARPA) 111, 113, 144, 146, 163,
    151, 266, 267
affective computing 169
agents 193, 205–7
Algol 88, 89, 250
algorithm 31–8, 130, 152, 154, 178,
    200, 233, 243, 244, 254
All-Purpose Electronic Computer
    (APEC) 260
ANITA 260
Apple 137, 147–48, 261
arithmetic and logic unit (ALU) 57,
    85
ARM microprocessor 71, 248
ARPANET 111–13, 116–17, 119, 121–22,
    126–27, 146, 149, 251
Artificial Intelligence (AI) 7, 10, 26,
    108, 150, 169, 181, 185–87, 190,
    194, 201, 205, 242, 251, 253, 254,
    271
Artificial Life 74, 194, 200, 205,
    223, 256

Ashby, Ross 193, 254, 256
assembly language 85–7, 103, 249
Association for Computing
    Machinery (ACM) 86
asymmetric key encryption 132
Atanasoff, John 51
Augmentation Research Center
    (ARC) 144, 146
Authentication 134, 136, 163
Autocode 87
Automatic Computing Engine
    (ACE) 26, 246, 256
AVIDAC 246

Babbage, Charles 51, 243
Bell Telephone Laboratories 43–5,
    48, 61, 75, 104–5, 107,
    150, 245, 251
Berkeley University 63, 125, 144
Bernal, John 'Sage' 219
Berners-Lee, Tim 123–29
Berthouze, Nadia xi, 163, 168–70
BESK 246
big-O notation 32, 243

binary coding 75, 107
bio-inspired computers 72, 248
bioinformatics 10, 217–23, 225
bit (binary digit) 76, 106
bitmap 153, 155
Black, Sue xi, xii, 28–9, 252
Blandford, Ann xi, 163, 165–66
Bletchley Park xiv, 26, 28, 51, 245
blocks world 187
body transfer illusion 160
Boolean logic 45, 47–8, 57–8,
       106, 175
Booth, Andrew 219, 260
British Computer Society (BCS) 90
Brooks, Rod xi, 191–94, 201
Burks, Arthur 197–98, 257
Bush, Vannevar 45, 142

C 89
C++ 89, 250
Cache 65, 128, 251
Catmull, Edwin 152, 253
Cellular Automata (CA) 206, 257
Central Limit Theorem 16
Cerf, Vint 111, 113, 115–6,
       118, 123
CERN, European Organization for
       Nuclear Research 109–10, 116,
       124
Chatterbot 186, 190, 255–56
Church, Alonzo 24–26, 45, 50, 88
Church-Turing Thesis 24
Codd, Edgar 'Ted' 92

Cohen, Danny 152
Colossus 51
compiler 89–89, 181, 250
complex instruction set computer
       (CISC) 81
compression 41, 107
computability theory 39
computer graphics 69, 110, 149,
       151–57, 171, 211–12
computer modeling 11, 99, 202, 212,
       222, 230, 257
computer network 2, 4, 5, 12,
       71, 104, 106, 110–24, 133, 135–36,
       138–39, 146–47, 149, 202, 251, 252
computer vision 228
consciousness 205, 207–08
Courtois, Nicolas xi, xii, 129–34
CPL 89
Crow, Frank 152
Crowcroft, Jon xi, 107, 116–18
Cryptography 75, 129, 133
CSIRAC 246
Cybernetics 174, 181, 255, 259

Damer, Bruce xi, 59
Dartmouth conference 181, 184
DASK 246
Database 91–5, 103, 124,
       179, 221–22
Davies, Donald 110, 112
Dayhoff, Margaret 220–21
Deep Blue 179
DEUCE 246, 260

domain name server (DNS) 120
dot-com bubble 7, 137

Eckert, Presper xiii, 52–3, 59–60, 75, 78, 102, 198, 249, 250
Eiffel 250
Electronic Delay Storage Automatic Calculator (EDSAC) 80–2, 84, 90, 109, 246, 248, 249
Electronic Discrete Variable Automatic Computer (EDVAC) 53–4, 58–60, 78, 198, 246
Electronic Numerical Integrator and Computer (ENIAC) xiii, 52–3, 58, 78–9, 198, 249
Encryption 129–35
Engelbart, Douglas 141–46, 148–49, 151, 162, 171, 251, 253
Enigma 26
ENQUIRE 124
Entscheidungsproblem 20, 24, 243
Estrin, Gerald 63, 251
Euler 250
Evans, David 151–52

F# 250
Facebook 128, 137, 166, 218
FACOM 246
fetch-execute 57–8
finite state machine (FSM) 243, 257
Finkelstein, Anthony xi, 99, 101–2
Flowers, Thomas 51

Forrest, Stephanie 200
Frames 186–87, 206, 255
fraud protection 136, 234, 236–37, 239
Freeman, Daniel 158–59
Furber, Steve 71
fuzzy logic 189, 234

G-15 246
genetic algorithm 100, 199–200, 213, 219, 234, 256, 257
genetic programming (GP) 202
Glennie, Alick 86
Gödel, Kurt 19, 24, 48
Gödel's incompleteness theorems 19–20
Goldberg, David 200
Goldstine, Herman xiii, 52–54, 58, 75, 79
Good Old Fashioned AI (GOFAI) 191, 200
Google 28, 136–37, 166
Gouraud, Henri, 152, 154
Government Communications Headquarters (GCHQ) 27, 132
graphics processing unit (GPU) 69, 248

Hail Mary ball 68–69, 102
Halting Problem 30
Hamming, Richard 251
Handley, Mark xi, 116, 120–22, 135–36, 138–39

hard disk 63, 65, 92, 247, 250
Harman, Mark xi, 100–1, 103
Haskell 250
head-mounted display 151, 156
Hebb, Donald 183, 197
Herbster, Mark xi, 30, 42
Heuristics 177–78, 204–5, 254, 255
high-level programming
    language 87, 95
Hilbert, David 20–22, 24, 243
Hinton, Geoff 203, 207
Hirsch, Robin xi, 30, 37,
    42, 185
Hogeweg, Paulien xi, 222–24
Holland, John xi, 196–201, 206, 208,
    256–57
Holland, Owen xi, 207
Hopper, Grace 250
Hounsfield, Godfrey 225–26, 260
Hulme, Daniel xi, 36–8
human–computer interaction
    (HCI) 163, 165–66, 168–69
Husbands, Phil xi, 192
Hyperlink 126–27, 145, 251, 252
Hypertext Markup Language
    (HTML) 125–28, 241, 252
Hypertext Transfer Protocol
    (HTTP) 126–28, 133, 241

IBM 60, 87, 92, 96, 150, 179, 197, 212,
    214, 216–17, 246, 250, 254, 258,
    259
IBM 701 system 197, 246, 254

IBM PC 148
ILLIAC 246
image registration 229–31, 260
imaging 10, 11, 225–27,
    230, 232–33
information theory 107, 129
Institute for Advanced Study (IAS)
    xiii, 48–9, 59–60, 63, 75, 79, 198,
    256
integrated circuit (IC) 61–2, 64, 95,
    153, 247
Intel 62–3, 71, 100, 247, 261
Internet 1–2, 6–7, 42, 102, 113–14,
    116–26, 129, 131, 135–9, 146, 165,
    241, 251, 252, 259
    Browser 1, 114, 120, 124–26
Internet Corporation for Assigned
    Names and Numbers
    (ICANN) 121
Internet Engineering Task Force
    (IETF) 122, 125
iOS 249
IP address 114–5, 120–23
iStethoscope Pro 261
IXICO 10, 232, 261

JANET 117, 251
Java 250
JOHNNIAC 246
Jones, David xi, 219–22, 224

Kahn, Bob 113, 115
Kilby, Jack 61

Kingdon, Jason xi, 233–40, 261

Kirstein, Peter xi, xiv, 105, 107–13, 115–19, 123, 131, 135, 137–38, 251

Kolmogorov complexity 40–41

Lamarr, Hedy 252

Lambda calculus 24, 88

Langdon, Bill xi, 202, 207

Langton, Chris 200, 257

Lanier, Jaron 156

Latham, William xi, 210–18, 258, 259

Licklider, Joseph 'JCR' 110, 111, 144, 149, 197, 252

Linux 89, 249

Liskov, Barbara 250

LISP 88, 185, 189, 250, 255

Logic Theorist 255

Lovelace, Ada 243

Mac OS X 89, 249

machine code 81–82, 85–88, 103

Machine Learning 169, 188–190, 200–6, 219, 230–31, 261

Manchester Small-Scale Experimental Machine (Baby) 248

Mandelbrot Set 40, 244, 245

MANIAC 246

Massachusetts Institute of Technology (MIT) xiii, 44–5, 48, 79, 81, 86, 87, 95, 107, 111, 128, 132, 144, 150, 185–7, 191, 196–7, 246, 251

Mauchly, John xiii, 52–3, 59–60, 74–6, 78–9, 86, 102, 198, 249–50

McCarthy, John 181–82, 185–87, 197, 256

McCormack, Jon xi, 213, 216, 259

McCulloch, Warren 175, 180, 182–83, 185, 188

memory 22, 24, 29, 33, 53–5, 57–8, 65, 76, 80, 86, 94, 100, 163–64, 175, 184, 193, 201, 231, 243, 247–9, 251, 253

microcode 60, 81–2, 85, 103

microprocessor 68, 70–1, 248

Microsoft 166

Microsoft Windows 89, 100, 125, 148, 249, 251

minimax 177–78, 254

Minsky, Marvin xi, 150, 181–89, 196, 255–56

MISTIC 246

Modula-2 250

Moore School of Electrical Engineering, University of Pennsylvania 52–3, 60, 75–6, 78–9, 181, 198

Moore, Gordon 62–4

Moore's Law 43, 62–4, 67–8, 95, 100

Moral Science Club 15, 17

Morcom, Christopher 15

Morphogenesis 28, 224, 257

Mouse 1, 2, 94, 125, 144–47, 162, 167,
251, 253
maze-solving 150, 173–77, 181, 184,
254 see also Theseus
MS-DOS 148, 249
multi-core 68–9, 102
MUSASINO-1 246
Mutator 213–15, 217, 260

National Physical Laboratory (NPL)
110–12, 246, 260
von Neumann architecture 58, 60, 219
von Neumann, John xiii, 48–55,
57–63, 65, 71–2, 75, 78–9, 83,
176–77, 184, 197–98, 204, 209,
246, 254, 256–57
neural network 71, 183–84, 187–88,
190, 197–98, 203, 206, 234, 255, 257
Newman, Max 17, 26–7, 51, 77, 248
Novakovic, Gordana xi, 215
Noyce, Robert 61–2, 247

Oberon 250
operating system 5, 12, 85, 89, 137,
147, 148, 249, 251, 253
ORACLE 246
ORDVAC 246

P=NP 34, 36–8, 42
Parnas, David 96, 99
Pascal 250
Patterson, David 63–4, 67–9, 91, 102
perceptron 188–89, 203–4

peripheral 11, 57, 117, 162–3, 249
pipelining 65–6, 247
Pitts, Walter 174, 182–3, 188, 198
Pixar 153, 253
Princeton University 25, 50, 183, 245
Privacy 104, 136, 167
Prolog 185

Ratio Club 180, 193
ray-tracing 155
recursion theory 39
reduced instruction set computer
(RISC) 82, 248
relational database 92–3
repetitive strain injury (RSI) 162
Roberts, Larry 111–12, 251
Rosenblatt, Frank 188
Russell, Bertrand 17–19
Russell's paradox 17–19

Samuel, Arthur 181, 254
Sasse, Angela xi, 10, 162–68
SEAC 246
Searchspace 235–36, 238–39
Segmentation 228, 260
semantic web 252
Shannon, Claude xiii, xiv, 44–5,
47–9, 58, 75–6, 104–8, 129–30,
132, 150, 174–79, 181, 184–85, 204,
209, 245, 248, 251, 254–55
Shawe-Taylor, John xi, 188, 203–4,
208
Shestakov, Victor 245

silicon chip 8, 61–3, 68, 247
Silicon Graphics 152
SILLIAC 246
Sims, Karl 196, 216, 256
Slater, Mel   xi, 157–61, 254
software engineering 95–6, 98–100, 102
Sommerville, Ian   xi, 96, 99, 101
sorting algorithm 31–4, 87
SQL 93–4
Stanford Research Institute (SRI) 111, 141–2, 144, 146, 251
Stanford University 105, 108–9, 186
Subroutine 82–3, 87–8, 249
subsumption architecture 191
support vector machine (SVM) 203–4
Sutherland, Ivan 144, 149–54, 156, 171, 181, 253–54
Symbian OS 249
symbolic processing 190, 256
symmetrical key encryption 130
systems biology 222

Taylor, Bob 111, 144, 146, 151
TCP/IP 113–17, 120, 122, 127–28, 139
texture mapping 155, 213, 253
Theseus xiv, 173, 176
Transistor 12, 61–5, 67–8, 88, 225, 246
transmission 43, 107, 113–115, 131
TRASK 246

Treleaven, Philip   xi, 234–35, 238, 240
Turing machine 22–4, 26, 29, 38–40, 49, 58, 243–44
Turing reduction 244
Turing Test 180, 190, 201
Turing, Alan   xiii, 7, 12, 13–7, 19–29, 38–9, 41–5, 48–51, 58, 62, 75, 77, 80, 129–30, 178–80, 190, 193–94, 204, 208–9, 245–46, 254, 256–57
Tyrrell, Andy   xi, 72

Universal Resource Locator (URL) 125–26, 128, 133–34
Universal Turing Machine 29, 243
University College London (UCL)   xii, xiv, 10, 30, 36, 63, 99, 100, 116, 118–20, 129, 157, 163, 226, 234, 241
University of Cambridge   xiii, 15–7, 49, 60, 77–9, 81, 84, 109, 112, 117, 246, 248
University of Manchester 26–7, 61, 71, 86, 246, 248
University of Michigan 44, 96, 198, 246
University of Utah 111, 152
Unix 89, 125, 148, 249, 251

vacuum tube 51, 58, 61, 184, 245
variable 84, 249
vector 66, 153–55, 174
virtual memory 247
virtual reality 11, 151, 156–61, 171, 258
visualization 171, 218, 230

Walter, Grey 193, 254
Web page 5–6, 70, 94, 125–28,
    133–34, 136–37, 165, 167, 241
WEIZAC 246
Wheeler, David 81, 83–4
Whirlwind 81, 197, 246
Wikipedia 240
Wilkes, Maurice xiv, 60, 76–84, 86,
    89–91, 109, 112–13,
    248–49, 251
Wilson, Stewart 194
WIMP (windows, icons, menus, and
    pointing device) 147–48

Wirth's Law 100
World Wide Web 6, 123, 125, 127–28,
    133, 137, 146
WYSIWYG (What You See Is What
    You Get) 147

Xerox Palo Alto Research Center
    (PARC) 146, 149, 253
XML 94

Z3 51
Zhou, Shi 117
Zuse, Konrad 51